Outlaws of the Purple Cow

and Other Stories

Outlaws
of the Purple Cow

AND OTHER STORIES

৯৯

by Lester Goran

THE KENT STATE UNIVERSITY PRESS

KENT, OHIO, AND LONDON

Library of Congress Catalog Card Number 99–13044

ISBN 0-87338-639-6

Manufactured in the United States of America

06 05 04 03 02 01 00 99   5 4 3 2 1

This is a work of fiction.

Any resemblance to persons living or dead is purely coincidental.

Library of Congress Cataloging-in-Publication Data

Goran, Lester.

Outlaws of the purple cow and other stories / Lester Goran.

p.   cm.

ISBN 0-87338-639-6 (cloth : alk. paper). ⊗

I. Irish Americans—Pennsylvania—Pittsburgh—Societies and clubs

Fiction.   2. Pittsburgh (Pa.)—Social life and customs Fiction.   3. Jewish

men—Pennsylvania—Pittsburgh Fiction.   I. Title.

PS3557.O6309   1999

813'.54—dc21   99-13044

British Library Cataloging-in-Publication data are available.

To

Julia J. Morton

whose skill and imagination have created

grand things for me

꧁

Contents

Contents

༄

Introduction

WHILE I WAS PREPARING this collection of short stories, in "The Notebooks of Henry James" I came across the following conversation James, as he so often did, had with himself in 1891 in Ireland. James was almost fifty then, a good many great works behind him, several monuments to follow. I found James had expressed to himself exactly what I would have said to myself had I his gifts for articulation, the ability to turn passion, even literary fervor, to eloquence so rare on a subject of mutual concern to us.

I must absolutely *not* tie my hands with promised novels if I wish to keep them free for a genuine and sustained attack on the theater. That is one cogent reason out of many, but the artistic one would be enough even by itself. What I call *the* artistic one *par excellence* is simply the consideration that by doing short things I can do so many, touch so many subjects, break out in so many places, handle so many of the themes of life.

. . . The upshot of all such reflections is that I have only to let myself *go*. So I have said to myself all my life—so I said to myself in the far-off days of my fermenting and passionate youth. Yet I have never fully done it. The sense of it—the need of it—rolls over me at times with commanding force: it seems the formula of my salvation, of what remains to me of a future. I am in full possession of accumulated resources—I have only to use them, to insist, to persist, to do something more—to do much more—than I *have* done. The way to do it—to affirm one's self *sur la fin*—is to strike as many notes, deep, full and rapid, as one can. All life is—at my age, with all one's artistic soul the record of it—in one's pocket, as it were. Go on, my boy, and strike hard: have a rich and long St. Martin's Summer. Try everything, do everything, render everything—be an artist, be distinguished, to the last. One has one's doubts and discouragements—but they are only so many essential vibrations of one's ideal. The field is still all round me, to be won; it blooms with flowers still to be plucked. But enough of the *general*, these things are the ambient air; they are the breath of one's artistic and even one's personal life. Strike, strike, again and again, at the *special*; I have only to live and to work, to look and to feel, to *gather*, to note. My *cadres* all there; continue, ah, continue to fill them.

His failure in the theater later has become famous and a subject of probing along lines of literary and historical examination. The collected edition of James's works sold poorly after that. He died,

I think it's safe to say, as unhappily and melancholy as in the worst time of a long life of disappointments. Yet who among us would not try to replicate those moments when James surveyed short fiction twenty-five years earlier and saw there the feel and touch, the extraordinary bounty of experience, too varied for length, too special for novels, too personal for anything but, if not the voice of the highest art, the exuberance and grappling with the truth of everything gathered over a lifetime?

PART ONE

Flowers in the Rain

ONE

Jenny and the Episcopalian

EVERY NIGHT's long walk to Jenny, after cleaning rooms at Haddon Hall till the late shift arrived at eight, was a journey to far places. On the streets at least there was no sadness that the war brought. Often in Oakland, where she walked, the streets were lively with people leaving concerts at Syria Mosque or Forbes Field baseball games. Her happy, solitary walks in darkness along yards black with night and buildings strong and quiet and no light showing were one of the few pleasures allowed her: work six days a week, church on Sunday, a very narrow stroll with her aged and mostly angry widowed mother up to the edge of Schenley Park, and back at work at ten in the morning to Haddon Hall Mondays without end.

She had, though, the feeling every night as she left Haddon Hall on Center Avenue after work, walked briskly down Craig to Forbes Street, and down the two miles to Craft Avenue and then across the Boulevard of the Allies to Joe Hammer Square where she lived with her mother that something soul-stirring could happen at any time. The war had not touched Pittsburgh, except for the occasional blackout; but the mills on the South Side made even ordinary nights mysterious and colored with flames and froth overhead, things under way in furnaces with molten metal being poured out of huge ladles and men without shirts dark silhouettes against fire. In the sooty air with all its ordinariness, Jenny thought that something was going to happen to her soon, something big.

Everywhere there was excitement. People who did not know each other spoke on busses and in church and at the hotel about the South Pacific and Hitler and Patton and the Axis and the United Nations. Battleships, huge floating armies on the water with guns big as houses and airplanes destroying whole cities in one night, and there were a million men at war and everywhere there was movement and surprise. She saw young women holding desperately to the arms of soldiers and sailors on the streets of Oakland and she wanted to be a sailor and she wanted to be a girl clutching at a serviceman's arm and to do the things that people in Pittsburgh, even thousands of miles from the fighting, did during a war. The women at work, Eva and Gert and Gilda, all had new stories to tell every night, discussions of the war and themselves and adventures common people fell into.

Some nights, as Jenny walked, she fancied she'd see a gigantic tank driving up the middle of Center Avenue, armored cars with four soldiers she recognized from newsreels or coming along Forbes a mighty elephant from India where American troops fought, and the great creature would kneel and she would board him for the ride home, or ride in the tank or shout defiance to the enemy from a bouncing Jeep. Usually she thought the elephant, trudging majestically with a tiger or lion trailing him, would arrive about the time she passed the broad, windswept part of Fifth in front of the University of Pittsburgh on nights when she was alone on the street. Other times she expected a magical bus with small men with beards and long caps who would pull up to the curb—near the Schenley Hotel with its glittering lights on the porches and in the windows still sending out brightness through heavy curtains—and the little men with rattles and bells would escort her home. All of it, in her imagination—tanks, elephants, tigers, soldiers and lions, the magical bus with music pouring from it like a merry-go-round that would never stop—would disappear about Craft Avenue. It would never do for her mother to see such things.

Her mother, quite simply, often believed Jenny was not all there. And the sight of the strange things that she imagined, even come to life through no fault of Jenny's, would be regarded as proof of her general loopiness. She had never seen an elephant except in pictures and never anything like a tank or a magical bus, but she knew, as surely as she knew her job folding towels and cleaning rooms at Haddon Hall, she would see incredible things one day. Foolish enough to mention this to people, her mother among them, when she was very young, she had been assured she was queer, harmless, and hopeless. So she stopped talking about what she expected to see.

She thought herself very normal for herself, maybe a little laughable sometimes, but, like people said, no harm to anyone and even, some days, when dressed in her best, as presentable as anyone, speaking well and slowly, thoughtfully and not startling anyone with a weird statement or a sudden glance during a conversation over anyone's shoulder.

"Jenny, in a lifetime of problems," her mother told her often, "you are the worst trial God sent me. I know we never are given more than we can handle, but Jenny, you are sometimes too much for me."

"How so?" she asked as a child. "Am I different? I don't seem different to myself. The kids at St. Agnes seem different to me— but not too different. They seem like me."

"You're not like them."

"How so?" she asked, meaning when she looked in the mirror she saw a person who looked like other people.

"It's nothing," her mother said. "Nothing. I'm just tired. You're exactly like other people. We're Catholic, and the Lord expects more of us than He does other people."

Her mother sometimes held her and said, "We're a prize pair, you and I, honey."

"Like other people?"

"Yes."

But her mother was vexed all day and all night and the weather was the cause that annoyed her or things on the radio and Jenny often made her rage too and her late husband who left her early with a queer daughter to raise and the neighborhood where they lived, Soho, on the fringes of Oakland on one side and the ghettos of downtown on the other, had gone to hell around her and that made her boil when she thought of it. With no one but Jenny to talk to, it seemed to the girl that her mother stored up her anger all day and waited for quiet moments with Jenny to pour them over the girl. Mrs. Virginia McEvoy believed in the church truth that all existence was divided into four parts, Life, Death, Judgment, Heaven or Hell, and if things were to be taken seriously only at the point of Death and then terrifying at Judgment and attended by choirs of angels or devils, as the case might be, in Heaven or Hell, why not treat Life, the first step, as important enough to be a dangerous, worthy forerunner to eternity? Wasn't Life part of eternity too and, surely, as sober a business as what waited?

Expecting little from Life, a preliminary to what else was going to happen for a long time, Jenny one night came upon a rare sight on her walk home from work. The night held a spring softness and a moon hidden behind clouds and the clouds dark and rolling over the streets where she walked, buildings like the Cathedral of Learning at Pitt strange, hulked presences under the sky. Thinking to alter her walk for variety, it being a dull week in a dreary month and the year not so grand either, by swinging down Craft Avenue to Forbes she saw from across the street a man sitting on the corner of Forbes on the steps of St. Peter's Church. He stood when he saw her and waved.

"Ho, Jenny," he said.

She would not have stopped but she thought it was a friend of her mother's. She walked across the street and looked long at the man and knew she did not know him, square-jawed, every hair in place, tall and slender, dressed clean in a white shirt and tie and dark suit. He was not the sort of man a person expected to see after midnight sitting on the steps of a church.

"I don't know you," she said.

"I don't know you either," he said.

"You called my name."

"Yes, I did. I don't know how I knew that."

"Good-bye, mister, you get yourself straight before you talk to women on the street. There's policemen around to protect people from your type."

He laughed softly. "I guess not," he said. "I'm not what you think."

She turned around and looked at the man.

"How do you know what I think? People are always telling me they know what I think."

A trolley going to the car barn on Craft made its turn, its familiar sound of gears and wheels and electrical sparks a comfort to Jenny. "No, I don't know what you think," he said, "but I do know you think I'm human."

"Well, what in the hell are you? You don't look like a cat or dog."

"I guess I'm a ghost, Jenny."

"Oh, sure, and I'm Pope Pius. And stop calling me Jenny if you don't know me."

"I don't mean to be familiar. My name is Woodrow Carter-Battermann."

He put out his hand to shake hands with her. She stood watching him. "Are you a crazy person?" she asked, not taking his hand. "There's crazy people on the streets all the time, talk to themselves, say things that seem to be they're talking to other people, but there's no one around."

"No, I'm not crazy. I'm a ghost—wait a minute, don't get mad. I don't know I'm a ghost except by being one. I don't know what a ghost is except from my experience. I'm sure I died. I'm positive. I remember my life, my death. I had a heart attack, not the first person in my family to go young, well, fairly young, I was forty-eight. But I guess once being dead, dying, and then being here must be that I'm a ghost."

"Excuse me, mister, but you're a crazy person."

She walked away quickly; and she wished she could tell her mother that she had met a crazy person who had said he was a ghost but knew her mother would become enraged and tell her that she herself was becoming every day more like a person who ought to be locked up.

She was not going to let the man frighten her. Jenny believed that men who spoke to strange women on the streets came and went in different places. She would probably never see him again, and if she did he would not be on the same corner before St. Peter's Anglican Church. When she boldly chose the same route the next night there he was. She ignored him when he called to her. But the next night when he called, this time from a rain-swept street, she crossed to where he stood and asked, "Are you crazy? You'll catch pneumonia out here calling to people you don't know."

"I'm dead," he said. "Don't you see? I can't catch anything."

"Crazy is what you are."

She avoided the church corner the following night, but the night after that she found him waiting for her as she left Haddon Hall on Center. "I'm going to call a policeman," she said as he fell into step with her. "How did you know where I work? I've never seen such a pest. Why don't you go back and haunt your church?"

"Well, I will. I think that's where I keep appearing, no matter where I disappear."

"You listen here, you go to hell."

They continued walking together and she liked it, him close to her, hearing his footsteps where she had so often walked alone and not talking but feeling there was a conversation under way. They passed a parked police car and she said nothing to the cops in the car. "Well, you know my name and I don't know anything but that name you gave me," she finally said.

"Woodrow Carter-Battermann," he said. "That's really my name, or was. I was the minister at St. Peter's, that church where I seem to be called to come, and I think I've been dead for five years and two months."

"Oh, yeah, oh, swell, tell it to the marines: what did you die of, if I might ask? And if it killed you, why does it let you walk around and bother women you don't know?"

"It was a heart attack, but I seem to be breathing okay. I don't know. Maybe I'm not breathing right. But I sort of feel my heart thumping and it seems okay."

She stopped at the Syria Mosque on Fifth, where the street was wide and broad, and said, "Say, don't you have anywhere to be? It's ten after twelve at night. Don't you have a mother or a wife?"

"Yes," he said, "I have a wife. She didn't die when I did, of course. Fact is, I'm still married to her, I guess, but she married someone else."

"That makes her a bigamist, mister."

"Hardly, I'm dead."

"Oh, Jesus, you're crazy. You go to hell. I'm going to walk by myself. Now leave me alone and the next time you see me pretend you forgot my name, okay?"

"I guess I could do that. But am I so offensive to you? If I wasn't a ghost would we be friends?"

"No! You're a married man, and I don't mess around—not with married men, not with anyone."

"I know," he said.

"You know? How can you know? You don't know anything about me."

"I seem to know. I don't know how."

"Leave me alone, do you hear?"

But she had to admit when she was alone in her room that she was thrilled; he had followed her, his footsteps soft behind her until the church. Then he called good-bye and was gone. She heard him no more. He stopped his pursuit of her at the church and she missed him. Really, any way you looked at it, a gentleman, neat and clean like a movie star: she dreamed of him, his chin and dark eyes, his neat tie and shirt. She did not care that he said he was a ghost—he had become for her like the sounds she heard in the night since childhood, like organs that almost played tunes she could recognize, shapes and colors that melted into waking until sometimes it was not until eleven in the morning she could recognize whether she was in a dream or awake. Sometimes the boundaries for her between what was actually and what lay in her mind from dreams and movies and songs and magazines and reveries in church came together until she could not tell one from the other; and, while the ghost was certainly of the real world (he was no dream), she did not know whether he had sprung into the real world from the place where melodies played whose names she never knew.

The next day, a Sunday, after Mass, she eluded her mother and went up to the church on the corner of Forbes and Craft and went inside, her first time in a Protestant church. She intended to ask if anyone there knew him, but she did not get her opportunity to play Sherlock Holmes. There was a picture of him there, up on the wall with other ministers in their full Episcopalian frocks, painted in oil, exactly the man who had been following her. Under that was his name "Reverend Woodrow Carter-Battermann" and the dates under that "January 11, 1890 – February 4, 1938."

She stopped a man walking past the portraits and said, "Excuse me, the dates under these pictures?" She tried to be vague, not pointing directly at the ghost's portrait.

An elderly man, he turned directly to look at the bronze plaques. "Yes," he said, "that's when Dr. Carter-Battermann was born and died. And this"—he pointed to smaller letters she had

not seen—"this is when he served at St. Peter's, 1932 till 1938."
He shook his head. "I did not know him. I joined the church
here only within the past eighteen months. But I hear he was an
excellent person. Died very young, as you can see. Are you a
member here? Were you looking for the minister?"

"No, no," Jenny said, running from the church. It was
enough that she had ventured there on a Sunday, perhaps enemy
ground, if her mother was to be believed. She hardly knew what
she would say to the present minister. "You know there's one of
you dead and hanging around here at midnight, I saw him more
than once with my own eyes." She developed chills at the in-
volvements in this odd place. She was pleased with her own
church, as who would not be? She had no interest in becoming
an Episcopalian, a religion whose ministers came back to haunt
honest, young, working Catholic girls.

Dr. Carter-Battermann explained to her Monday night, after
she had completed work, that he understood nothing at all about
his condition except that he knew he was certainly there on Center Avenue, walking with her down Craig toward the University
of Pittsburgh, that he could touch others—he took her elbow—
and she seemed to be able to touch him; but where he went as
daylight came or why he was anywhere at all and aware he was
anywhere he could not explain.

"Do you mean you vanish in the morning?" she asked, not
knowing whether to believe him or not.

"I don't know. I just know that there are periods of time I
don't seem to be anywhere and then other times I know I'm
here. Until I saw you walking down Craft toward St. Peter's I
had been standing there at various times, very lonely, because I
knew I was a ghost and wouldn't be real to other people—I seem

to disappear in certain lights or times of day—but I knew you'd
talk to me and be friendly. I just knew it."

"I'm still not sure I'm friendly."

"Of course, you are."

He took her hand, and she did not shake him off. She let him
hold her hand, enjoying his grip and the movement they made
together, he very well dressed, a little lightly for the cool April
night, and she in a maroon cloth coat. She should have been
tired from work, but she was not. His touch made her alert and
easy. She swung his hand slightly.

"Imagine me," she said, "holding hands with a ghost."

And it was true: occasionally in the lights of an automobile or
passing through certain shadows he became very, very pale or in
deep darkness seemed to blend into bushes or trees, a lawn on
Fifth behind him.

He told her later that week he loved her, standing before the
church and holding her close, pressed against her, the smell of
his beard and hair thick on her, his hands tight against her back
and she wanted him even nearer. "You don't," she said. "It's only
there's nobody else in Pittsburgh you can talk to—I'm like the
only woman on a desert island for you."

She kissed him hard and he walked with her partway to her
home. She rattled on, elephants, tigers, merry-go-rounds. "I
knew it," he said. "I just knew it."

Her mother said, "Jenny, you're acting like you do when you
get sick. Don't lie to me. I'll know. What is it? What's happening?
Tell me, I'll help you. It's a man, I can understand that. If it's a
man I'll understand. You'll bring him home and we'll all talk."

Jenny said, "No, I'm not bringing him home, not now, not
ever."

"Oh, my God. Then you have a boyfriend."

She told her mother, yes, she had a boyfriend, and her mother said quickly, "Bring him by. If he's not too good for us. Is that it?" And when Jenny did not answer, her mother said, "Jenny, you know you're not ready for these things."

"I'm twenty-three, ready enough. If I was a man I'd have been drafted when I was eighteen and already five years into the army and war."

They lived in a three-room apartment and it was not easy to escape each other.

"Something wrong here," her mother said. "I see all the signs. Is this fellow married you don't want to bring him by?" When Jenny didn't answer, her mother said, "Well, is he old? That it? Some man twice your age?"

Jenny said, "Stop asking questions!"

"Jenny, is this fellow a Protestant? Have you picked up with someone not of your faith?"

She fled to her room, and her mother came to the door and said, "It's happened to girls a lot smarter than you, Jenny. Nobody's so smart they figured this one out. Stay with a Catholic boy, someone not far from you in age—and don't get mixed up with a married man. They always go back to their wives, and you wouldn't have wanted it otherwise. You're a good girl."

Jenny put a pillow over her head, trying to drown out her mother. Why did the woman know everything? All her mother hadn't correctly surmised was that the boyfriend in her conjectures might be not of this world: *sweetheart, don't give your heart to a ghost, they disappear in the daylight or when a car's lights hit them head on.*

In a week the closeness of Woodrow as they walked and leaned close together in the alcove of St. Peter's was too much for Jenny, and when he asked her to go with him to a certain small hotel in East Liberty she went. He laughed as they left the taxicab, she paying as he had no money at all, was never hungry, never ate, and thought it absurd that he might vanish at the check-in desk of the hotel. But he did not, neither there or upstairs with her when she came in and joined him in the tiny, musty room. Not having any other man to compare him to, she could not with any certainty describe even to herself what it was like to make love to a ghost. It was still Woodrow's body, his skin, the scent of his arms when he held her, the bristles on his chin. She did not know what he was supposed to feel; she herself felt afterward complete, funny, and eager to laugh and joke with him. As car headlights caused him to waver to her vision and he to look in amazement at the transparency of himself, they both giggled like children. She wanted him to be happy. She cared about nothing but him. This was what people talked about all the time and when it had come to her it was him she thought of and remembered in her first time, hardly herself and her kisses to his neck and cheek and chest. His eyes in calm delight, his hands not sure and then careful and right, his walk across the room with no clothes as if the two of them were Adam and Eve in the Garden. Before evil or words or experience, she held on to the nakedness of him and his sighs and his breath and his mouth rather than any memory of herself.

"This is love," she said when they took the cab back to Oakland.

They went to the hotel, the Chateau Hotel, once a week for the next ten months. They always laughed and always felt a lingering sadness; she did not know to ask of him or herself, Where's this going? Or, Why am I doing this? It was he who told her she should think of those things. He did not know why he was still around, why he had come back five years after he died and when he would leave. He had no control of any of it and because he loved her, he said, "Jenny, I may be gone at any time. It's not you. I don't know why I'm here. I don't know when I'm going. We are going nowhere, I think. I love you and that's enough for me—I think I'm supposed to love you. I didn't understand it really when I was alive because I didn't believe I was going to die and what there was should have been precious. But you have long life ahead of you and think about us. There's plenty ahead for you without me. I'm a million to one freak occurrence in your life. Please, don't count on me. It scares me."

"Listen, Woodrow," she said, "nobody knows when they're going. I could drop over one day at Haddon Hall and go someplace you'd never see me. And isn't that what all the soldiers say to all the girls? I hear it all the time: 'I don't know where I'm going to be next week. I follow orders and go where the army sends me.'"

"But that makes sense. People are supposed to die and leave us forever, and the army is supposed to order soldiers to get on boats for other places."

"No, no," she said, "dying and going to war doesn't make sense either, Woodrow."

She had one friend at work, a woman named Gilda Snapp, shortened from Snapplewski, and she told her, as she was Polish and knew more than enough about life, everything about herself and Woodrow, emphasizing his educated speech, his easy walk, the beautiful tailored clothes; then, the two of them sitting in an empty room at Haddon Hall, smoking cigarettes and drinking black coffee, she told her the rest.

"Oh, Jesus, a ghost, you're sure?"

She had had two husbands, drinkers and sullen, woman

chasers both of them, but not ghosts! A new one on her. "Jenny," she said, "it's a new one on me."

Jenny became afraid. It was all so much. Gilda was still a fine-looking woman and had known many men. If what Jenny was now involved in made Gilda uneasy, it had to be something beyond anyone's ability to make sense of it. She liked when Gilda said at something she saw or heard, "Same thing, old story, honey." That she was stymied by Jenny's romance was scary, a weight as large as a hotel on her.

"And it's not that he's married that's the problem, like older than me, a Protestant, and a minister."

"Well, things like that usually count for a lot, but I think the ghost thing is the big drawback. Men act like ghosts sometimes with women, doing that vanishing act, but I don't think it's because they're from the spirit world. It's because they're big bastards."

"Woodrow is no big bastard, I can tell you that. We talked about the Virgin Mother and he said he wasn't too sure about that, but it's a difference of opinion between us. He's no bastard."

Her mother talked to Jenny of her boyfriend in terms so familiar, Jenny might have thought she knew him. While Jenny walked with her in the park silently after Sunday Mass or listened to her when she finished work at Haddon Hall, her mother spoke of men who were married and were always ready for a little on the side, smooth talkers, the gentlemen ones the worst of all. "Give me a snorer and a man with grease spots on his shirt every time," she said. "You know they'll be where you left them last week. Who wants them? There'll be no takers, trust me. The handsome ones with the elocution lessons and the never no ain'ts in their conversations, gone with the wind first chance they get. I know what you got yourself into, Jenny. It's a Protestant dragging you down, deluding you, no Catholic boy would do it to you. Only this isn't a boy. I can see in your eyes this is a man practiced in the world. He's old enough to be your father, and that's right, show me the truth of it, by getting up and walking away from your mother."

Jenny by 1945 had begun to think that she would live in a world without end right here in Oakland, always Woodrow Carter-Battermann, his hands and voice and herself tall as a sky-scraper with telling him of her tanks on the streets and elephants and busses that played sweet music and he listening and nod-ding, always saying in approval, "I knew it, I knew it." There would be no end to it, and it was in moments rich and full and by months valuable as the most precious diamonds. Even when her mother gathered her friends around her on certain nights and her mother led the conversation into tales of ruthless old men and snake-oil salesmen and married men out for a fling, each woman swearing it was all true, all looking under their lids at Jenny. She sat like a soldier. She knew what she knew.

At work at the hotel, Eva, who was Irish, Mrs. Carmody now with her married name, and her husband a soldier in the South Pacific, said, "My own sister ran off with a Baptist, a Southern Baptist, and he ditched her in two months."

The women gathered for coffee and cigarettes, once a fine time of night for Jenny but now a half hour when it seemed only she was under discussion, not Hitler or the second front in France, but Jenny McEvoy. She had told each of them bits and pieces of her story with Woodrow, withholding a few details but hoping too to hear some truth to reassure her. There was none in the air in the smoke-filled rooms where she sat with her friends on their breaks.

"I know a certain Mrs. Flannery's story," Gert said, Irish too. "It wasn't a Protestant took her life, it was a man old enough to know better and he tricked her into leaving her husband, and she came on hands and knees, crawling to return, but Flannery says, 'Stay out there in the wilderness, it was your choice.'"

Jenny's head rang with the sins of men. But it wasn't Woodrow Carter-Battermann.

"Get out of it," Gilda told her in private. "I'm sorry, it's unnatural."

But she stayed, secure in her love, until the hot August day that the atomic bomb was dropped on Japan. People talked of it everywhere; and she could not contain herself waiting for work to be completed, to rush to her waiting minister and ask him the meaning of these things, sharing terrible and triumphant times with him. But he was not at Haddon Hall to walk with her; and he was not at St. Peter's Church to greet her as she passed from streetlight to shadow. The church sat in the summer heat still and dark, the ivy on its walls drooping with the season, worn out with waiting for rain.

There was an emptiness on the night. There would be no swaying shadows that spoke. Tonight elephants would not parade along streets where electric trolleys ran. Nothing was here but what was here.

Confused only for a moment, Jenny knew without the details to affirm her loss, he was gone to places never described, in words not invented. He had surely known, coming from where he'd been, that one day she would be alone on streets where he should never have been; but she stopped her thoughts in that direction. She trusted him. Had he been able to stay on these familiar night streets he would have. Whatever the orders were, he had to follow them, not knowing where they came from or much past, Be here, or be there. Straight with him, no good-byes called for, for eternity if need be, she laughed softly to herself as if he were at her side, not even here now ghostly and fading to vanish as trees cast their branches in odd light on the sidewalk.

She smiled at the memory of the man turning red with a beer sign or blinking white in circles of bubbles announcing wine sold here.

So sure was she that orders had come, things settled about the two of them and matters now were beyond their common dreams that she did not change her path to walk down Craft past the church the night after he had appeared to her like a shadow come to life on the sidewalk, the one in a million chance that he might be there. She knew that if he could he would find her wherever she was, not on a certain street or at a certain time. He was gone.

"He's gone," she told Gilda. "The matter settled itself."

"I'd be scared," Gilda said. "What if he comes to snatch you in the night and carry you off? Don't it scare you when you think of the great unknown and dangers you were bumping into without a sign from nowhere what you were doing, right up there between the life and death, the gray country there's been no one visited and no one returned?"

"I don't think of things like that."

Clouds hung around Jenny's mind that she could not dissolve by thought. There were plain truths somewhere in her she could not put words to in the rush of her feelings.

"Don't say that, everybody thinks of things like that," Gilda said.

Jenny took another puff on her cigarette and held in the smoke like women of experience did. "Maybe for someone else to be scared. But being called queer all these years," she said, "I finally found a man cared for me and my mother said he was too old for me and that was bad news and he's a Protestant and people saying that's no good. Then he's married and never been divorced and that's my eternal soul heading for hell. And next he ain't of this world but a spirit and that's all wrong! All I know, if he ever comes back or I get a chance to meet him again in Heaven we'll work out the being Protestant and the business with his wife and it'll be happy days are here again for the two of us."

"I'll say this for you," Gilda said. "You do have your own mind."

Gilda could not know the thrill of it, the purpose, knowing one day the minister, Jenny's true love, might, any day, any night at that, step from the shadows on an ordinary street and be there again with her as blinking neon captured him in the movements and reflections from windows on storefronts and render him half here, the other part into thin air; and she thought, But all of his soul hers again.

TWO

Keeping Count

On a foggy morning in April 1959, a bus swerved to miss a man lying drunk on the bridge to downtown Pittsburgh, and, not killing the inebriated man, the bus broke through the railing down to the Allegheny River and plunged like a predestined rock the hundred feet to the water below. Seeing the tragedy, James Thierry, in the bus for Oakland, behind the doomed bus in the water, ran across the bridge and over the embankment to the water and swam out to pull to safety any survivors. For a man of his years, he was still a strong swimmer. He showed his police badge to officers from the river patrol and emergency ambulances who came to the rescue of the victims on the bus. He was allowed to move freely in the water and on the riverbank.

James pulled from the Allegheny at least three people, maybe more—he did not keep count. The newspapers credited him with five; he could not testify to any of it, only the swimming out and return exhausted to the riverbank. Too tired to move after a long two hours, he sat, vaguely sobbing with fatigue, aware as people were brought to the bank that some were dead. He could not avoid the score in his mind as he watched each boat come in with its cargo, living and dead. No one knew how many had been on the bus; no one could be sure how many had died. Divers worked for days and the agreed account was two dead.

The drunk on the bridge had gone to the broken railing, leaned on it watching the commotion below, and left. No one knew his name.

But the hell with him anyhow, James thought, he might as well have been a lightning bolt or a black cat: the fate of the dead people lay in the depth of the river, the suffocating bus. Perhaps the number of rescued or dead amounted to a meaningful score in some celestial count, or maybe there was no cosmic meaning at all to it. James knew he himself would never know the meaning and, a believing and practicing Catholic, did not by habit care to confront riddles that had perplexed other people with better minds than his for thousands of years. There were purposes, and mostly his own, those dimly perceived, were what he tried to make matter. Live decently enough and expect the world to go nicely to hell all on its own, no hardness in himself if he could help it, few illusions about goodness behind every tree.

But there was something unfinished in the bus's fall. The last brave cries of fear and outrage had allowed no time for a reckoning, unless as the people toppled downward in those brief seconds before the cries of astonishment, grief, and terror their minds had summed up the scores of their lives. James had tried to imagine his own possibly last thoughts. What would the people on the bus think to enumerate, children, lost loves, money in bank accounts, great athletic contests, women or men they had held in promise and reward? What did they note as final just before they sank into the water or was it all a jumble and nothing ever there first to last except period-end-of-story with the whole idea of anything ever finished and tallied a fairy tale?

Falling to my death, what would I count? James asked himself as he walked to another stop for a bus to Oakland in a light rain that had started after the fog, comfortable and enclosed in a fireman's raincoat.

Nothing would come to me, I imagine, he thought, things pretty well accounted long before my descent into the mighty Allegheny. Two wives had died, respectable farewells made, love lingering over each departure, enveloping memories to console him at their loss, but gone with no regrets of words unsaid, misunderstandings to gnaw at thoughts of them that occurred at times bidden or suddenly there. And two children had left him with barely a final nod good-bye, but absent now as if their unceremonious farewells had been an occasion of the times and had nothing personal in it, a letter from Nepal, snapshots from Morocco: he did not care about them enough to wonder about their well-being. He had been orphaned at ten in Pittsburgh, lived in foster homes, and had given the children all that he could and when they left, each in turn, he thought, Well, they had it better than I did, shoved off, and I did okay, so will they. There was no monument of emotion surrounding an unsettled tab sheet about any of it.

The bus's leap from the bridge kept him awake that night.

A soft rain still fell as he went to the window of his apartment and considered again what he would account for at the end, given as he was now, not the few seconds of shocked fall over the railing of a bridge but perhaps a relatively long time to consider such things. An accounting was in order, had been missing from his sense of who he'd been, he decided, no matter the length of time ahead, heart, kidneys, liver, and lungs sort of in a rhythm of descent whether it was over a bridge or not. James, at four in the morning, took a pencil and hastily a subscription card from a news magazine, and, after staring at the wall for a few moments, began quickly to jot down in the white margins the names of all the women with whom he had ever had sex. Pleased with the smallness of the idea that had occurred to him—to make a list of trifles in the absence of anything complicated that might muddle his convictions about his life, interesting enough and, he thought, well lived—he became more involved with the work in progress the more names he remembered. The card soon was filled; he scratched down identifying qualities where he did not know a name. Philly, 1946; shoulders like R. H. (That would be Rita Hayworth, and what else did he need to remember?)

James had worked with a carnival when he was a boy, a runaway at fourteen, and there were many small towns whose time in his life was illuminated by the faces of young women as surely there lay before him in a long tunnel of time from youth to now the tumbling electric light bulbs of the Ferris wheels, Janie, Margie, the Guess Your Weight, Pitch-the-ball, Ruth Ann, another Margie, Come See Hazel the Lady with a Beard, and more than one Ginger, Tonya (a false name but a memory of a night in snow banks at the carnival grounds in Wheeling), and Jenny and Kay and Susie and Lulu.

The card was soon filled. Names and abbreviations crawled up the margins and between the words printed on the card in red and stark black. He stood and took a legal pad from his dresser which also served him occasionally as a desk in his small apartment. He found a fresh ballpoint pen and continued. He had worked with ice shows after the carnival. He had met many women when he worked in hotels and then he became a policeman on a beat when he returned to Pittsburgh after years on the road. He had gone from that to Juvenile Court; he was now a captain of police, Capt. James Thierry, a name on his shield, an identifying plate on a desk. And everywhere he had met women and had sex with them: a lust in boyhood, a passion and a proof later, a habit, a way of life between wives, and then a source of wisdom, a large—perhaps not—reference work to which he could turn at times when human nature confounded him. He had never thought to count up the women until the bus and its passengers fell to their moment with destiny and it occurred to him that some accounting was necessary. He did not care if the number was relatively large or, given his bountiful opportunities, small. The sum total had no meaning in size; its importance was that it had happened and was real as a statement from what was in a certain bank account, neither to be assessed rich or poor but there to be considered. Sometimes he stopped at his list when he could not remember a name, initials, or even a city or a characteristic, only the sense of a woman, darkness perhaps, a lost cap left under a bridge in the encounter, a morning in another town whose name he hardly knew. He paced, recollecting.

He walked around the two-room apartment, occasionally going to the window to watch the rain on the street outside. He worked frantically until daylight came in the windows, scratching names as they came to him, alive to himself now and at the time of each woman, enveloped by them and the scent of cotton candy in the room, himself then in rolled-up sleeves hauling tarpaulin, cheap perfume on him nights and days, dark, stained nights with dime store powder, all youth and lovely. Outside it was raining in the morning light. Trapped indoors with the list and the paper he felt an intense communion with the two small rooms and the completeness of his shallow vision of what whimsically constituted a summing up of his life.

Brought up by religion to suffer guilt at too many of the names and initials on his list, he still repeatedly smiled to himself at the length of the list he had amassed in life and on the legal pad. He had forgotten about himself and what led up to the moment of the disaster on the bridge and the sudden death in springtime, all that sat with him in the bus behind the terrible one that swerved for a drunk as he heard the screams of horror; and now he had a list of women, and perhaps other summations to be considered in time before he himself crashed into an Allegheny River of his own. He had been a lonely bastard in the last four years since his wife died. He missed his wife. He did not feel anything at all in the absence of his children.

His daughter might as well have spoken Chinese to him, so little did he understand the points she seemed to be making; and the son—the less said the better, no record necessary there, drugs, drunk-driving arrests, flight with embezzled funds, an irony. Captain Thierry regularly dealt with problem children like his own, a liaison officer at Juvenile Court, famous for saving troubled youth, but not his own. I'm probably going more bonkers by the day, he thought, going out into the wet streets Monday morning, numbers of women, clients at the Juvenile Building, times I tried to talk to my own kids and failed. No list in my mind finished: I'll descend to my death with not one thing completed.

He usually walked down Forbes to work, but today he stopped to adjust his umbrella on the sidewalk and something in the brisk, certain snap and movement of the umbrella brought something to his mind. He returned to his rooms and counted the initials and names of his fifty-seven years, and then counted them again. There were ninety-nine. In his raincoat he sat at his desk and tried to think of another woman, rather desperately, the challenge of a completion of sorts in the number one hundred. But not another woman would cross the bridge from his past to the present rainy Monday morning. Well, well, he thought, something demonstrably unfinished, but given my years and fatigue and general lack of interest in little that I see and hear these days probably doomed to be that unsymmetrical number forever. And, again, perhaps given my splendid adventures I may have easily forgotten at least a certain woman somewhere around Morgantown or Asheville. But there was something disquieting about the irregular number—he had slightly more than three months to go before his early retirement, and it almost seemed, he thought as he walked along in the rain, he would not be able to die without that woman rounding off things, not able even to retire sensibly, as if there were unfinished business with his work, a mutilation in his life that required some statement.

He counted to himself things all morning at Juvenile Court: broken noses on mothers created there by sons with cocaine habits, prostitutes under fifteen he had known as he sat at his battered desk, fathers of sons who had stolen family cars and wrecked them, boy bank robbers, child purse snatchers, alcoholics under eleven. The bruises, the scars, the lines of zombielike parents all hiding something, days on the job and nights staking out warehouses suspected of receiving stolen merchandise, twenty-seven years a cop and he had nothing but lists bothering him. One anyhow: who was that other woman? Surely she was there. Had he compiled his lengthy list, in the grip of the death feeling, only to see it turn to nonsense?

In his work he often went to the courthouses in downtown Pittsburgh to plead a case, testify against some youthful murderer. Downtown he had come to know secretaries, deputies, mayors themselves and had been assured of any one of a number of jobs with the city when he retired with the Juvenile Court: the water department, highways, fire inspection, or just on one of the staffs in the great, blossoming bureaucracy of city hall. Anything, he thought, except that long, steadily moving, absurd line that advanced on him night and day. This was not just today's failures of systems and society he looked at daily in the face; these were children with long lives in front of them, and there the promise that things were not only rotten today, but wait till tomorrow! The enemy was nonsense that ate at his will to help the lost: that none of it, plantiffs and defendants, bustling clerks and policemen, lawyers and doctors come to put bandages on broken heads or to sew fingers back on severed hands, himself, none meant anything.

The suffering line would be there every morning and on into the night, a parade with no music to keep them in step.

He looked up at a young woman in police uniform who stopped at his desk.

She was in uniform and darkly beautiful. "Excuse me, Dara, I was daydreaming," he said.

"The Dirker kid," she said. "They're not going to try him as an adult."

"I guess it's justice."

"Except the punk ought to hang," she said. "He tried to set

the cab on fire with the driver in it. Let him go up with the grown-ups where they go when they do things like that."

"His father made him swallow lye soap when he was six," James said.

"Send his father up with him."

"Okay, Sergeant Bear."

As she moved away he watched her calves in their sheer stockings. Wouldn't it be a prize to his foolish list to make her one hundred. "Dara," he called, but when she turned he said, "I'm sorry, I'm just tired. I know Dirker wasn't a kid toasting marshmallows at a high school football game. He'll be robbing cabs and assaulting cabdrivers when he's ninety."

She turned away quickly, and he realized she thought he was being sarcastic. Well, he had not thought of her as Miss One Hundred even before he spoke, too young by decades for any interest in him; but there'd never be another woman in his life unless he let go of the agony of thinking that nothing meant anything. He tried to remember one more woman, but none came, and he put his list into his coat pocket, realizing he had counted several women twice in his ambition to conclude with a symmetrical hundred. He scratched out a name. He had called her blondie and Betty Boop, but she was one person, a saleswoman for a pots and pans company he had met in a bar in Harrisburg.

At the Irish Club on Saturday there were four of the old-timers sitting at a table in the corner, and James joined them. It was after midnight, and he had fallen asleep working on his list, filling in by a word or two further descriptions of the women he had summoned up from the past. He thought that in the more than thirty-five years since he had been a boy in pursuit of women he might find that he had mistakenly remembered the same woman more than once: he would have been pleased to see his list fall to eighty-two or ninety-four. He enjoyed the recollections that swept over him. He had not remembered how he had enjoyed being the young man in a torn undershirt pulling up ropes at fairgrounds or donning a straw hat to call pitch and toss games, the whole soft summer atmosphere of youth and strength came back to him in the embrace of women.

At the Ancient Order of Hibernians the smoke that lay on the place usually was the zone of neither here nor there, lies not quite crafted, the past in the dull grayness of cigarettes and cigars never gone further than the last person speaking: decades were honored in recitals well told and stumbled over but not ever buried while one man or another remembered. At midnight at a far, dark table, as frequently happened in dreamlike hours before dawn, things lost in World War II returned in all their poignancy. There were men who had fought in the Pacific at the table, and Europe, and brothers were celebrated who were dead, and hapless youths who had left the home streets and not been seen again. Jeeps crashed again, submarines sank with innocent boys from Robinson, Dunseith, Terrace, Chesterfield Road, and Darraugh drowning, blown apart, or on fire. The casualty lists from France and the Pacific in the *Pittsburgh Press* had held high school pictures of boys who had lately been altar boys at St. Agnes: only moments ago, they had been wearing white gowns and cardboard angel wings in the annual Christmas pageant.

James listened, nothing to add. They had joked at the table about his heroism at the bus crash, but no one let him pay for a drink. He drank a white wine. He lost himself in the converging shadows of the other men's lives. They rang like peals on a great bell their sorrows and fears, enumerating the long flow of the years in tales of moments and people.

He had known some of them when they were children. He had gone away, naturally returned. Where was there to be other than here where nothing that happened to anyone was not understood by everyone?

"She married me for my allotment check," Corny Sullivan said, "and when I came back and it stopped she and me run down like a clock not been wound."

"Your clock wasn't wound years ago, Corn," Dully said.

"That's a great one talking," Dickie Trent said. "We went to the whorehouse one week after Lent and Dully says he wants two girls and he takes two upstairs with him—they were three dollars a girl in those years. Five minutes later they all three came down, and the one girl says to me and Clarence waiting, 'Your friend didn't need no two girls, half of one would have been enough. He was satisfied on the steps going up.'"

"Clarence Meagher," Arn Hurley said. "It's been fifteen years since he and I sat at this table and he said he knew he wasn't coming back from the war."

"I said it myself," Dully said, "but here I am."

"Religious boy, I doubt Clarence ever was with a sweetheart, maybe a prostitute, but never a girlfriend."

"Think of all the women didn't get to marry all our boys lost at sea and buried in France," Corny said. "Must have been in the thousands."

It was after two and James had a full day tomorrow. He stood slowly, reluctant to return to leave the truth of the unreal world in the smoke and old visions.

"You're not leaving, James?" Dully asked. "You just got here."

"I am," James said and finished his wine and in measured stride walked home to his apartment on Neville in the night with as much summer to it as spring.

He slept in what he thought had been a deep and restful repose, but as the morning became clearer to him on waking, he thought of his restless dreams. He had walked, he remembered, down long labyrinths of alternating stations of light and dark, cheerfully enough, clutching the hands of children. The children had at first skipped and run and hid in bushes and behind trees.

He knew the trees, giant sequoias he remembered from a trip to California: as he observed the ancient trees he had been moved to a tearful solemnity at the stillness that lay on leaves and undergrowth, all inanimate grass and roots in a long, dark, forever-silent forest. Sunlight fell between the trees in his dream state and he and the children stepped from light into shadow and then again into dappled light. In the dream, Thierry himself was not apprehensive, but the children were terrified at each unfamiliar turn in the maze. The huge trees frightened them and eventually James felt a panic in himself at the great unmoving sequoias, living and broad and imposing and somber as death in their stolid immobility. Captain Thierry said to each of the children as he took one by the hand, then the other, "Take it easy there, don't be bothered, kid. The Captain knows the way." But in the confused twists through the labyrinth, over roots and bumps, the path through the trees took, the children began to sob, and James was overcome by what they felt and saw. The turns were dark and the trees tall and lowering, danger lay in every shadow, things clutched, moaned softly, spoke in sinister whispers beyond words.

He reported into Juvenile Court on Forbes, then took a bus for the north side. He walked up Federal and turned down a street of old rooming houses: no streets for a child. The grand old homes owned by the Irish ancestors who had come here almost a hundred years ago still stood majestic and painted, the porches and columns reflecting the morning light; but where he went was the other north side. The morning sunshine on the narrow street mocked the garbage cans on the sidewalks, the dangerous doorways and the sagging door frames. Toothless people stared at him. He nodded. He knew the tug of war ahead. Mrs. Dubrinia with one son sentenced to an indeterminate time in Thorn Hill, the juvenile facility for lawbreakers under eighteen, would wrestle with James to have her fifteen-year-old daughter commited temporarily to a mental institution and returned home in ninety days. Otherwise, the daughter's drug use and kleptomania would have her incarcerated like the son for an indefinite period with a prison record on the young woman's already long, sad history. She argued, as did many of the parents James saw in the course of his interminable failing efforts, to keep the child out of jail on the less than persuasive argument that they were better off at home. There was no Mr. Dubrinia, perhaps in this case an argument for a more stable home situation for his daughter of record: Mr. Dubrinia held up gas stations by trade.

James walked up the unpainted wooden steps to her second-floor apartment, and Mrs. Dubrinia cleared off the dishes and cigarettes from breakfast on the kitchen table.

A tall woman in a housecoat, she ran to change, indicating she understood the formality of Captain Thierry's visit. Her apprehension had the theatrical quality, James thought, of the make or break about it. Winning the lottery. She fluttered and looked at him: having the daughter home was important to her, maybe redemption for the daughter loading up a stolen suitcase in Gimbel's with perfumes and small radios and trying to walk out the front door.

"You know, Captain," she said, dressed now in a cotton dress of large sunflowers, "nobody in their right minds would do a thing like that, walking through them revolving doors like they were going to Monte Carlo for a vacation. She was begging to be caught, given medical attention and tranquilizers to calm her down from antisocial conduct."

"Or stupid," James said. "Stupid is not crazy."

"Stupid is a kind of mentally impaired."

"Then we build more pharmacies and give up the prison business altogether."

"Murderers and the like: put them in jail, not kids like Donna. She needs pills to calm her down."

"But Mrs. Dubrinia, even taking pills, you know this isn't an environment to raise a kid. You don't have a job. You're on welfare, Donna has no future—maybe jail time will give her a trade, some sense of responsibility."

He was performing; he was stressing, however inadequately, the mother's responsibility in saving her daughter, giving the woman an even more important finish to her drama. She must understand that there would come a time when there would be no further chances for the girl, defeat staved off but near. He had already decided to recommend psychiatric evaluation, perhaps a month of counseling, and then the daughter's release to her mother.

Mrs. Dubrinia began to softly weep. "She'll come out a hardened criminal," she said.

"Don't cry, Mrs. Dubrinia."

"Call me Irene, Captain, please."

"Okay, Irene, don't cry."

"Captain, have you ever been lonely, do you know what loneliness like a bug in your hair feels like? You can't shake it?"

"I know the feeling."

"I have it now."

"Let's have a cup of coffee. I'd like a cup of coffee."

"You would? So would I."

She had long blond hair and twenty years ago she had been handsome. Her features still held the last of a purpose to them, the nose and chin amounting to a face of the sort in old movies, resolute but wounded, stark and not deceptive—but plenty of chicanery in the eyes, quick to watch the movements of his hands, his posture as he sat at the kitchen table crossing his legs. On a fine morning with few preliminaries he quietly had coffee with Irene Dubrinia, a woman waiting to be one hundred on his list.

"I know what it is to be lonely," he said, reaching across the table to touch her neck where it met her chin.

She quickly took his hand and kissed it.

He stood and went to where she sat and leaned over her to kiss her on the cheek, but she turned her face and kissed him on the lips. He slid his hand down her shoulder to her bust and realized with the movement that a strangeness had fallen on him. He had never in his attempts to enter with mercy and justice the lives of his desperate clients really entered the living, breathing air of their misery. Protecting them had been a vigil observed through a bulletproof window. He could only pretend to be with them; at the end of their particular drama he was still himself, Thierry at the Irish Club, in his apartment, attending Mass with his own memories of failures, real enough but nothing with the hot breath of endless catastrophe in it. Kissing Irene, touching her, there was no barrier between their wretchedness and his safety.

She clutched his hand. "Can I call you James?" she asked. And she stood and held him close and he held her too and stroked her back and then let his hand pull her closer.

"It's fine, honey," she said, pulling him toward the bedroom. They walked to the bedroom, and she said softly, "James."

He let her remove her dress and underclothes quickly and somberly, in too much thought, sat on the edge of the room's double bed. The stark metal lamp on the table became real to him. There was a dresser. He saw every scar in the old wood. In the mirror over the dresser he saw on the glass clouds framing it. No sharp image would ever reflect in that dime store mirror. He closed his eyes, knowing this was wallpaper he would remember a long time, and realized for fleeting seconds now that he was counting again, tumbling, but now with a miser's passion, coins piled up as foolish treasures, women numbered, days left till retirement and till death itself.

A person could not really, he thought, stop that earthly parade of injustices that approached, bowed in recognition and moved on to allow further grievances and laments to take their place in line. Only the promenades in memory of things loved could hold off the brass lamps in north side apartments, dressers with torn clothing and the shadows of erring and wandering children eternally under the threat of lifetimes of paying for the sins of gas station bandits. And the sight of himself, now in the long line to be counted with the broken noses.

He stood and said, "You're beautiful, Irene. Another time. I can't do this today."

She stood looking at him from the bed. "Is there something wrong?" she asked.

"Not with you."

"Sit here with me, honey, just relax."

"I'll sit," he said, "but it's not that."

"What is it?"

She made no move to cover her nakedness.

He sighed, and said, "Me."

"You're not just saying it."

"No, it's me."

"You don't smile much, James."

He pulled her up and to him and said, "I used to be a skater. I used to dance. I was good enough to get paid for it in the ice shows." He danced with her in the narrow bedroom, the bed and overhead lighting fixture too real.

"You really can dance, can't you? I'll bet people called you Jimmy back then."

"No, I was always called James. I guess I'm a James type."

She seized him and kissed him, and when she released him she said, "I used to be called Lulu, can you beat that? Imagine getting Lulu out of Irene; but my mother's name was Lucille. Maybe that was it: Lulu."

"I knew a Lulu."

She smiled at him and held her hands up, not reaching toward him but as if she were displaying herself as a saleswoman might, demonstrating herself with her hands. He was speechless. "Well?" she asked. "Not bad, huh?"

"No," he said, wondering whether it was James or his twin who stood in a badly lit room, shadow and Japanese screens veiling corners and tables, or was it Captain Thierry of the gliding motions and absolute confidence? He did not move, torn between desire to touch her, rub his hands along the small of her back, stroke her shoulders and push her hair forward. She watched him under heavy eyelids, looking up. "Right here," she said. "Or on the bed, James, I won't mind. You're the handsomest fellow; I swear you could have been a movie star if you wanted. There's not many like you around and I'll go places with you. James, we'd look good together and after that," she ran her hands down her body, "there'd be all this too. Honey, I'll make you happy. Lock the door if you like secrets. Go ahead, lock it, it's been yours for months and you never noticed."

He could not move, only a hand toward her.

"Don't be shy, lover, take it," she said.

Shivering, he put his hand on her shoulder, knowing he was at last where all the clergy had said he would fall if he listened to temptation, reaching to touch a woman meaningless to him but for legs, breasts, a sturdy neck, and glowing eyes. It was a hand on her neck—in a darkness more final than any he'd ever entered. But excitement there with the numbness of wrongdoing.

"Hot stuff," she said.

She was white and full, rising out of the dim room. He felt his legs tremble with emotion. He pulled her to him and said to himself proudly, You're a man ready for anything, and was interrupted in the heat of his flight by a sound. A housefly buzzed at his ear; in the gesture of driving it away he became the James Thierry he recognized, a lover of women as freely belonging to himself as in any moment of his life.

Stepping back, he said, "Oh, God." He heard the housefly somewhere else.

"I'm going to get it," the woman said, clutching at him through his pants. He jumped back and pushed her away from where she blocked the door.

"Haven't you heard of the sexual revolution?" she asked.

He had blundered with Irene into a place barely visited, even at this late date. It was not the territory of lovemaking and the women he had known from breaking into automobiles to find a place to embrace or in the time of his marriages. This was a place without him at all in it and no promise that there was the remotest quality of love there, maybe at best only the excitement of bodies, no search for the warmth at the heart of returned youth or interest beyond an undaring act. It was a damned dreary place, and he wanted to leave it, aware now all numbers of hope for him had been counted and the ceremony of counting itself could cause the sun to fog over with neglect for the immediate that sat all around him.

At the door to the steps leading out, Irene said, "You'll do what you can for Donna? I know you will."

"It's not up to me; but don't worry."

"I'll call you Jimmy, and you call me Lulu. You have a friend in me, okay, Jimmy?"

"I know," he said, thoughtful that he knew so little about what to count before passing.

Was that it? As the bus hurtled to the cold water below did what we imagine in final seconds tell us of the best that had happened? In the sorting out there to appear in brief seconds who we finally were. Walking down to the street from the wooden steps, he remembered the other Lulu from long ago: she had been ten years or more older than he was and had come in nights bright with electric bulbs on Ferris wheels to him in the room in a boardinghouse in Akron where he lodged with two other carny workers. Knowing she was coming, the two other men had agreed to stay out of the room until two in the morning, when the local bars closed, to allow James and Lulu their moment. The air on the north side as James walked to a bus stop was ripe with the promise of the coming summer. Light and soft, it shone on the porch railings and brass ornaments on the front doors of the houses he observed, the day not bowed under age or failure or remorse, on the air only the innocent pleasures of things beginning to bloom with the season.

"You're really something, James," the first Lulu had said, sitting up afterward in bed one night and looking down at him. "You look like Ronald Colman."

He had been saddened, as he so often was with compliments he could not fathom. "I used to be something," he said, dreading staleness even then, running his hand through his hair.

"Used to be! God's sake, kid, how much could you have been once, you're still a boy now? You're not twenty-one yet."

"I am twenty-one," James said, "this year," grappling even then with the mysteries of accumulation. "You don't know how many things I've done."

"Sure, baby, sure," she said. "Ain't we all?"

THREE

The Big Broadcasts

"THE STATUTE OF LIMITATIONS has run out a long time ago,"
Dickie Dunn said one night in 1956. "So I feel as safe sitting here
telling you about a crime as I would if you were all deaf and
dumb."

The uproar that night at the Ancient Order of Hibernians
wasn't enough to cause the roof to collapse; but one more shout
the length of the hall, one more foot-stomping polka, and the
pitchers would have jumped from their shelves and the electricity would have failed from loose wiring. It was a starry April
night and the excitement of weather on the loose was in the great
hall: tales told best among the members were rendered against
the sounds of a jukebox blaring "Four Leaf Clover," Sammy
Krushkin's three-piece Polka All-Americans, shouts of beer accidentally spilled in someone's lap. A quiet moment, a solemn assembly, not on this field of fable: here one competes with the

raw currents of life itself, not the literary dormant stillness of story time.

"Did you kill someone, Richard?" Pal Mahoney asked. He was necessary to a really well told story, that former Jesuit: he knew when to ask the pertinent question to cut through digression, abbreviate description, steer a man away from an excess of emotion by a curt refusal to listen to another word unless someone stuck with the facts.

"Let him talk," Cleet said.

There was general agreement among the others that Dickie be allowed to tell about the crime at his own pace in his own fashion. "Now, let's remember my statement," Dickie said. "I didn't say I committed the crime, but I don't say my testimony is hearsay either."

"In other words," Mahoney said, "there'll be no human judgment."

"What's that mean?" Cleet asked. "What has God to do with Dickie's remembering a crime?"

"There happens to be only one authority for whom any crime isn't hearsay. It's all ultimately hearsay or make-believe or interpretation, if you please: murder in the first degree, second? The murderer himself doesn't know. You know damned well who knows."

Cleet said, "I ought to get a white collar, turn it around, and call it a vocation for all the religion I get up here with my Iron City." Cleet's arm was in a bandage he would wear for two more months full time and periodically the rest of his life, the silver wire in his shoulder dancing about when rain threatened. He would never use the arm right, never play football again—or sleep a whole night through. He sat with the rest of us, each for his reasons, until dawn.

"You all know Georgie Granek?" Dickie asked and looked with great significance at me.

"The loudmouth," Vernon Scannell said.

"The Big Broadcast of 1949," Pal Mahoney added. "You can hear him six blocks away. He called my name once and I turned around as if he were at my elbow and he was a mile down at the police station on Forbes and I was at the Juvenile Court building. They call him 'The Walter Winchell Show.'"

"You know he's a gambler then," Dickie said. He bent forward across the table, his quick black eyes following us one to another. Blessed with a choir boy's angelic expression, Dickie had once played the young Oliver Twist in a play at St. Agnes and caused, so the story went, every nun in the house and even Father Farrell, that tough nut, to break into audible sobs. "People have been saying he's a high-powered gambler since I was a kid," Dickie said, "and saying he carries huge sums on him, saying it since I was a baby and I was hearing it and thinking about it."

Pal Mahoney said, "He was no real gambler. He bet a five on the Pirates when Dale Long was at the end of his home run streak and Long didn't get a hit the next five games."

Jack Hanley, the lawyer, came silently to the table and joined us, nodding about.

"I was a kid I'm saying to you," Dickie said. "This was seven years ago: I was fourteen and Clifton here was—what were you?"

"Fourteen," I said, unhappy to be called to witness to Dickie's strange tale, as everyone turned to look at me.

"Clifton can vouch for every word I say," Dickie said.

"Wait a minute!" I cried. "I don't know what you're going to say. How can I testify to what I haven't heard?"

"You know what I'm going to say," Dickie said. "Indeed, you do," and of course, I did.

If ever a man demanded to be murdered, it was generally agreed, Georgie Granek, the Walter Winchell Show, was the prime candidate. It was not in his appearance. Standing flush to the corners where he orated nightly, he seemed, snapshot-posed, to be like other men of his age and time. Returned from the U.S. Navy in 1945, later still unmarried at fifty, to spoil the flat truth of a snapshot, he was balding, barrel-chested, muscled, and held by day a foreman's job in a grimy tire warehouse. He arrived in Oakland every night like an on-stage prima donna in full-throated aria, clean and barbered to repudiate the day's toil with his Niagara of talk, talk, talk. And that money he carried, so undeserved by the bragging lout, was where the homicidal impulse was stirred even in men like Pal Mahoney or the saintly Billy Noonen, who left Oakland young to be a missionary as if to establish early what we all knew to be his heavenly credentials.

Granek was a terrible loser and fought the name as if it were a dragon with hot breath on Forbes Street. Women, dice, World War II, age (he'd offer once a night to fistfight some youth three decades younger than he was on some offense of manner, not requiring substance to be challenged), family, geography—he made himself contemptible in all our eyes. While the rest of us gave a frequent but faint bow to the possibility of success beckoning us in some ripe maturity that lay ahead, I don't think we deceived ourselves. What else was the lesson to be learned from the life around us at the Irish Club? Even the brilliant minds at that moment six blocks away at the University of Pittsburgh Medical School discovering vaccines against polio or hitting eight homers in as many games for the Pirates that season at

Forbes Field. Why, quite simply—it was almost stated—life was a series of postponements, hedgings against the moment when we all had to accept it that we hadn't accomplished much. We believed in Heaven as a last resort.

Georgie Granek argued with the menace in the night air breathing too close on his prejudices: Pittsburgh was the finest place to live; women, he had never met one who wasn't a whore at heart; family, he came from men who worked at Jones and Laughlin sixteen hours a day, drank six more, and slept two and toiled, whored, and drank till their eighties, and that was good; and, deadly to his future on the planet, his love of money. He claimed he carried around never less than two thousand.

Of course, generations grew up wondering how they could separate Granek from his cache.

It fell to Billy Noonen and Dickie Dunn to try to make the dream of acquisition a reality. A meditation as sweet as honey: one night as Granek staggered home after talking for four hours about his meager accomplishments, to leap from a doorway, one holding his arms, another quick as a bat dancing about his body, into his pants pocket, removing his belt lest the cash be there, pulling off his shoes to see if they concealed his fortune, and like the brilliant summer lightning of our youth making arcs over our heads in ripeness and promise of unending Junes, vanishing away in darkness, now rich, even noble to have bested the braggart. By the time the boys revealed the scheme to me it had grown in their imaginations until the money had already gone to deserving mothers and sisters without dowry, nephews with teeth that needed straightening, and perhaps a cashmere sweater for themselves as agents of such good.

"He'll fight like a tiger," I said, postponing my flat denial.

"There'll be three of us," Billy said. He was a frail youth, thin-chested, and his curly brown hair made ringlets about his pale triangular face.

"Two," I said. "I'll be sitting right here listening to the Polka All-Americans while you two start down the road for twenty years at Blaw Knox."

"Come on," Dickie said, "we're asking you because you're a logical mind. Can't you see it?"

"No."

Billy said, "There's nobody at the Irish Club we hold high like you, Clifton. If you turn us down we're lost."

Put that way to me at fourteen I felt myself imperiled: I could turn my back on larceny. But could I disrupt their dreams and mine of a man to be trusted in a pinch?

"No."

"My nephew goes through life looking like a monkey," Billy said, tears coming to his eyes. "It would take three hundred dollars to give him a future. It's killing my sister: she says it's a curse from her being born to my father. Visited, you know, on little Louis."

"Oh, Christ," I said.

"Georgie won't complain," Dickie said. "The man in question won't say a word about it. First, people'd think it was the usual lie. Second, we'd be heroes if it ever got out—which it wouldn't. Third, mind, he'd be too ashamed to admit he was bested and, fourth, if anyone ever heard of it, Mister Mister would be a target for every tramp kid in Oakland who needs two dollars to go bowling at the Strand. Clifton, it's a matter of six minutes' work and as safe as the sidewalk out there."

I said, "I'll think about it."

Two weeks passed and mercifully, I didn't hear a word from either boy. I thought, I'm saved: they forgot it. Or one fell in love. Or was able to borrow a season pass to the Pirates games and I'll never hear of it again. But, no, on Saturday night, two days after the Fourth of July, the two conspirators pulled me to a corner table at the Oakland Cafe and Dickie clutched my forearm. "We ain't forgotten," Dickie said.

"No, we ain't," Billy said.

I see Billy's face before me: he left for the seminary about a year after these events and his face as he shook hands with all of us, his widowed mother sobbing as we said good-bye to him at the bus station, was no paler or more lit with spiritual claims than at that moment. Poor Billy looked saintly at birth and he left us celebrated for virtue, probably with only a vile thought or two about Georgie Granek, untouched by the world as if he had been chosen for a certain, kind eternity for his spotlessness. Looking at me with those eyes already marked with the grand beyond, Billy said, "We've been putting together a modus operandi. We've been following the boaster about, estimating his comings and goings. We got him pegged. He shows up in Oakland at seven-thirty, quarter to eight every weeknight. He takes a trolley home to the South Side every night at a quarter to eleven except for Wednesday nights. Wednesday nights he walks home. Don't ask me why. Wednesday nights he sets out down Forbes and walks home."

"How do you know he's going directly home?" I asked.

Billy looked about in astonishment. "Where would he go?" he asked. "Where's he got to go on foot?"

"Maybe he has a girlfriend down in Soho," I said, stalling.

Dickie sat back. "We have to follow him this Wednesday, Billy," he said. "Clifton, you have a logical mind."

I felt slightly relieved again, but the following Thursday I stayed away from the usual places, walking through the Carnegie Museum till it closed at nine, then taking a trolley for downtown. But as the trolley rode down Forbes, stopping at the Gammons at the corner of Atwood in Oakland, there stood Billy and Dickie Dunn. "Clifton," they shouted. "Clifton—boy!" I walked to the front of the car and alighted at Coltart and slowly walked back to Atwood where, I thought, my fate lay.

Telling the story precisely as I have related it here, Dickie Dunn looked at me closely in the Irish Club seven years later. "Is there a word of untruth I've uttered thus far?" he asked.

"Not one," I said. "Remind everyone though that we were fourteen."

"We were fourteen," Dickie said. "Damn it, millions dead since then. What's it all mean?"

I saw Georgie about in the following week after I had talked to Billy and Dickie and I tried to discover where he kept his money by the way he stood or walked. But there was no method of getting past his harangue. "She stood, you know, like this," Georgie said as I moved forward to listen, "and I almost knocked her teeth out right there—did she think I was off the farm not to know what she was selling?" He usually owned the corner before the Briar Bowl on summer nights, his eyes following the young women from the university, occasionally interrupting himself to snort at one in appreciation or disdain. "I said," Georgie declaimed, "'How much?' and she said, 'What do you mean, sailor?' and I damn near threw her right through the window of that Hong Kong saloon. 'Why, it's the way you smell, lady,' I said. 'I can smell three-dollar whores when our ship is out to sea five miles.' You can, you know, you can smell them if you got any kind of experience at all."

I backed away into the crowd, hearing Granek say, "They don't fool me."

He was big and moved gracefully. I wondered if the three of us, given Billy's precarious state, Dickie's uncertain passion, and my reluctance for the task, would be enough to subdue the man. Would we become some part of another miraculous tale of his, to be brought out and displayed on the Briar Bowl corner long after we were gone from Oakland, a fragment in the uncanny year in which he had whipped three punks who had tried to assault him? Caused them to crawl bleeding and finally in handcuffs up to Number Four where they sat in a cell without bail? The prospect was not pleasant and I spent a restless week and met Billy and Dickie the next Wednesday night.

They were both pale. It was a warm night and their faces glowed with perspiration, the Irish Club relying on its open windows, air-conditioning not having arrived yet. The overhead fans mocked the low-lying heat in the room. A weeknight, the place was empty except for us.

"He disappeared," Dickie blurted.

"Oh," I said, thankful that the loudmouth had resources for evading pursuers. So that was to be the path by which we eluded our ill fortune; Georgie would simply escape us by stealth, allowing us our dreams with none of the penalties of reality. "Then he's up to tricks, the bastard?" I asked, not quick to douse the fire finally. "We should have known. Well, it seemed too good to be true."

"No!" Billy cried. "Dickie is saying he disappeared."

"Vanished," Dickie said.

"Gave us the slip," I said, as if ruefully.

"I'm saying to you one second he was there," Dickie said, "and the next he was gone."

"Oh," I said, "hearing your footsteps, he found a doorway and quick as a wink he dove into it. Faster than the eye could see."

"No," Billy said, "it was on the Brady Street Bridge to the South Side, him and all that money walking along, fast down Forbes to Soho, the rat nests down there with all the unsavory types on their doorsteps watching him, and us eight feet behind him, and then on the bridge. Then, as we watched, he disappeared."

"Well, he didn't jump over the bridge railing," I said.

"He didn't," Dickie said. "He did not."

"Where did he go?"

"He vanished, I'm saying to you," Dickie said. "Mister Mister just disappeared. In the middle of the bridge he was there same as the three of us this minute and the next he wasn't, Billy and me alone on the bridge with only the Allegheny River under us and the sound of the 77/54 streetcar somewhere."

Seven years later, at the table where we sat in the Ancient Order of Hibernians, Pal Mahoney asked, "Excuse me, is this a ghost story you're telling us?"

"How do I know?" Dickie asked. "You tell me."

"Well—" Mahoney began, but Jack Hanley, who had gone to Notre Dame while Mahoney was at Lowain, said, "Just a minute, Pal, we're not ready to classify Dickie's tale yet. It seems to me a vanishing isn't a ghost story. Where's the ghost?"

Mahoney said, "Why, the real fellow, the braggart."

Hanley saw an edge. "We haven't heard the whole story. I don't usually make up my mind until I have all the information." He had become a lawyer at Notre Dame and Pal had returned from his Jesuitical studies to become a travel agent. The two men grappled over who had the facts until one could almost see data assembled and collated before one's eyes, tossed about like a bone between two dogs. Once they had argued all night: I woke and slept, woke again, and they still battled. It was 1944, I remember, Mahoney said it was a vital question for an intelligent person to deduce, knowing how many angels could dance on the head of a pin. It was a question of individuation. Knowing the size of an angel, a person might accurately learn to have some insight into the proportions of God. Or the spiritual dimensions of a man. Hanley had slammed his fist into the table, knocking over a pitcher of beer, shouting, "Look out at the dancing angels on the floor, you jackass. That's the only proportions you're ever supposed to learn!" Awakened from my drifting sleep, I saw Nora Flynn dancing a two-step, by herself appropriately; she was a widow, both of her children having left her; Corny Cornfield alone and swaying to a three-in-the-morning melody in his head; a boy named Paul Rabbit near virtual penetration whispering into the ear of a girl with smudged lipstick whose name I did not know. It was the usual fairy dancers who drifted to the juke-box tunes to hold off the dawn even as the rest of us drank beer and debated; and, indeed, to this day, I wish I knew the dancers' proportions better.

Of course, on the following Wednesday, my curiosity eating me, I went with Dickie Dunn in pursuit of Georgie Granek. Billy strolled eight feet behind us. As absurd as the notion seems today, I silently prayed Georgie would disappear so that the three of us would not have to fall on him. And then I offered another prayer: that he would not. If the braggart vanished, what became of natural law? The parting of the Red Sea? Were miracles so cheap in a universe that went untold miles beyond the Milky Way that they could occur on the Brady Street Bridge to a despicable half-ape like the Walter Winchell Show?

The bridge lights shone in the darkness and the air was thick with soot. It was not, in truth, a perfect night for visibility; but we could see him well enough, wearing a jaunty white cap, white shoes, distinct in the thick night. The stars were obscure overhead, but lights from the South Side rippled with the water's flow below us. The Allegheny made a slight murmuring sound and there before us, yes, the loudmouth vanished.

"You three had committed a crime of the heart," Vernon Scannell said. "But you were saved."

"Clifton will testify," Dickie said, and I nodded. "It happened."

"You were all three scared to death," Cleet said, "and you suffered a mutual hallucination that allowed you to get out of robbing Georgie."

Jack Hanley shrugged his shoulders and said, "It's not a ghost story with a meaning to it."

Pal said, "Indeed, it is. Georgie Granek is, as the saying goes, all talk. It's a rare case: I believe the man disappears when there's no one about to listen to him."

Hanley wore his customary suit and tie. He liked his appearances at the Irish Club to be viewed as sort of ceremonial visits as if the rest of us were there as inhabitants and he was a visitor passing through, groomed, pressed, on his way somewhere else. "Do you see that fellow there," he said, and pointed to an old man sitting in a corner alone none of us knew except by sight. We all nodded; was he going to disappear? "His name is Roscoe Fallon," Hanley said. "And perhaps thirty years ago you'd have known him by name and sight. He used to own a tailor shop here in Oakland, and he took bets on baseball games, nothing serious, but he was a bettor. And you know in the thirties Babe Ruth hit all three of his record-breaking home runs in Forbes

Field. Well, the Babe took a liking to Roscoe, used to come into his place—it used to be next to the Cozy Tavern in the thirties, on Oakland Avenue. Babe Ruth took his suits there to be cleaned and he struck up a friendship with Roscoe and one day he told Fallon, 'Bet the farm on it, kid, I'm going over the fence tomorrow.' Well, Roscoe put together every cent he had, about forty thousand dollars, quite a sum for those days, and took bets anywhere he could at three to one, which was sucker's odds, it should have been ten to one. The rest is in the books: Babe Ruth did it. And the night before he broke the record two years later for the most home runs in a season, he came to Roscoe, and he said, 'Put your money on it, kid, I'm going to make history to-morrow,' and Roscoe put together a hundred and fifty thousand dollars and took odds of five to one. The last record in 1938, the Babe came in to the shop on that morning and asked Roscoe, 'How you fixed, kid?' and Roscoe said, 'Fine, Babe, fine,' and Babe Ruth said, 'Well, I ain't feeling as great as I was last time I touted you, but knowing you trust me means a lot to me. Mort-gage it all; I'll do it today.' And Roscoe became a millionaire. He never said a word about it and I only know because he told Ned Rafferty, who was his nephew and up at Notre Dame with me and one night as Ned and I are walking across the quadrangle at Vespers he tells me this remarkable story. Well, look at the old fellow. He's been everywhere. Ned says he was with Jean Harlow and Mary Pickford out in Hollywood and he and Douglass Fair-banks used to go boating. Mary Miles Minter, God rest her soul, the rest, Roscoe knew them all and was one of them. Howard Hughes, him. Lindbergh called him in a bad time. But he's a quiet man, enjoys a drink in peace, and he came back to Oak-land. Ned says he saw it with his own eyes when he was a kid, in the parlor, Governor Duff and Roscoe having a whiskey one afternoon. Ned's the only family he has, and here he sits, a few old cronies, Duddy McCabe, old Doc Pierce. Sits by himself mostly. It's like his mouth is sewn tight. I've been watching him for years and I never heard him utter a syllable. It's not a story well known. I don't know if he has fifteen cents put away or he owns this city block and comes here to look over his property."

Seeing us all turn in what must have been wide-eyed amazement at the toothless old fellow, he stood unsteadily and made his slow exit to the door, doomed to carry about with him, tight against his skin like his none-too-clean shirt, the enchanted truth of his adventures, all glimpsed in a thick haze and never really known. Perhaps he waved. Or perhaps it was an old man's gesture, coat too big for him, shoes too large, he adjusted himself to antiquity and blessed the smoky room in passing with an airy gesture of his hand, mute and glorious. I listened for his footsteps, but Doris Day sang "Sentimental Journey" on the jukebox and I heard only the sense, not the sound, of the life of the never-to-be-recorded.

Walter Winchell has passed from a radio time when his urgent words brought millions to him in a spell: all the big broadcasts alerting us to Nazis, sinking ships and airplanes ablaze over foreign soil, and all of it somehow connected to living rooms in Pittsburgh and Kansas City. And scandal holding listeners prisoner, promised and implied, the majesty of the born storyteller, not much point to the terror and awe inspired beyond that of the moment's paralysis of will as auditors shrank to less than themselves in the listening and expanded too gripped in the consciousness of another's story, in thrall. Other claims are made on our attention, one dead bard replaced by other voices on the air as we are connected to disembodied stories: Georgie Granek, corner impresario of lies as transparent as air and yet gifted with the mesmeric enchantment that follows the teller like cigar smoke after the person reciting the terms of our bondage has passed.

We watched Roscoe go, bobbing between tables, each step as he hit the wooden floor requiring a bounce and a shuffle. How strangely the unheard melodies of old Roscoe's silence fell in the raucous music of the Walter Winchell Show's forgotten women, named by him nightly; Georgie's cousins and a sister, who had betrayed him; his father, who was celebrated on street corners on the hour for beating him when he was a boy with unearthly punishments; sailors he had cold-cocked; and bosses he had insulted on leaving a job, all to be honored loudly each in turn while he declaimed them, lost rhymes to speak now only in the voice of the wind, as unenunciated as one dusty particle from another. "Mother of God," Cleet said, watching old Roscoe shuffle, sag, right himself, and stagger to the door, the weight of wealth and experience and importance invisible in the sad, almost gone all-time winner among us, "I'd have given the old bum a quarter by the look of him and never knew anyone in this place ever had a connection to history."

Mum's-the-word Roscoe, finally too a well of only echoes, all of the proud fermentation of green shoots and moonlight that raises by morning flowers and men of the purest sun and none of it, like the true history of Cleet, Dickie, Pal, Corny Sullivan, and me, ever to be recorded, not spoken, remembered less by the minute in one failing memory or other.

FOUR

Adventurer

RODERICK SHEEHAN was born with a heart that ran to a meter of its own, beating away in a rhythm known only to itself, and, as a result of his infirmity, he was coddled remarkably by his doting mother and his aunt Alys. He never played roughhouse games with other children, instead allowing his mother to invite small girls or frail boys like himself to their house on Ward Street. They played bouncing jacks and card games, dressed up in costumes, and there were cupcakes and milk for everyone at five before the children were promptly ushered out. A widow, Roderick's mother stood at the window waiting for him to come from school; his maiden aunt had followed him surreptitiously home from grade school to junior high for years, protecting him against street hoodlums, other youths his age with stouter hearts, and automobile traffic too strenuous for his incapacity.

When he was thirteen, he fell in one Saturday afternoon in

October with a group of older boys, Toots Kiley, Bronco Kelly, Regis Parkes, and Lenny McLeod. He joined them near the Morgan Street cemetery while they plotted a raid. They would swoop down from Allequippa Street and attack the enemy at Pitt Stadium. Gathering momentum in a pack, they would assail the boys from other neighborhoods who sold football souvenirs in front of the stadium. It was the Friday before the Pitt–Notre Dame game, and it rankled the boys from Robinson, Dunseith, and Allequippa that strangers from other parts of the city came into Oakland—onto the streets where they lived and walked every day—and sold things to the people attending the games. It was not the crowds coming to witness the game (although there might be a fight picked there with a spectator from time to time, someone who was acting too smart for his own good), it was the day of the Notre Dame game itself. The annual excitement rose as the two schools of everyone's youth in Oakland clashed in autumn: a secret, uncomfortably good feeling when Pitt, the home team, won—with the bad spell that fell on a person at the same time to know that a great Catholic football team from the best Catholic school in America had been nationally disgraced. The joy and fear, the blood ringing, the big day brought down the boys who lived on Robinson, Dunseith, Allequippa, and Terrace, that awful sense of being left out more than ever. They played no part in it. They would not attend Pitt; they had no part of the girls and the corsages, the ruddy-faced men in overcoats with fur collars who trudged like a conquering army up the hill to the Pitt Stadium. And they were not of the parties who piled out of automobiles from Ohio and West Virginia, as far away as Wisconsin and Michigan, to cheer on Notre Dame. The boys did not know who these people were. They exuded power in their Irish bearing, bluff and short-nosed, and their women carried green scarves and green pillows to sit on and, Roderick knew the bad feeling, between the two schools' partisans he and the boys were as invisible as the dust that blew alongside the curb that ran up the street adjoining Pitt Stadium.

But if they could not fall on the people who went to the Pitt–Notre Dame game or one of the other Pitt contests, they could in a howling body attack the boys selling souvenirs. There was no permit or license necessary. Anyone could put together a few strips of wood, tack a cloth to the strips, and pin on the Notre Dame or Pitt buttons or little footballs with a ribbon of green or blue and yellow. The strangers sold them for whatever they could get: usually fifty cents a souvenir or a dollar for a pennant, varying, selling drunks the pennants for five dollars and a football for a dollar. Convincing themselves that the boys from other neighborhoods were crooked—Jews, Syrians, and Italians—and they had somehow to represent honor in Oakland, they annually planned raids. Sometimes they schemed in a body to rob the other boys of their ill-gotten gains, sometimes merely to humiliate them by ripping up their boards, throwing their souvenirs about and landing a punch or two. On the day of the game, Oakland boys sulked, parking cars and jeering later at the crowds from a safe distance seated on the hoods of automobiles. They grumbled at the day while police moved them on.

Listening, Roderick knew this year a historic raid was going to happen before Pitt Stadium in a wild outburst that would be talked about for years. People would remember this run. At thirteen he was the youngest boy present. Lenny McLeod, who was sixteen, had done it before three times, and when the subject of the Pitt–Notre Dame game came up, he was always listened to with respect as an authority who had fought the marvelous battle himself. He had become a part of the lore of the game. "Lenny was there," someone would say, and Lenny'd comment not only on the rush before the stadium but the scores of the game and the quarterbacking. So on the morning of the game Roderick went to the small empty lot on top of Dunseith, where it met Morgan near the cemetery, dressed in a jacket and a heavy scarf. He wore gloves, for punching if need be.

Only Lenny and Lenny's cousin, a boy slightly older than Roderick named Bobby, were there. Of the rest who had made plans, one would say later his mother had insisted he take his sister to a dental appointment; another said he had injured his ankle and knew he would be a burden to the attackers and sat with his foot elevated to prepare for a raid on the strangers when Southern Methodist came to play Pitt; and Toots had overslept, not waking until four in the afternoon. Alone on the windy hill with Lenny McLeod and his cousin, Roderick knew the afternoon had failed, but Lenny insisted they make the run without everyone being there. "These bastards have to learn they ain't welcome," Lenny said, rubbing his knuckles.

Running wildly down the hill alongside Pitt Stadium, the three boys shouted like Hopi Indians, Roderick feeling that this night he would know what being a man meant, but with the exhilaration as he heard his feet pounding on the pavement, the tightness in his chest, the twisting of his head, and the startled faces of people walking up the hill, it all still had the same taste of being a kid to it. This was the way boys ran. This hill belonged to those slow, laughing people with the women in lipstick and rouge and wearing green corsages—and to the peddlers selling them souvenirs. He was still a child running loosely, waiting for an adult to call him to order. He ran to a child's purpose. Adults in fur-lined gloves with women in heels watched and were distant.

Lenny seized a boy selling souvenirs and twisted him about. His cousin punched the boy. Roderick ran past them and shouted, "Cops, it's the cops," pleased to see Lenny and his cousin leave the souvenir salesmen and join him. The three ran through the throng making their way up the hill to the gates. At the foot of the hill they ran across Fifth and did not stop until Oakland Avenue. Leaning forward in spasms of breath catching and coughing, they regained their bearings.

"I'm glad you seen the cops," Bobby said.

"I saw them the same time Roderick did," Lenny McLeod said.

"Big bastards!"

"He was making right for us," Roderick said, thinking perhaps there had really been a cop. He himself had seen no one approaching but had realized as they ran he was parading the little-rat feeling on Notre Dame Saturday that had possessed him since he was a young child. It was no way to be one of the boys he admired: to dash about in public display to show the world you didn't belong there. Roderick got credit for knocking down one of the peddlers' boards, making up the crash and the look on the fellow's face and maybe telling a good story was how a boy got to feel that he was welcome to sit at the table with older people. It was Lenny McLeod who baptized him later that day, on the football afternoon of confusion and fabrication. "You should have seen Ramrod go through the mutts," he said of Roderick to the other boys. "They was scattered like bowling pins when he hit them like a fullback."

Roderick himself from that moment on was "Ramrod Sheehan," believing a dozen enemies had tumbled before his mighty
charge on an afternoon when he was only thirteen.

With the daily adulation from his mother and aunt, their
repeating choice things he had said and pasting up the crayon
drawings he made, Ramrod grew into a stout young man,
hunched with thick, fat shoulders, unable to play at athletic
games and wandering about the Irish Club nightly or prowling
on Forbes on weekends, asking any of the regulars, "Hey guys,
what do you say we go out and get some girls?"

At home, he sat daily listening to his aunt and mother discuss
him, content to be with them. "Roderick always had the ability
to remember things," Aunt Alys said. "He used to see a person
once—and he couldn't have been three years old—and he'd ask
a month later, 'Where's Mr. O'Brien?' He was a little man, not
at all like a toddler." Aunt Alys had her chances but she wanted,
it was said, a man as religious as herself but with a sense of humor. It was not a common combination; she and Ramrod's
mother had shared a dour father, and Ramrod's father himself
had taken life very seriously. His mind was like a cabinet with
shelves and small cupboards for everything. When he departed
at quite an advanced age, having married late, many people
thought he had left in his eighties because it was an orderly time
to go. Sober, he stood in a picture on the piano before a potted
palm in a dark brown room, serious (one child, no more), a
hardware business behind him where every lock and screw was
known to his mind, and a wife at arm's length after thirteen years
of marriage. He left Ramrod's mother with an adequate sum—
she did not work—and a capacity for love that had never been
fulfilled in the old man's time on earth. She loved Ramrod with
the passion of a sweetheart and the devotion of a wife. She felt

for him the abiding concern of a mother and the wild reckless-
ness of one of the Boylan sisters, who all had loving hearts. Between Aunt Alys and his mother, Ramrod grew to search and
pursue welcome and appreciation from the very air itself.

He was sixteen when he told his mother and aunt he was now
a man and he'd choose his friends, but he knew he was wanted
only for his Ford, the only car available to his classmates and
drinking partners at the Irish Club. Not that the young men he
traveled with could have owned cars if there were not a war in
Europe and the Pacific: he was the magnet around whom the
boys moved. He drove about the make-out artists, the athletes,
the restless, the scufflers, and the pool sharks who had a livey out
in East Liberty and needed a ride. He was delighted to chauffeur
the fellows who just liked to take a drive out in the evening
during the war years and to shout out the windows at girls on
the sidewalk.

"Say, baby, is that real or are you carrying cantaloupes home?"
Dinky Cairns would shout, and, without waiting for a reply,
Ramrod would jam the accelerator, and away down Brookline
Avenue the Ford would fly. Never would Ramrod know such
laughter, tears of pleasure in his eyes, the car loaded with boys
pounding each other in glee. Praying weekly for the souls of dead
servicemen, he felt a great guilt wash over him that these were
probably the happiest days of his life.

Prohibited from taxing his frail heart, Ramrod became the
equipment manager for the football team at Schenley High. He
was with the football players in adversity and victory, cheered
and known by name as if he had run a hundred yards with an
intercepted pass. Accounting for the towels, the shoulder pads,
and the jerseys and seeing to it that all was counted and sorted,
he still had a privileged seat in the afternoons in the bleachers to

watch the team work out. He listened carefully to the coaches' instructions to the players. He remembered each injunction. At home before a mirror he practiced putting his shoulder down and blocking an onrushing tackle. He saw himself as an offensive guard. He wore football jerseys with the team's maroon-and-white colors and the name "Ramrod" on the back.

In the twelfth grade at the awards banquet at Webster Hall he was awarded a letter for football and given a jacket, which he wore proudly night and day.

They were days of sweet company, always a guy around to talk to, fellows to ride down to the big Isaly's on the Boulevard with and drink milkshakes in a host that took up three tables. Later, in his Ford, he returned each of the players to his doorstep with a wave and a "Watch your dong!" On Saturday, as night gathered, he asked around for where the guys were going to find girls and with the regulars, or maybe a football player from school, drive up to Webster Hall and hang around the wedding parties there or go downtown to the Roosevelt Hotel and crash an office party or a wedding, out to the South Side in the Ford to one of the Polish Falcons' lodges or maybe to the Irish Club. Inquiring "Where's the girls?" Ramrod landed first on arrival at the bar wherever he went and then, while the others danced and made come-on talk with girls, Ramrod noisily drank himself into a stupor. He made friends at the bar, he argued baseball statistics and yardage, he described Steeler games he had seen, movies he had witnessed, told tall tales to strangers about women he had had, and with every breath savored the time of his life in a whirl of people who didn't know him for the mama's (and auntie's) boy that he was.

Dutifully, he would drive the friend he had come with to the home of the girl his friend had picked up, wait patiently as if it were his adventure, and then drive his friend home, listening to the details.

He woke late on Sunday mornings and, shaving for Mass, had the feeling that he had had a wonderful night the night before. He did it Saturdays all through the twelfth grade and on to the summer after he graduated. Waking Sunday morning hungover and tired, his mother's and aunt's eyes censorious, he basked in how he looked to the world: a fellow who got around, friends, a fast life, drink, new places, sturdy, strong looking with what must have appeared to a stranger's eyes thighs and calves like an oak tree, bull-necked. Holding his stomach slightly in, he walked on his toes like a man carrying about dynamite in his shoulders and fists, explosives too volatile for him not to walk any way but with an athlete's grace lest he cause havoc by a sudden movement. He strode about like a panther on the prowl Saturday nights and Sundays through the long summer after graduation, seeing his friends scatter into new jobs, a few to college, and some into the army.

When he himself went to the U.S. Army office in the county court building to answer to his draft notice he was—as he knew he would be—turned down because of that heartbeat that had made him dance to its erratic tune up to that moment. He went across Grant Street to the U.S. Marine recruiting office and insisted he wanted a physical. He told the story many times afterward. He had tried to enlist in the marines, had offered to serve in any way the corps wanted to use him, but had been turned down.

Coming home at four in the morning in the summer, he felt annoyed to find his mother and aunt about on mysterious errands, knowing they had waited up for him, but he let himself be pacified by them as they made him eggs and bacon and talked about his dead father and an infant daughter his mother had lost: on the balls of his feet, walking about the familiar living room on Ward, like an untamed horse, he thought, he felt most himself as his mother and Aunt Alys watched and approved of what a fine man he had become. The nighttime Ramrod and the mama's boy were one in that big room with the picture of the Madonna over the mantel, the fringed lamp, and the ship in the hallway painting battling against an ever-angry sea.

His aunt bought him underwear and when his mother washed the shorts and undershirts she starched them. Ramrod liked the tight underwear, the feel of its closeness. It gave him, he thought, an edge. It was a reminder of something strong; it made him feel complete. The smell of the starch, the closeness of the fit, the sureness of the Jockey supply: Aunt Alys had bought the shorts and undershirts for him since he was a toddler and they were to Ramrod somehow part of the real him under the jerseys and the athletic jackets of his manhood. Often, when he went with the boys to a white whorehouse out in New Kensington, before he climbed into bed with the prostitute, he lingered about in the blue shorts his aunt had bought, the tight clean undershirt that showed off his shoulders, but the whores never noticed. No one ever knew, he supposed, what he was really like except his mother and aunt, and even they saw only part of the complicated picture. For the rest, no one, he thought sadly, knew him.

But he put aside the vagrant melancholy thought when he took a job out on Neville Island. It was patriotic work. He became an apprentice machinist, wearing overalls to work every day and a white T-shirt—and making big money. Every two weeks he took home five hundred dollars. The waves of quiet he felt on Sunday morning consumed him sometimes all through the week. "Here we are," he'd say to a stranger at a bar, "lapping

it up while our boys are dying. I tried to join the marine corps—
more than once—and I'm still living off the land and our boys
are out there this minute." He occasionally was revolted by the
good feeling, the rolling in honey mornings and nights he lived
in, the noise and dancing, the great times—never to be repeated
when Hitler fell—while the world outside of Ramrod Sheehan
had sons dying in the flaming North Atlantic. He thought of the
split in himself between the good times he was having and the
terrors of the war as the great sorrow of his life and then, at a
wedding at the Polish Falcons' Hall on the South Side, met the
girl of his dreams. He was, he told everyone, ready to get married
anyhow. The bachelor life wasn't as free and easy as people made
it out to be.

He married Stella Bialek of Dormont in May 1945, two weeks
after the war officially ended in Europe. He took it all as somehow connected, leaving behind his carefree youth with a good
marriage, the joys of friendships, and being an adventurer in
Pittsburgh during World War II. It all came together: the end of
the terrible war and the dawn of responsibility as a husband and
father. Above all, Stella understood him: she knew he wasn't the
roughneck of the big shoulders and the athletic grace, a tough
guy, the two-fisted man's man as so many people saw him. The
first time he had danced with her during the wedding of a girl
she worked with (she was small, golden-haired with ringlets
framing her pale white face, and with a slight limp), she said she
thought he was very sensitive. She herself read a great deal and
she liked to talk about books. She worked as a cashier in the
restaurant of the Pittsburgher Hotel downtown and, like Ramrod, lived with her widowed mother.

He talked to her all night at the Polish Falcons and gave up
his friends in Oakland, driving nightly over to Dormont and

sitting with Stella and her mother until late and talking of every-thing. Stella knew all the latest songs; she often sang to him.

He moved in with the two women after he was married. While his mother and aunt would have chosen someone Irish for him, they could not object to the devout Catholic home Ramrod lived in. Stella's mother went to Mass daily, kept Lent as rigor-ously as a saint in a children's storybook, and crossed herself be-fore the numerous crucifixes which hung in the family home. On Sundays, Ramrod drove over to his mother's, at first with Stella and later by himself, to sit with his aunt and mother and tell them of his week. He phoned daily. Stella, it turned out, seldom wanted to leave her home: her short leg had made a re-cluse of her and Ramrod could not budge her from her habit of hiding away. When she walked, she swung one leg, the shorter one, in a slight arc that wasn't at all unattractive in its steady rhythm. A person could see something wrong there, but it was not, Ramrod thought, as if she looked like a woman with an infirmity. Her face was beautiful, a half-blind man could see that, and she had a merry ring to her laugh and she laughed often. He felt protective toward her, imagining threats life could offer her and in his daydreams defeating her enemies. At work she sat on a high stool at a cash register and felt protected. Get-ting her to leave her mother's house was another matter: after a time, he no longer asked. She subscribed to the *Reader's Digest* and read him funny sayings and sometimes articles. When she looked at him with her soft brown eyes, Ramrod saw the same love there he saw in the eyes of his mother and Aunt Alys and felt himself a very, very lucky man. He inspired love in good women. Relishing now even the half-hour trip from Dormont to Oakland, he went to visit his mother and aunt alone in his new car, a four-door Buick.

They still sat in the familiar living room with his father looking out at the three of them, old, sober, not quite disapprov-
ing. They rehearsed the ancient tales of Ramrod's remarkable
memory as a child, his sweet smile that caused Dick Powell once
at the Enright Theater to bring the little fellow on stage and do
a dance with him. "He had a natural tendency," Aunt Alys said.
"All us Boylan girls did. I never saw a hint of it in your father."

"Oh, my, no," Ramrod's mother said. "Andrew wasn't op-
posed to it, but it wasn't for him. I'm sure gaiety in Roderick is
from the Boylan side. And the good looks. Now, the brains I do
think were partly Andrew's."

Lost and consumed by the gentle side of his nature in well-
known surroundings, Ramrod took home the laundry he had
left with his mother the week before. As always, without asking,
his mother and aunt had starched his shorts and undershirts and
Ramrod wore them close to himself all week, feeling the presence of his good mother and his saintly aunt about him like a
religious medal at his throat.

In the spring of 1948, after Ramrod had switched jobs at the
Dravo Corporation, now a time keeper instead of a machinist
but still wearing a hard yellow plastic helmet to work, Stella mis-
carried. Attending her when she returned from Allegheny General, Ramrod felt guilt over his thoughts when he learned she
had become pregnant. He had wondered if he would love the
child if it had a heart as timid in its beat as his or had one leg
shorter from birth as Stella had. He decided to monitor his
thoughts more carefully and attend church more frequently, but
within the month of Stella's miscarriage he met Jimmy Nevin on
Craft Avenue on one of his Sunday visits to his mother. Together, Ramrod and the old quarterback from Schenley had
strolled up Craft as if they owned the sidewalk, up to the car

barn on the corner, turned up Forbes remembering games and memorable drunks, and up to the Irish Club. Eloquent and thirsty and filled with high regard for the past and now, there they drank until the time ordinary people woke for work. Toots Kiley was there, boyish as ever, drinking two beers to everyone else's one and remaining as slender as when he was ten; Jimmy himself treating Ramrod as if he had been first team all those years; Cleet Cavanaugh in rare high spirits, repeating rumors about Shirley Temple; Bill Stewart, now graduated from Duquesne in psychology; the Moran twins; Donal Crowley and his wife, Hoagy Carey's sister. All of them, Ramrod thought happily, now reassembled as if they had never left boyhood on the same tables and chairs. About were the same old-timers, young punks at the bar, dim light unfailing and homey in the large third-floor hall. When the jukebox played "Mr. Sandman" Ramrod almost wept with the rightness of the night. It was a song that he was certain would be around for another twenty years like the favorites from the war years; he and the good times would not die with old age and responsibility. Twenty-six might just be starting out for some men, and look at what Ramrod Sheehan had already seen and done.

He began to attend the Irish Club as he had in his youth, loyally arriving on Oakland Avenue in his Buick at eight. If it was not the exact old boys from his first return at the bar or their old tables, there were others he had known: Sid Smith and Donald Carpe, who had been in Korea; Billy Spare; and Joe Bailey, who had once in a personal matter knocked cold an assistant swimming coach at Pitt. Toward morning, Ramrod drove home once more the regulars who hadn't a car of their own, and two months into his return to Oakland, Ramrod was in third gear again, athlete's hidden power in his step and glance, powdered and spruce, his hair held down by Wildroot, murmuring, "Let's go out and get some girls."

He went to new places like the Copa on Liberty, downstairs, and the Carnival Lounge across the street. But the places were too strange to him, dark and swept by unknown currents. An evening there, even nursing drinks, could run ten, twelve dollars and it left him feeling sorry when he returned home and climbed into bed with Stella and she turned sleepily and asked, "Did you have a nice time?" At such times, Ramrod promised himself he'd cut out the dancing with women and the spending money, but the next weekend he'd be off again, holding his stomach in even as he made his way out his front porch down to his car at the curb to pick up Jimmy or Don, who was once said to have hands as fine as Y. A. Tittle. He hardly knew where it would end, but he felt alive and fresh again. He was eager for days to pass and the weekend to start: all of it right, the great friends and prowling and drinking on Saturday night and sitting with his mother and aunt the next day and talking about his father's family and remarkable things he himself had done when he was five. Once, in Oakland, Abe Simon, who had fought Joe Louis, saw him as he walked past where Ramrod and his mother stood waiting for a streetcar, and stooping down from his great height said, "That kid's going to be a boxer, lady, a light heavy at least." His aunt Alys clapped her hands at the memory, not having been there but having attended so many recitations of the event that she now applauded.

Ramrod began to feel like a man who had cheated time, and then on March 17 he met the famous Jane Sullivan, whose husband was Jack Sullivan, the fire captain. Not knowing who she was, he danced with her on St. Patrick's Day at the Irish Club, propelled by the noise and the crowd that extended out from the bar at the Ancient Order of Hibernians, Division No. 9, to the dance floor and on to where the dancers struggled to move around the walking wounded. After the first few dances, Toots pulled Ramrod aside and asked, "Do you know who that is?"

"The queen of hearts," Ramrod said, woozy from the beer and merriment that clung to him, hot and sweating.

"Jack Sullivan's wife. She pulls in trouble like a thirsty daisy."

"I'm doing nothing but dancing. Who the hell is Jack Sullivan?"

"The fire captain."

"I'll buy him a drink. Where is he?"

Ramrod felt in control of the night; he had nothing to hide, well known far and wide as a good egg. If Mrs. Sullivan—she had told him only her name was Jane—was up to mischief that was between husband and wife. He himself was a quiet man who sought no trouble. But, he thought, he wasn't running away from a scrap either.

"He killed a man in the service," Toots said.

"A murderer?" Ramrod asked.

"Yes," Toots said. "But he got off with a mental. They said the man had goaded him into a homicidal rage. He came home and joined the fire department, worked his way up to captain in ten years. He's a smart fellow. Watch yourself, Ramrod. He's mean."

"I'm not up to anything," Ramrod said. "This man he killed: were the circumstances known?"

"Sullivan was a colonel in Africa and the man was an Algerian, on our side you know, and the man insulted Sullivan's outfit."

Ramrod felt himself surrounded by mystery: Africa, Algeria, a war that had never touched him. He sensed his heart uneasy.

He had carried about nitroglycerin tablets since he was a boy, dutifully replacing each tiny tablet every three weeks for years. He touched them in his pocket. Under the heat in the room he felt cold as if parts of his life were coming together in a clammy union that might erupt.

"Well, the hell with him," Ramrod said, the words bolstering him. "I've done nothing to give him offense."

"I didn't say you did," Toots, a bare-knuckled fighter who could use his feet too, said. "But I'm not the one making the decision, Ramrod-lad. She's been in the center of more than one brawl."

Ramrod danced with the woman again. He saw she wore a wedding ring. He asked, "Is your husband about?"

"Elizabeth, New Jersey," she said. "He's up there for a convention."

Ramrod's heart dissolved into a small dance of its own as he pulled her closer. She was a fine-looking woman, not young, but as he held her he felt her softness and smelled the shampoo in her hair. And she held him close too—there was no mistake in that. Held him and ran her cheek against his and whispered words to songs from the jukebox in his ear as they slow-danced and pushed her crotch against him and, unashamed, erect, he did the same. She went to the ladies' room, and Cleet Cavanaugh took him by the arm. "Do you know what you're doing, Ramrod? That's Jack Sullivan's wife, the fire captain."

"The hell with him," Ramrod said.

"He ain't normal," Cleet said. "He committed murder in Africa."

"Cleet, I'm not interested in history. I'm not up to any harm."

When she came back, Jane said, "Let's leave."

Ramrod, feeling he was perfectly in his rights to drive a

woman home who had no ride on St. Patrick's Day, helped her with her coat and made his way to the door. "Ramrod, is your head on your shoulders straight?" Toots asked in an urgent whisper, pulling him aside and taking Ramrod's arm. "The man is out of control. He's in a fight once a week. They say he carries a gun. He's going to kill someone. He and Chris Cairns fought each other bloody two years ago and it was over her." Toots pointed to the woman standing a flight down on the stairs and looking up.

"He's in New Jersey and I'm taking care of fires in Pittsburgh," Ramrod said gleefully, punching Toots. It was a remark, Ramrod thought, that would go down with the great ones for devil-kiss-my-foot boldness, and when Toots stepped back, Ramrod knew he had scored. "So long, sucker," Ramrod said, joining Jane.

She had put her hand on his knee as he drove. At her door she handed him the keys to the house. It was two stories with an attic in the neighborhood around Schenley High School, once called Schenley Farms. He locked carefully the doors to his Buick. Trees in stark branches stood around in the late winter cold as he fumbled with the keys to Jane's door, then opened the door. He had wondered who lived in these houses as a boy, and now he would know. From the ground up, he thought, caressing Jane's hips as they walked into the house. "Can you see?" she asked. "Shall I turn on the lights?"

Seizing her, he kissed her hard in the center of the floor and held her, running his hand up the back of her leg.

"I'll take you upstairs to my place," she said, "my very own place."

She took him by the hand and climbed the stairs with him to a small stairway that led to the attic and a tiny room three stories up. Ramrod could see the top branches of the trees outside as he looked out of the room's one small window. He turned and she had taken off her dress and in a pink slip sat on the bed, careless about the folds of the slip as it crept up her thighs. By the window's light and a small lamp she beckoned him, one leg under her as she sat. He threw off a sweater he had been wearing and his pants and his shirt. He kicked off his shoes and bent to pull off his socks. He stood before her in his underwear and said, "I like your place."

Distinctly, he heard footsteps on the narrow stairway to the attic.

"It's him," she said, starting to rise and collapsing back onto her pillow. She made a sound like a small, lost dog.

"Ah," Ramrod said, letting out all the breath in his body that had accumulated over twenty-six years of good fortune as he prepared to pass through the door to another side where an ill fate lay.

"Oh," he said, breathless as his heart roared inside him. There was a closet in a long drapery that was stuffed with women's dresses to his right, but he could not hide in the crowded closet. Crouched among the hanging dresses and the burgeoning shirts, the overpowering scent of perfumes, Ramrod knew he would die there. He could see himself with his knees clutched to his chest, curled up in death like a man asphyxiated by smoke inhalation. There was only the window. The woman sat on the bed, her petticoat now covering her thighs, her eyes following him. She covered her mouth as Ramrod spun about in first one direction, then another.

He ran to the window in a panic and looked down at the street below. "Jane!" a man called. "I know you're up there." The sidewalk two stories down was flat and as Ramrod looked it seemed to grow white under a streetlight. "What shall I do?" he turned to ask the woman and saw by her panic there would be no answer. "Stop him on the steps," he said, his voice cracking. He waved at her, gestured her toward the door in the room.

He felt in his tight shorts and undershirt like something bound and packaged on a supermarket shelf, too clean and dusted; he soon would be in his starched shorts with their blue polka dots shattered like a thing toppled from a shelf by the handle of a careless janitor's broom. Unless he moved, he would die in this room, and he went again to the window. Down there on the cruel stone hovered the dread of crushed ankles and knees torn into pieces, perhaps a split skull, but if he did not crack his spine or his head in the leap he could call out for help once he lay on the sidewalk.

Someone would come. Witnesses would be down there to protest against the husband murdering him as he lay bleeding. He could crawl to his car and there broken and ruined hide on the floor. No, the car was locked, and the seconds for thoughts of safety from his terror had fled.

Mama, he said to himself, you used to sponge me with cool witch hazel when I was overheated. And Aunt Alys, good aunt, greatest aunt, you read Roderick the comics on Sunday morning front to back with Captain Easy to keep me calm. And you two know I meant no soul on earth any harm.

His leap from the window into darkness ended with a large, dull thud and he was filled with a wave of sickness, but, hot and aching and trembling, he was alive, spared. He slowly stood, nothing broken, his ankles in sharp pain but useful. And then he heard the footsteps of the fire captain approaching, his voice hard on the air between them. Ramrod screamed.

Holding up his pistol directly at the man's eyes, Captain Sullivan wondered what possessed the chubby little guy. "Stand there," the captain called again, his gun plainly in front of him, while the young man, head down like a maddened bull, charged at him, limping on ankles damaged from his leap. He flailed at the air and shouted words the captain could not understand.

The captain fired.

FIVE

An Old Man and Three Whores

"WELL," Ned said to Warren when the news first broke of the scandalous conduct of his old uncle and the three young women out in East Liberty, "I suppose there's worse sins an old man can commit. He could have poisoned barking dogs on the street or thrown himself in front of trolleys to collect insurance. Seems kind of a gentle way to edge into senility, in the company of lust and foolishness."

Ned was trying of course to ease Warren's shame. Warren was a well-known perennial choir boy, boasting of his years before the altar: he had married late and never spoke for five minutes without bringing up the subject of "my good wife" or "my kids, now." But Pal Mahoney overheard Ned and turned his innocent remark to his own purposes. Mahoney had been passing the table at the Irish Club, his coat on, his scarf around his neck, but his head spun at the word "sin." It summoned him to confrontation: the old, honest word, a token of the language of truth in the air of hundreds of cigarettes and lies.

"Is that so?" Mahoney asked. "You are on record as approving of prostitution, Ned, a victimless crime, is that the turn your strange mind is taking?"

"Not at all: I'm drawing a comparative. Warren's Uncle Mumpie is to be understood, his age, his health, his past life. And maybe there's more to the story than the newspaper printed."

"Yes, there is," Mahoney said. "There's the words the newspapers don't run: gluttony, lust, pride, envy, and crazy-old-man. You'd think that there wasn't a soul on the streets of Pittsburgh not guilty of any of the seven deadlies, so little are they in the *Sun-Telegraph* as a reason for the hourly mayhem. No, it's bad-home this and drunken-father that, not clear and resounding: 'Cracked old fool filled with lust and pride,' like it ought to say. My apologies, Warren, but a lie isn't in me at this late hour and what I'm saying now in public I'll say at dawn in private. If your Uncle Mumpie must be judged, let him be judged fairly. He had to be in the grip of demons thinking he could handle three whores all combined in age not equal to his own." Knowing the answer but then pausing as if he were still weighing judgment, savoring his moment, Mahoney asked, "How old is the buffoon in question?"

"Eighty-two."

"A joke," Mahoney said, as if relieved he had not been impulsive. "A dirty joke. At eighty-two a man given the grace to go on with life ought to be tending a vegetable garden, a few tomatoes, vines on a trellis, maybe a glass of wine about five in the afternoon as he gets ready for a bowl of cabbage soup and bed at seven."

Mahoney waited to see if anyone at the table accepted his combative tone as an occasion for stopping his homeward march.

No one spoke, and he put up his coat collar against the wind outdoors. "Might as well be addressing hyenas as this bunch," he said, walking away. "Mass is at eight tomorrow, monkeys and degenerates. See you in church."

When he was gone, Dickie Dunn said, "Last Word Mahoney strikes again: Warren, your uncle is a man and men make fools of themselves, it's in the order of things."

Warren had tears in his eyes. "This don't help me none," he said. "Don't men slow down at all, say, at age sixty-five, the legal age for retirement in most professions—or give the beast his due of another ten years to wind down, shouldn't Uncle Mumpie be ready to throw in the towel and quit the snuffle and snort game at age seventy-five? There's something to what the Last Word says: Uncle Mumpie is a scandal to my wife and children, to say nothing of me who used to love my Aunt Sally, God rest her soul, seeing her defamed posthumously now by a lecher."

Ned said, "Wait a minute, Warren, none of us knows what the old man was doing with them three whores. We were not given battle reports hourly by the Associated Press, like the taking of one hill or another there in North Korea. For all we know, Uncle Mumpie was teaching the girls how to further their education by elocution lessons, or maybe showing them how to pour tea should the occasion occur. Or how to hold a badminton racket in a ladylike way in case anyone wanted to play a game with one of them."

"Maybe how to plant geraniums," Quigg Saterly said, laughing, too open in his derision for Warren.

The disconsolate young man stood. He looked around at the

table, friend and foe, and said, "Mahoney was right, I'm among the beasts of the wild. Go to hell, all of you, and I hope there's not a one of you ever knows what it's like to have an eighty-two-year-old uncle living in a whorehouse with three whores."

There was a decent interval until he reached the front door of the Ancient Order of Hibernians, Division No. 9, and then even Warren on steps down could hear the merry chorus that rose behind him in the great hall of shouts, jeers, prayers, programs, and babble insistent enough to cleave the roof and bounce back downward off the red clouds over Pittsburgh.

Uncle Mumpie had been arrested at his home in Monroeville on a quiet suburban street where he had resided with his wife, Sally, for the final fourteen years of her life. They had been married for more than fifty years when she died, and people had said at the time of her demise that his devotion for her—and her love for him, and concern—meant his days were numbered. But not two years had passed before cars began to pull up in Uncle Mumpie's driveway, there was the sound of laughter at irregular hours for the tranquil street, young women in large cars and wearing sunglasses at night strode on high-heeled shoes to his front door and admitted themselves with their own keys. The investigating officers from the Allegheny County Task Force on Nonviolent Crimes never were able to ascertain that prostitution was actually occurring in the little house, but by assigning decoys to the case it was established that the young women were using the place as a headquarters for an escort service, one of the first in Pittsburgh trading in the ancient crime, and certainly the first in the suburbs. And when the whores were brought in for booking, with them stood tiny Uncle Mumpie, seemingly as friendly as ever, nodding to strangers, taking from his pocket an orange wrapped in a handkerchief and peeling it, offering a slice to the judge, one to a policeman, another to a whore standing at his side to be photographed for the morning papers, to the shame of his nephew.

Uncle Mumpie could not plead that it was not his house. He could not claim he did not know the young women's trade; it had been under way for more than a year and he had greeted customers on the phone and occasionally drove one of the young women in his old Buick to a trysting place. He was charged, perhaps unfairly, with operating a house of prostitution. But the three young women did not get off easily either; they were held for outstanding warrants on other crimes they were alleged to have commited—burglary, arson, assault and battery on police officers—each crime of theirs another thorn in Warren's flesh. That his old uncle could have fallen, perhaps loosely and willingly, into such company and there, seemingly without remorse or great thought on the subject, thrived, a sorrow to all McBrides living and dead.

Warren hired Daly Racklin, the local attorney noted for cheating justice and not his clients, but Racklin, with all his skills, still could not keep Uncle Mumpie out of jail. Racklin protested the man's age, his exemplary record, the chronic hardening of his arteries, but it was to no avail. A mood of vengeance had settled on the case. The neighborhood had been changed by the introduction of the waves of license that Uncle Mumpie and the three whores had brought to Monroeville, one of the prostitutes had caused seventy thousand dollars damage in a hotel she had attempted to burn to the ground. A campaign for district attorney was being waged at the time, and Uncle Mumpie was fortunate to be let off with six months in jail, to serve, it was understood, no more than two months. The prostitutes were not as fortunate; they were assigned variously to eighteen months, a year, and eight months. Contributing to the dishonor that lay on the affair, Lila, one of the dark-haired prostitutes, was photographed in the very act of kicking in the shins a bailiff she insisted had treated her too roughly for the occasion, another, Tanya, shouted at reporters that they were all hypocrites: "Our customers are businessmen, reporters, judges, and priests." But she was quoted in the morning papers as exclaiming, "Our customers are priests," and it was another thing Warren had to live down—the jokes and asides that Uncle Mumpie had joined the Church and was doing good works in servicing its clergy.

Warren visited his Uncle Mumpie once a week in jail, and at the Irish Club even Pal Mahoney said there was something fine in Warren honoring his old uncle. But others were not so understanding. It was said, not within his hearing of course or that of any other members of the McBride family, that Uncle Mumpie had a considerable sum of money put away. Money there was that came from the spoils of whoring and Uncle Mumpie's frugal lifetime of savings and thriftiness: he had owned a fish wholesale company in his early years, delivering for decades frozen fish to restaurants the length of Pittsburgh. And he had driven the same automobile for years, a Buick no less than thirteen years old, and before that a Pontiac for seventeen years. The sum varied in the telling, and Pal Mahoney said he was sick of every kind deed a person exhibited being cut down to dollars and cents.

"Warren doesn't know what his uncle has any more than anyone at this table," he said one night before Uncle Mumpie was released from jail. "Chances are good those girls took it all away from him ten minutes after they moved in."

Given the old man's advanced years, there was not much suggestion of specific lewdness in the Irish Club discussions of what Uncle Mumpie did at night in the company of the women—

or for that matter did during any other part of the day. Was there some exotic adventure beyond previous imagination of the sexual powers of an octogenarian unfolding in Monroeville? Could new boundaries of what was possible between men and women be breached in an examination of Uncle Mumpie under one roof with three robust if law-breaking women? It was not discussed explicitly, but certainly Warren's shame held in it some moral failure of his old uncle beyond that of cashing in on the ill-gotten earnings of prostitutes.

But Warren was there for the old man when he was released from prison, head down, shuffling, friendly with the guards, seemingly unaware he was being ridiculed. One whispered something to him as he left, and when Warren asked what the guard had said, the old man said, "They tease me, you know. They make jokes. There's no harm in it. They're a good bunch of guys. I learned my lesson."

"You caused Aunt Sally to turn in her grave. *In her house, Uncle Mumpie!*"

"It breaks my heart to think of her. I thought of her every night, all day."

He was allowed to live with Warren, his wife and two children, during his year of probation, and in a couple of months the furor about him stopped. No reporters came, no television stories; he became another old man in Oakland, sitting on a porch when the weather permitted, at Warren's house on Bates Street. He nodded at strangers, and when Pal Mahoney stopped to take him out to Wilkinsberg on Wednesdays for the occasional bingo night, Uncle Mumpie seemed grateful. He walked with Warren's children around the block, he sat at the window in cold weather. He took up cooking again, simple soups, salads for Warren and his wife, Sundays waking before anyone else and beginning huge breakfasts of bacon and blueberries and pecans and pancakes he devised from trips to the Giant Eagle he made all week long. The pecans and blueberries, Warren remembered, were from the old days when he had gone to Aunt Sally's and Uncle Mumpie's. Uncle Mumpie called the pancakes his specials, and Aunt Sally used to say she wouldn't eat again till next Easter after a particular Sunday of fine times.

"Do you miss your late wife?" Pal asked.

"Like my right arm is gone."

"You regret your conduct?"

"I would go to jail ten times longer if I could make it all like it never happened."

Feeling confirmed in all his thoughts and being, Pal announced Uncle Mumpie's recantations at the Irish Club. He took the old man's self-recriminations as proof of something much larger than the situation at hand. He would cite Uncle Mumpie frequently as an example to one erring youth or another. "A man's never too old to slip," he said, "or too old to see daylight either."

Warren brought the old man up to the Irish Club on St. Patrick's Day, and if anyone snickered it was done so furtively it might never have happened. Eyes down, looking up gratefully when anyone spoke to him, laughing heartily at anything like a joke, Uncle Mumpie was loved. He was accepted. The younger men invited him to their tables, older men struck him on the shoulder in passing and said, "Hey, Mumpie, looking good, boy."

He nodded, Yes, yes, yes, benign and distant, thinking what thoughts beyond the obvious pleasure at the ending to a terrible time. A woman named Alice Graldon shook her finger in his face in mock reproof as she passed his table, and she swore he made a snapping gesture at her as if he would bite her. She was assured by Mrs. Mary Donegan who was at her table that she had witnessed the scene and Uncle Mumpie had simply nodded at her in an awkward, old man's tilt of his head and there was nothing of the beast there who'd snap at a woman being playful with him.

"I don't like the look to him," Mrs. Graldon said.

"Nonsense," Mrs. Donegan said. "He's got a look like a grandfather, he's got a walk like a grandfather—the old man's a grandfather! You read the papers too much, they turn everything sour. With diseased mentalities in every doorway in Oakland plotting murder on honest people, putting that old man in jail ought to be a crime itself."

But what transpired in Uncle Mumpie, boiled like the simple soups on Warren's stove, thoughts as he walked the children, himself leashed to the kids as he seemingly led them, could never of course be known—not for a great, great distance high above where judgments were made nightly at the Ancient Order of Hibernians, Division No. 9.

Where to look for clues, even by Mahoney who swore human beings made no sense, that remained the last question. But he did not believe his own protest, constantly arguing in word and deed the opposite. The fortunes of Uncle Mumpie confirmed him daily in one philosophy or another. The old man planted a small garden at his nephew's house, he raised radishes and tomatoes, and he sold the house in Monroeville, a garden surely a sign of stability of mind, a permanence, and the sale of the tainted suburban dwelling a form of renunciation, a casting off of the site of his contamination and fall.

"It's a story-book ending," Mahoney said one evening to a group who had mostly lost interest in the old man. And when no one responded, more eagerness on the night to take up a certain rumor about a pitcher from the Chicago Cubs who reasonably gave up home runs in obscure baseball games because no one watched the team, Mahoney said, "But it's nothing to take as a given: there's not a man here not ready to fall to error if temptation comes along."

"Not you," Ned said. "I expect you'll never fall, Last Word. I expect when I'm doomed and not even on the books anywhere you'll be somewhere setting the standard."

"Not so, not so, I'm human. It's just the terms of the temptation that's the question. What's to tempt Mumpie or for that matter me? You, Ned, or Corny here, anything at all, a smile will do. But Mumpie: how are you going to tempt a man who has lived with three whores and is too old for money to have any meaning? I say, it's a victory for rationality—the old bastard is just past temptation and will now live his life out like a reasonable old nut."

Mahoney was of course as perplexed in detail and broader philosophy as was everyone else at the turn the old man's saga took.

One day, Uncle Mumpie vanished from the house where he lived with his nephew Warren. It was assumed he had, in the manner of a failing man of venerable years, wandered away. Police drove through sidestreets looking for him, and a squad of volunteers from the Ancient Order of Hibernians had separated into three cars, Branigan's Oldsmobile, Cleet's Ford, and Corny's old Henry J. And they had gone looking for him the length of Oakland and out to East Liberty, scanning the streets and alighting at various bars where he might have stopped. Father Farrell said he hadn't seen him since the previous Sunday, and, in truth, no one paying much attention to him, it could never be determined who it was exactly who had seen him last. It was as if the poor old criminal had never been there at all.

Within two days of his disappearance, though, it came to the attention of the police that someone had broken into Uncle Mumpie's house in Monroeville in the absence of the new tenants, away on vacation. Warren, with Paul Kerry and Pal Mahoney, drove out to the house to investigate and there found Uncle Mumpie in police custody once again. He had been sleeping in a back bedroom.

"Loose wiring at that age," Mahoney said. "Things fly around up there with no regard for time and place."

"He went to where he thought he'd find Aunt Sally," Warren said.

"Poor soul," Mahoney said. "Life and death all run together past a certain point. He was trying to recapture the good, lost years with his longtime dead wife. It's a burden to be human, I tell you: walk the straight and narrow and time throws barricades at us when we try to get from here to there. And add into the guilt Mumpie McBride has to feel for his recent bad conduct and you have a desert with quicksand every forty feet going on in a man's mind."

Mumpie, occasionally sobbing, was driven home and told he had worried his family and friends, to talk things over with Father Farrell, maybe his doctor, not to ever try to right things by reliving the past. Aunt Sally and the wonderful years were gone.

"You don't think he was looking for the whores up there?" Cleet asked when Warren had safely left the Irish Club.

"That would make no sense at all," Paul Kerry said. "He knows the girls are in jail; and he knows the place in Monroeville is sold and they'd know it. No, it was no real meeting Mumpie was going to, it was a meeting in his mind, living and dead. He just went up there as I figure it for a good night's sleep like he used to have when he was a young man."

After he had been in Warren's care for another eight months, sitting on the front porch at his nephew's house one day in spring observing a fine rainfall, Uncle Mumpie watched to his astonishment Lila pull up to the front curb. With some difficulty—these particular stairs downward to the street were always a curse on his knees—he rattled down to her Mercedes. "Lila," he asked, "is that you?"

The light rain had stopped falling on the street and the quick sun from between clouds now caused the wet stones to shine with a brilliance to the eyes that made Mumpie squint. The street lay before him in a shaft of sunlight, and he felt a spray of water from a bush in the front yard as it brushed against his cheek. He did not wipe at the water but let it linger cool on his face. The freshness of the day and the young woman spoke of youth to him, himself striding into grocery stores carrying in each hand sixty-pound bags of shrimp and cod, honoring Fridays and Sally and the family and the delights of powerful wrists and the universe in place and laid out like a red carpet before him.

"Uncle Mumpie," Lila said, her long dark hair falling to her waist, sunlight catching strands to make them bright, "sure, it's me. I'm out now. I've got a place on the north side."

"And you remembered me?"

"I did. We were buddies, you and Delores and me and Tanya."

"That's what we were, buddies."

"Do you think of us? I'm here for old time's sake, Uncle Mumpie."

"I went up to the place in Monroeville. You said if we were ever separated, thick or thin, there'd be the mirror in the back bathroom with the hole behind it and we was to put a note to each other or Tanya or Delores in it if the heat was on. So I went there, I sold the place, and I broke in and there was no note; and I left a note with the address here and the telephone number."

"I heard you sold the place."

"So you came without seeing the note I left."

"You gave me your nephew's number a long time ago. I figured you'd be here."

"Lila, where are you staying?"

"It's a place of my own, up Troy Hill, later when she gets out maybe Tanya moves in with me. Like old times."

Savoring the sweet scent of her hair and arms, the tilt of her neck, he leaned for privacy into the car window, not that the children could hear or understand. Who could?

"Lila," he said, a man drowning in misconceptions about himself and life in general. "Lila, I'll move in with you this afternoon, tomorrow if need be, and Tanya when she gets out and Delores. All of us together. Honest to God, Lila, it'll be the greatest mercy you ever showed in life. We'll play blackjack like we used to and you and the girls will come in my room at night and throw shoeboxes full of twenties down on me again while I'm sleeping and we'll have a whisky together and I'll get a car and drive you where you're going and no harm will befall you with Uncle Mumpie at the wheel, and I'll make us breakfasts with blueberries and pecans and pancakes again every Sunday. I have the money from the house and twenty-two thousand more put away not a soul on earth knows about except me and now you. Remember the times we had, and give me your number quick now, they watch me like hawks on a rabbit. What times we'll have again!"

"Uncle Mumpie, you're a rascal!"

"I am, I am, bless us all."

"What's your nephew going to say? What are people going to say?" Lila asked.

"There's not one as miserable as I am so they better keep their traps shut or I'll say plenty about them."

Never again would he sit at a window in a frost-bound winter enclosed by the ice on the pane in front of him, given a small porthole in the ice's design where he had warmed away the ice to look out at the street from his nephew's house. People passing, looking up, would see him and they would wave at the man in the cleared circle in the ice. He would nod, he would smile; and now not ever on this earth would there ever again be such moments worse than death.

When she did not come to fetch him in a week, Uncle Mumpie called Lila at the number she had given him, but the telephone operator said the phone had been disconnected. Rather than wait for their inevitable reunion, he stole his nephew Warren's car and set out for Troy Hill to find her and knew he would, once having stumbled on happiness, it could not be removed from a man's life this easily, and, missing her, there was always the last opportunity, taking himself to the banks of the Monongahela River and throwing himself into the water with heavy rocks in his pockets. There to die but have dropped from himself old age like a lizard in a skin he no longer needed and be reunited again in eternity with the scent of their perfumes and the movements of their bodies when Lila and Tanya and Delores came and would be as he remembered them at their best, bold and unconcerned where they stood or dozed like cats, strolling into the lamplight of his familiar house and shadows he had never known beautiful before them, bringing him back to a youth he had never tasted either, waiting for the bus that never came and was rediscovered now and forever in their company.

SIX

O'Casey and the Career

CLARICE CUNNINGHAM'S maiden aunt Olive, her mother's respectable sister, died when she was seventeen in 1950 and left Clarice all her fortune, a sum of close to twelve thousand dollars, provided, no strings attached, she attended the University of Pittsburgh with the money. Aunt Olive had worked for the Board of Education for more than forty years. She had accumulated plaques and a large cup for her years of service, no absent days in all that time. Her name was frequently in the newspapers, one of two assistants to the various superintendents of schools who retired or died while Aunt Olive went into her next decade.

She had taken, unmarried over her long career, several night classes at Pitt, one particularly memorable with the editor of the *Bulletin-Index,* a local weekly cultural and business survey, and, without a college degree anywhere else, she came to think of Pitt as her alma mater.

Pitt, she often told Clarice when the girl came to see her in her apartment in Oakland to touch her for a dollar or two, gave people opportunities to better themselves beyond anything known in Ireland, anywhere else in Pittsburgh, and perhaps all of America. Had she to do it all over again, she said, she would have washed walls to go there, rather than taking the secretarial courses that gave her the chance to rise at the school board but left her feeling like an outsider when discussions became philosophical or called for knowledge of the geography or history of the world.

Clarice had not imagined when she daydreamed aloud that she would receive funds from Aunt Olive to fulfill her visions of an unrealized college education. Aunt Olive made no stipulations on what Clarice should study.

Clarice had been thinking vaguely she would work in a library or at Gimbel's department store. The nuns at St. Agnes had delighted in the little tales she wrote in grade school and said one day she would be a great scholar, even a nun with her way with words; but being a writer put no bread on the table, and she wasn't cut out to be a nun, too ambitious in the world, she supposed, too eager to prove herself.

She planned with the inheritance to study accounting at Pitt. She was at the time the only person living in Terrace Village Two, a government housing project, walking down the long hill to Oakland and Pitt, reassuring people as she passed familiar landmarks of childhood. "I was never going to be a nun," she said often to people she knew on her route. "No great loss."

Clarice feared change; she wasn't unhappy with accounting, the sensible profession for most of the young women and men she grew up with, no rocking the boat there. Change always meant trouble, her mother falling from a bar stool and twisting her back and wheelchairs and doctor's visits and tears of pain in the night and her father in an encounter with a policeman, himself Irish, but having it in for Irish taxicab drivers and being jailed for three days. Clarice and Kiley, her solid older brother, almost trembled when the telephone rang. Kiley, called Riot, never missed a day at work at the warehouse on Penn Avenue where he loaded produce trucks, steadily accumulating money and offering Clarice all or any part of it when she was accepted at Pitt.

"You're not that old, Kiley," she said. "You'll need the money when you go to school. And there's Donnie."

In a miracle, more of human connection than the intercession of the divine, her mother had given birth to a late baby boy.

"Donnie will be fine between us, and I'll die happily under crates of grapefruits one day," he said, "and you'll all be sued for damage I did to Florida fruit."

With all that she had seen, the daughter of Tommy and Joanne Cunningham and people on the streets and in apartments and the Irish Club who crowded her brain with voices and movements hardly remembered, she knew herself to be a moody young woman but edged with suppressed laughter. She was not popular with young men, she felt, because she had a habit of listening to them too carefully and sometimes when she became too comfortable attempted to read poetry to them at the oddest times. Strolling in Schenley Park after high school classes, down toward the Panther Hollow Bridge, she misunderstood the moment and began to read aloud with passion Keats or Byron. She knew her excitement over the language she read was foolish. Kissing under the bushes in the park needn't have been celebrated with an "Ode to a Nightingale," but at the time it always seemed to Clarice that it was not really a true moment of romance unless it soared to poetry. She astounded the young men. She had once more lived up to her reputation for peculiarity. If they were boys from the government housing projects there fell astride her eccentricities the locally familiar image of her father, drunken and with his shirttails flying, chasing down Robinson Court after a beer truck and her mother running in another direction to catch the truck at the foot of the hill if her father missed it before it made its turn. Riot, being older and male, took the family's public reputation in stride. "Nobody's going to like us more if the old man was sober as a judge," he said. "And nobody was going to hate us needed to see them making fools of themselves to pass the word on us. We are what we are, except you'll be more."

The change in Clarice toward solidity in her own eyes started one afternoon in a sophomore lit class. The teacher said she had complimentary tickets and if anyone was interested, out at Carnegie Tech they were performing a play of García Lorca's. *The House of Bernarda Alba* was being read in class at the time and one might understand the play better having witnessed it staged and in costumes. Clarice and two boys and a girl from the class went to a student performance on a Wednesday night, the first stage play Clarice had ever seen. She staggered home alone, drunk as any Cunningham in history on alcohol but with words running through her brain and arms and legs, the sidewalk unsure under her feet. She felt like shouting at trees the grandmother's words of defeat and defiance: "She died a virgin!"

She went to Tech every afternoon the rest of the semester. She devoted long afternoons to anything like a rehearsal, auditions, and dramatic readings. She lost herself in the people on stage, leaning forward tensely as if she would jump from her seat and join the actors. She attended alone every night to whatever was being staged: Noel Coward, Tennessee Williams, Molnar, Sophocles, and O'Casey—above all, O'Casey—and in the spring, on Aunt Olive's money, she switched her major to drama.

She did not explain to her advisor that she did not plan to be an actress and she did not envision teaching dramatics in high school: she was going to be a playwright. Her advisor, a woman named Burke, said, "You have a good way about you, work hard, and you can have a long career in acting. You're not the glamour type, but they never last. Your type lasts: you have a nice look, kind of open, fresh, and your hair is beautiful. How would you describe it? Red?"

"Yes, red."

She read O'Casey daily and at night she wrote plays. She worked on them in geology classes and in Economics 101. As she wrote, she could not keep up with the cadences in her head of her father too quickly dictating lines to her, all unintentionally, her mother answering her father, voices interrupting each other at the Irish Club, accusations of blasphemy, and dire oaths.

Once she stumbled from a class as the teacher spoke of the westward migration of peoples—laughter inside her at something apprehended that morning as she walked to school, too inane to repeat or write but too precious not to cause her to strangle over the spell of what she'd heard. It was a look that went with an expression. It was the furor in a face that contained mixtures of various red rages and alternately benign smiles chasing after each other in a moment: faces and voices that came to be one voice and face that stood behind her and whispered words in her ear. How could words embody the whole terrific comedy just on the walk down Robinson, then up Fifth to the university? She tried not to smile at the presences in her mind: men mistook her inward smile when she passed them for something else directed at them. Seeing a man smile at her in that quick burst of something-doing, she changed her expression. Two options for a woman who wanted to translate the world: get a reputation for strangeness at the eccentricity of her good humor or keep the smiling to yourself when men might be lurking.

Clarice sat nightly at the kitchen table in the government housing project and wrote plays. She knew her subject as surely as if it were a special delivery letter the mailman had handed her at the front door. It was her times sweeping down Robinson Street like the spring wind past the elementary school on the corner attached to St. Agnes, the voices rising in noble foolishness at the Irish Club nightly, slow afternoons where there was no war in the world outside, no mother clamoring to disturb her tranquillity. She tried to listen only to the directions inside herself: absorb like rain falling on her tales of gallantry and lies at the Irish Club so long recited they had become more fixed than the truth of certain matters.

She watched the semesters at Pitt trickle away, a pause between the time she worked at Woolworth's behind the counter in high school and when she'd probably find herself behind another counter at Gimbel's after graduating college. Nightly it seemed to her that her theatrical career at Pitt would turn out to be as fantastical and failing as the adventures she heard all around her from her brother and his friends and in the taverns and clubs. Her career so far: not belonging at Pitt writing plays and Saturday night discourses at the kitchen table where her father held court for anyone caring to drink Virginia Dare wine with him until dawn. Gaunt with long white hair, her father's strength was in his raspy voice. Whatever had died in the man, extinguished by drink, had come to reside in the voice which orated tales of the cabdriver's life all night long, while her mother, seeming not to hear a word, a once handsome woman, tried to match him but fell to bed hours before he did. The old man, holding on, continued narrating, sometimes alone at the kitchen table with phantoms who came unbidden to the empty kitchen. Often Riot, coming in from his night in Oakland, led him to bed, while Clarice, having given up the arguments years ago, had learned to sleep while he carried on his discourse at the table.

"Where do you get the strength?" she asked Kiley one morning after a particularly loud argument her father was winning with himself the night before at the kitchen table and she had heard Riot come to save him.

"It's in the situation," Riot said. "Left up to me he'd be there still, but he is the father and I am the son and that's the mother and Donnie's sleeping and it's the sister, the playwright, needs her rest. So I do what the situation demands."

"Like the job in the warehouse. You ought to be going to college."

"Not the situation."

In Clarice's third year simultaneously the Drama Department held a play-writing contest for one-act plays and she fell in love with a young man in her modern theater class named Tim Cairns. Together with Tim, a tall, bright, dark-haired boy who wanted to be an actor, she read her plays over, aloud, each taking various parts. She wrote scenes for her one-act plays about Terrace Village bedrooms where old grandmothers were too ill to get out to shop and a man in a grocery truck came to bring them food and stole their change; ribald misreadings of Irish legends rendered on St. Patrick's Day by men who had once eluded the black and tan but had now become confused with movies that they had boozily witnessed; and her mother, her brother Riot, who was being buried alive because of duty in a warehouse, and small dramas that began on the corner of Oakland and Forbes and ended on the corner of Meyron and Forbes, two blocks away, three years later.

Tim wore a long storm coat in the winter and lived in Fox Chapel in a house with chimes. The few times Clarice had gone there with him, holding his arm up the long walk to his stone house, large enough to be a chapel in a foreign country, she felt small and colorless. Neither his father nor mother paid much attention to Clarice beyond a perfunctory greeting and farewell.

Tim's amazement and disbelief at her stories began to cause her alarm. Was she lying? Or, as they said at the Irish Club, adding yeast to the mixture to cause it to rise?

Tutti Dunne before the Betsy Ross Restaurant had said one day, while she waited for Riot when she was thirteen to take her to the movies, that the best street fighters used their feet as well as their hands. Tutti, a small, shy young man, then about twenty, did not mean graceful plunges and spins to the feet or leaps and landings; he meant that as one's hands flailed away at an opponent one kicked and kneed at the same time, into the shins, the knees, as high and as hard as one could go without falling off balance. He showed the group who stood with Clarice before the restaurant the quick forward attack which had made him famous, a blur of arms, hands, legs, and feet that was irresistible in moving back or dropping an enemy. He smiled when he was quickly done, not meeting anyone's eyes.

"You could kill someone," Wade said. He was short and broad-shouldered and carried beer cases for a distributor. He had been arrested once for throwing eight bottles of beer at two policemen. "I never saw someone go through a person like he was butter like you, Tutti."

"I don't kill no one," Tutti said awkwardly. "I don't fight unless I have to."

Gerald said, "Street fighting is in the mind—you beat a man before the fight begins or maybe with the first punch or two. The rest is dessert."

Gerald, Riot's closest friend, had once been known as the toughest fighter at the Irish Club: tall, with hair stiff and black, short-nosed with a chin that protruded, and long arms, he was a baseball player in high school with prospects and so swift in his hands that Johnny Ray, Billy Conn's manager, called him "Irish" and said he could make him heavyweight champion of the world. Gerald seldom fought. When he did he swarmed an opponent and beat him across the long dance floor at the Irish Club, starting at the rear tables and blanketing the man until as if all in one motion they were at one end of the room and then in seconds one heard the sound of the crash at the cigarette machine sixty feet away across the room as the man came to earth. His almost mystical air of ferocity touched them all. Clarice knew she'd never punch like any of them, even Riot, who was called that because he was so quiet and gentle; but she thought, even as a young girl, wasn't it in Riot's idea of the "situation" that she be there to tell of what she saw and heard?

Chesty Moran said, "Fighting's for dogs. Human beings should find some other way to settle their differences." Everyone nodded, Gerald, Tutti, Clarice, Riot, and two other boys on the corner. Chesty Moran had a glass eye and if the fight was serious he'd pluck out his eye and dash it on the sidewalk before the battle. Perhaps it was as Gerald said: someone planning to engage Chesty Moran turned and fled, hearing the glass eye strike the pavement and seeing the awesome street warrior, one-eyed, coming at them.

"But men have to fight," Tutti said. "It's in their nature."

"How do you mean?" Clarice asked.

"Well, where's drinking to go? Why's a body set up to be drunk if there was no plan for the alcohol to be discharged somewhere? And anger? Are you supposed to beat your head on the wall if you're angry?"

"I'm glad I'm not a man," Clarice said and felt close to all of them, but she knew she had never somehow belonged with them or their sisters, a spy, one of them down to the bone, counted in their numbers although they had always been good to her, protected her, and did not argue with her or Kiley or let others threaten them. She knew that she embraced them most when she wrote about them, loving each lie and vision and invented history, putting it down so that someone else could hear it, love the teller and the one who had become the teller's storyteller. She held her mother close in her writing, forgave her father, sent up pages and pages for her brother Kiley and all the nuns at St. Agnes who had spotted early the key by which Clarice could open the door to her love for the human race.

The boys scattered after awhile and Clarice and Kiley and Gerald walked down Forbes to the Pitt Tavern where the boys had been drinking beer since they were fifteen. Clarice would order a Coke at thirteen, enraptured to be with them, the movie forgotten.

At twenty-one Gerald and Riot knew all the regulars and were, legal age now, greeted by the two women owners. Gerald brought two Iron Cities and a Coke over to a small table and sat staring into the smoky room without talking. Before he came down to Forbes Gerald sometimes had to find his father in various wildernesses that ringed Oakland: other times, while his three younger sisters sobbed, he had to leave his government housing apartment and go search for his mother. He had taken to street fighting as kindly as another boy might discover chorus in high school or the photography club: a sure place with kindred spirits where there were no unpredictable parents or hidden meanings to language.

Gerald said as he inhaled his Camel, "I'm done fighting. I'm finished. What happened Saturday night was that a greenie bumped me on the dance floor. He was six inches shorter than me and he wore a suit made out of potato sacks. His hair was cut in a ring around his ears and it made his left ear look two inches higher than his right. The greenie couldn't speak English and when we collided I said politely, 'I beg your pardon,' and the greenie said in his brogue, 'You've insulted my cousin Gladys. Stand back, Gladys, I'll assert your honor.' Well, I made a move to push away May Wells with whom I was dancing and I said, 'There's no hard feelings, cousin,' because he was little and I thought I would kill him. He said, 'Put up your hands,' and, you know, Clarice, Riot, those are words that I accept as the first blow. I went for him. I hit him in the face and came forward expecting I was about to clear every drink from the bar with his hurtling body. But he didn't move an inch. I hit him again, and then again with my other fist. And what he did was this: he jumped in the air and hit me on top of the head. It's a trick they brought over from the old country. I went down like a snowman in the sunshine. Something lethal descended on me and I collapsed. He was the victor. He bought me a drink. I staggered to my feet and I was a new man. I will never raise my fist in combat again."

Clarice turned into the play competition twelve one-act plays and the other aspiring playwrights at Pitt combined turned in eight between them. Of the three plays to be produced two of the plays chosen by the judges were by Clarice. "We would have chosen all three by you," Mr. White, her modern theater teacher, said, "but it didn't seem right. All twelve of your plays were better than anyone else's." Mr. White's hair lay flat on his head in broad strands like Dr. Caligari whose movie he showed every semester in class.

While waiting for her plays to begin production, Clarice walked in Schenley Park with Tim and talked, hardly catching her breath for two hours at a time. They read each other Wordsworth and passages from O'Casey: she thought even as she recited the gray and golden lines that though she had not witnessed a civil war or any battles in her time on Forbes and up Dunseith, she knew things. No, Clarice said to herself, reciting by heart "The Eve of St. Agnes" to Tim, I have a definite calling sure as the claims of being a nun or a certified public accountant.

She worked on a three-act play, long into the night at the library in the Cathedral of Learning and then back home at the kitchen table on weekdays, relinquishing the table to her father on Saturday nights. Her father had been barred from the Irish Club, creating a disturbance there one Christmas Eve that toppled a Christmas tree into the jukebox and somehow setting afire Paul Kerry's visiting aunt's blue taffeta gown, for which the old man, Tommy Cunningham, paid well enough and apologized but was barred for life. He was the only person in the history of the Ancient Order of Hibernians, Division No. 9, to be so banned: usually the committee that met on unruliness offered a suspension of six months or so and never kept track of the miscreant afterward. But every doorman at the Irish Club knew Tommy and when he showed himself once or twice to test the ban, imposed in 1940, the door was firmly closed on him. "People who steal forty million," Tommy often said vaguely to himself at the kitchen table, "get a chance for parole but not Hard Luck Tommy Cunningham," and even later in the night, "I'll appeal the ruling; I'll run it right up into Boston. I'll put a lawyer on them, win the appeal, and then never show my face there again in this life."

When Clarice asked her father what was the point of this revenge he would exact, the old man once said, "That a man with four grandparents who are Irish has as many rights to have a drink among his own kind as does an Italian wandering in off the street." He loitered, lonely, in the kitchen and tried to read what Clarice wrote at the table. Clarice kept it covered or moved to another room.

Clarice's three-act play moved by fits and starts: sometimes the old man took up twenty minutes, dominated scenes where he was supposed to be sitting in a corner in a stupor; other times her mother stopped and said good night to a kitchen full of late night debaters while they ignored her, causing the play to take a dreadfully sad turn. She wrote until daylight appeared in the sky over the square, rectangular government housing apartment buildings across the court.

She put Aunt Olive in the play and took her out. She wrote in the great fight upstairs when a sailor returned from Japan and found his wife in bed with his older brother Max, and then his kids upstairs running from the apartment and randomly banging on doors crying for admittance as the sailor pursued his wife and brother with a pistol, firing and leaving scars in the hallway. No one was killed, and the sun rose over the trees that ringed Terrace Village in the morning.

She gave the play, when she thought it was completed, to a girl who sat next to her in Speech 202 class. The girl said she loved writing, couldn't do it herself, but would type Clarice's manuscript. She was an actress but wasn't in either of Clarice's plays and said she'd settle for designing sets or teaching costuming. She had straight blond hair, richly dark at the roots, and black eyebrows with dark eyes. Clarice found it remarkable that she had, with a simple announcement, become overnight a playwright and was interesting to other people at the university, one of whom she devoutly planned to marry.

The aspiring set designer's name was Helga Black and she worked as a housekeeper for a family in Squirrel Hill while she attended Pitt. Clarice had never learned how to type and was grateful to Helga for undertaking to type her play.

She secretly called the Greyhound bus station proudly for the price of a round-trip ticket to New York and planned to take the play when it was typed to Tennessee Williams's agent, whoever she was, and go to Josh Logan's office in New York and show somebody there her play. Making plans, jotting down the numbers of the bus station, the times, the return trip, working out where she would stay—the women's Y seemed the best place—she felt as if the earth in its turning had dislodged her and she floated in stellar space. She had felt before the writing like an incomplete child. Now promise lay in Helga Black's typewriter and the stage of Stephen Foster Memorial Hall where her plays were to be presented at the beginning of April. She recited Eliot and Shelley and kissed Tim passionately at strange, inopportune moments. She ruffled Helga's hair and laughed and Helga said, "You're crazy, but I don't blame you. I wish I were you."

The night her plays were to be put on, Riot assembled his

friends and their girlfriends, all of whom Clarice knew a lifetime, at Coyne's, downstairs to the Irish Club. They teased her by saying, "Can I touch you?" and "Will you remember my name tomorrow?"

Pal Mahoney bought everyone a beer and then Corn Sullivan bought beers for all of them. Her brother's friends wore white shirts and ties and their girlfriends, Marcie and Mary Jo, Bunny and Gin, had their hair done.

Clarice wore a thick sweater, heavy and big, of the sort she supposed O'Casey would wear at one of his productions. They had met at seven and left Coyne's a half hour later, all of them, waiting for eight-thirty. They walked out across the Panther Hollow Bridge, singing "Did you ever get that feeling in the moonlight?" timing it so that they arrived at eight-fifteen at Stephen Foster.

Pal Mahoney, Riot, the girls, a boy named Scaggs, Corn Sullivan, who harbored a desire to be a composer, Gerald and Clarice and the others walked in twos and threes slowly through Schenley Park, Clarice savoring the moment. "We'll sit away from you, we'll only make you nervous," Pal said.

"What a night," Corn said.

"It's Clarice's, make no mistake," Pal said.

Pal was himself theatrical with his bristly brows and gesturing hands, having been trained by Jesuits to make a point, but he would have been bound in chains and dropped in the Allegheny River rather than step on a stage.

Corn Sullivan said, "I think the reputation the theater has for attracting degenerates is unwarranted."

"Well, you're not there," Bobby Scaggs said as they walked along in the haze of night falling on shrubs and trees in the last of their youth, "so we know all the degenerates aren't in the theater."

"I'd settle for a degenerate," Gerald said and ran a few steps looking back to see if the invisible baseball which might come at any moment was aloft.

"You wouldn't know what to do," Mary Jo said.

Gerald snagged the invisible ball with a great leap on the Panther Hollow Bridge and turned and pegged out the runner at home plate. "You know, given all we know about war and the rest," he said, "I never cross a bridge I don't think of my cousin Eddie Spears and what he told us when he came home from France, how him and the other paratroopers leaped there into the darkness over the channel in the invasion. I look over this bridge and the idea of jumping scares me until I taste the beer we drank in my mouth. Them boys leaping into nothing, just jumping into darkness and clouds and trusting their parachutes and their guns and their officers and God to see them land feet upright on the ground."

"It makes me dizzy to think of it," Clarice said. "The uncertainty."

"You think we have troubles this minute," Pal said. "For blackness all around, think of the frogmen who used to dive in the cold water during the war. Remember Ken Donnely, he was one, swam out to a Japanese destroyer with his bombs, planted them, and was never heard from again."

Clarice and her plays were not cheered at the end of the performances. The old man and her mother hadn't come but Tim had brought his mother and father. The three of them left without talking to Clarice, and, ominously, Helga Black wasn't there. She had promised Clarice her typed play a week earlier and when

Clarice called the place where she worked the woman for whom she tended house said she had returned home to Steubenville, Ohio.

Clarice had asked why and when was she expected back, and the woman said, "I wouldn't know."

Clarice had imagined Helga appearing the night of the performances at Stephen Foster with her play crisp in a manila folder. It was called *The Hard Way.* She had thought that all the constellations of her longing and youth would gather together that night under the soft chandeliers of the narrow carpeted hall and she would be at last whole in other people's appreciation and her own sense of having gathered together everything she was and might be in one marvelous girl with a very bad beginning. Riot gave her a bouquet of flowers, and she tried to shelter them from the rain as they all walked, but the rain was hard. At the corner of Oakland Avenue and Forbes, she put the flowers into a receptacle can. She thought, Without the rain the flowers die and too much of it kills them just as surely. I guess it's pray for rain but not too much of it.

On a deserted Forbes in the rain, she felt abandoned with Riot and the girls and Corn and Pal and Gerald, and Pal finally said, "Up on stage you made a fine pack of jackasses out of us."

Clarice said, "That wasn't my intention. I tried to write what I knew, what was funny. Didn't you laugh? Wasn't there humor and truth in it?"

"If you weren't against us there might be something there," Mary Jo said. "It's the way an enemy would see us, boozing, talking about fighting, foolishly daydreaming."

"Bearing old grudges," Pal said. "Like old ladies washing clothes at a mountain stream."

Gerald said, "You made your mother out to be a drunk. It's your mother I'm thinking of. Riot, that was your mother on stage and you know it."

"It was an actress," Riot said. "It was a made-up character in a play. My mother's home this minute."

"Mrs. Costigan my mother?" Clarice asked. "How can you say that? She wasn't intended to be our mother. She had the characteristics of ten women in my neighborhood, and you choose my mother to pin it on."

"If I was your father," Corn said, "I'd lock you out of the house. You could have called that noisy reprobate George Washington and a blind four year old would know you'd put Thomas Cunningham up on stage for your Pitt pals to laugh at. Who else broke his leg chasing a beer truck in our time?"

Riot put his arm around her as they walked down Oakland Avenue to the Irish Club and whispered in her ear, "Being a playwright's brother ain't all it's cracked up to be, but don't worry about the family's good name. There ain't none."

She drank beer with Riot and his friends until late and no one mentioned her play again. The Korean War was in the smoky air of the Irish Club and they discussed it. While an early spring rain began to fall the boys and girls dispersed on Oakland Avenue in the new light and Riot and Clarice made their way through the drizzle up Robinson to the housing projects.

Gerald called that week and said, "I want to talk to you, Clarice, not Riot."

"Me?"

"Are you too good?"

"You know that's not the case."

"Well?"

"Okay, go ahead, we'll talk."

"I mean, over a drink."

He was eight years older than she was, and she supposed she had known for a long time that he was interested in her, in something of her more than Riot's sister.

"You sure, Gerald?"

"Of course, I'm sure."

"Gerald, I go to the Carnegie Library every afternoon at five. Could we meet over there? A cup of coffee in the downstairs cafeteria."

"The library?" he asked, and she knew that she was not making it easy for him. There was an unmanly quality to the library, and it was across the street from Pitt, the core of the danger zone for Riot and his friends who regarded that block as a haven for enemies of much they held dear: rich boys, homosexuals, communists, and women who considered themselves superior to the Oakland boys.

"No," she said, "on second thought, I think they close the cafeteria early at the library. How about the Betsy Ross?"

Wrong again: the restaurant was across the street from the Irish Club, too public and not particularly an Irish hang-out, owned by Greeks and patronized by men with thick mustaches.

"I was thinking along the lines of the Schenley Hotel," he said, "the bar there."

This was as direct an invitation to a long-term commitment as if Gerald Durgan had offered her marriage in writing, notarized. The bar was expensive and no one went there except on extraordinary occasions, even engagement parties.

"Okay," she said. "Sounds good."

She met him the next day and the bar held the manner of a vacation place.

People obviously not from Pittsburgh were in the booths and

at the oak tables, well dressed, tanned, loud in a foreign way, not the slow, sure, silence-punctuated rhythms of the native saloons. Gerald wore a crisp Hawaiian shirt in reds and yellows and he almost visibly perspired more by the minute.

Make it easy, she thought. Make it good, make him win.

They spoke of old times and St. Agnes and the Irish Club, and after awhile he said he thought she needed a friend. She had insulted almost everyone. People were angry with her. She needed a strong man to defend her. In her bad condition, he wanted to tell her right now he'd stick with her forever, not ever let her down — and not just because of his friendship with her brother. He had never talked directly like this to a woman, but he was going on thirty, and he had good prospects at the post office. He could even plan taking business courses at Robert Morris.

"Well?"

She knew she should act surprised. Me, Gerald? What are you saying?

Instead, she said, "You think I'm in a bad condition?"

"Yes, you need a friend. And are you acting now as if I'm not capable enough?"

"No, I'm meaning to listen more than talk."

"Well?"

"What if I continued doing the things that brought down all the anger on me? What if I hadn't a friend in the world but you for the evil things I wrote?"

"Couldn't happen. Clarice, I think you're brainy as well as beautiful, but you're not so brainy you can't see the truth of plain arguments. I'd show you by talk and example that you shouldn't be taking the path you're taking. What you're writing isn't evil, just hurtful. Between the two of us, we'd find another way for you to use your intelligence, us together. Going into business, a bar, an Army-Navy store, a good home, kids. You'd forget all this other stuff in a year—and, if you didn't, well, do it nights and weekends. But don't plan on building a life around things that damage other people. Well?"

"Maybe I'm too far gone."

"No, I know that underneath all that double-talk people hear in college in you there's still the beautiful kid with red hair I used to see bouncing down to church on Sundays, excuse me, surviving your mother and father, doing good despite the bad breaks fate put up for obstacles. But you come through: now I'll come through for you."

"You sure can talk well, Gerald," she said. "You could sell gloves in hell if you set your mind to it. And had you said this to me two years ago when I was crazy about you"—a lie—"I'd have leaped at the chance, like all the other girls in Oakland mad for you. But right now I'm in an unclear time in my life, as you know. Let's not talk serious for now."

For now! She had gone too far.

"I have too many things to work out, Gerald, okay?"

They were quiet over their wine, long and persuasive periods of failure hanging over the enterprise for him; but she was not unhappy with the deadly tone their conversation had taken. As her feelings mounted in her about his sullen thoughtfulness, she knew she was angry. She did not feel at all in a bad condition; she did not require comfort and unwelcome promise for the future. She knew what Eddie Spears's cousin leaping from the airplane in a parachute understood: better this choice in the skies than that.

She and Gerald shook hands on the sidewalk outside the hotel, and she walked quickly down Bellefield to Forbes and the library.

When she called Tim the next day he did not come to the phone. His mother said, "He's not here," and when she began to ask about him, his mother said, "You've failed your heritage" and hung up on her.

At the registration office at Pitt a clerk gave her Helga Black's telephone number in Ohio and she called her. "I'm getting married," she said while Clarice shifted at the public telephones on the basement floor of the Cathedral of Learning.

"I wish you the best," she said, "but I'm concerned about my play. I gave it all to you in pieces. Did you type it?"

"I sure did," she said. "I'll call Mrs. Shermer and tell her you're coming. I'll tell her exactly where it's at." She gave Clarice an address in Squirrel Hill.

"Good luck," Clarice said. "You're a friend in a million."

"I just know you're going to hit the big time," Helga said.

After taking a trolley in a heavy rain, Clarice made her way up to the Shermer residence with an umbrella, careful not to slip on the wet ground. A fine-looking woman, warm from the heat in the house, pale with flushed cheeks, and an expensive beige silk blouse, admitted her. She stepped back as if Clarice had come to do work there. She pointed up the stairs.

"Helga's very impetuous," Clarice said, and the woman didn't answer.

In a desk drawer in Helga's former room where Clarice expected to find the newly typed manuscript there sat the scraps of paper on which she had scrawled scenes, half pages, some on wrapping paper, wisps of paper with numbers on them and three words, a rolled-up sheaf of paper with handwriting on both sides. "She told me she would type this for me," Clarice said, fumbling with the scraps. The woman looked at her without changing her expression.

She thrust some into her raincoat pocket, asking O'Casey to remember that things were not always easy for a third-year dramatist at Pitt, then other sheets into her purse, and then some into her blouse to protect them from the rain. The woman said nothing but this time let her precede her down the stairs.

"Thank you," Clarice said at the door.

The woman closed the door quickly and she heard her bolt it. Careful not to fall, she tried to stride purposefully toward the sidewalk, then sure of her footing on the pavement she began to walk faster. Clutching her play closely, a passport to astonish New York, she fell into a slow run in the rain with her precious cargo.

It was ten blocks on the streetcar back to her brother and Oakland and his friends and their mothers and sisters in Oakland, the boys probably at this moment sitting in a back booth at the Betsy Ross or the Pitt Tavern yawning and stretching and the women young and old with conversations on the phone and maybe plans for bingo and going to a movie, all, no matter the years, dwelling on their youth blurred before them this minute: as if what was happening now was so good it was already kindly memory. At first she ran and tried not to jostle the scraps of paper which nestled in her pockets and against her body. She would die, she thought, if she lost a syllable. Then she asked herself what did a one-act play or two, even a three-act play, matter. She ran faster heedlessly. She was herself, however bad and offensive to public decency, in a situation of being a playwright in an April rain and an amazement before the world, a woman from a government housing project, with all she knew and had seen and heard and remembered. And, finally, with all the unintended insults and damages, wasn't putting it down on paper really an afterthought for someone like Tommy's daughter who was drunk with love going nowhere?

She carefully boarded the wet, slippery steps to the 67 Swiss-vale and the familiar streets of Oakland ready for the terrible gasp, the breath not there, the plunge into clouds and space or black water that being a playwright like García Lorca or O'Casey meant every hour of the day. Days and nights of sweet danger, and no particular friends to hold your hand. It was no subject for tears but the thing to do—listen to steady Riot Cunning-ham—and no personal regret for her in it, only the leap and air and maybe never ever touching solid ground.

SEVEN

The Priest of Storms

AFTER THE Hungarian Revolution of 1956 there came to the United States a young man from Budapest named Joe Tapir. He had been in the square where Stalin's statue was overthrown. When the Soviet tanks came in a few days later he had to run for his life from his native country. He swept into the embracing, open arms of Americans, who saw him a survivor of things they cherished and a promise of eventual victory against the godless communists in Europe and the Soviet tanks that supported their mischief. Cardinal Mindzenty had been freed by his captors and for a while as the year closed it appeared there would be great changes in Europe.

Tapir came to Oakland, about twenty years of age, and was honored everywhere. He was treated like a long-lost brother and son by the adults and boys from the St. Paul's Cathedral district and St. Agnes's parish, down Fifth. He was outfitted in suits and ties, sport shirts with huge flowers on them, and given a car by the Knights of Columbus. At the Ancient Order of Hibernians, Division No. 9, he was celebrated with toasts nightly by men who swore they wished they had been there that day to see the beginning of the end of the hated communism represented by Stalin's head in the gutter rolling away from the body of the statue in Bem Square. Until he could learn English and make deliveries, he was given a job in the office of Bowyer and Brown, All City Truckers.

The fervent anticommunism in Oakland assured him a long, happy life of free beer and dinners for decades. As people later remembered him, he had green eyes and a firm chin and had sturdy arms and was neither tall nor short but had a solemn steady look and an earnest attention when he was spoken to.

He became acquainted with a young woman named Alice Quarles, and the people who discussed such subjects assumed she would marry him. She was short with bobbed hair and bangs on her forehead, looking more like a grade-schooler than a young woman who attended Mt. Mercy Academy. Altogether Alice was a good catch, scrubbed and clean and intelligent; an elder sister had married a man who managed two movie theaters for Loews in the Pittsburgh district.

Alice and Joe Tapir looked good together, both moving with confidence in their smallest and largest movements, he in a borrowed tie that was never knotted properly at the neck and not talkative but interested in conversations and she wearing her finest clothes when they went anywhere: downtown to a movie, the Irish Club, sometimes with her family out to a bingo game in East Liberty. Joe Tapir was with her every night. Weekends he worked in the small yard behind the family house on Ward Street.

He lived on Craft Avenue in one room, and he walked down Forbes to see Alice every day, nodding to strangers, sober but friendly. He fit in, talking to children, polite to adults, never flirting with any of the young women on the streets of Oakland.

This ability to move comfortably with people, from the Masses at St. Agnes to the occasional stroll Joe and Alice took through the Carnegie Museum on Forbes, later became of interest to any number of people who said they had known him and, further, drawing a conclusion, it goes to prove something, no one ever really does know anyone else, do they? If that was the lesson.

As easily as he had fallen in step with Alice Quarles, one day he stopped seeing her.

"I called him, you know," she said to people who asked about his absence, immediately after he was gone. "There hadn't been a fight or anything. He was here one minute, underfoot, my mother said, and the next he was gone. He said he would explain. Later. He said he'd be in touch. He'd call, I guess I thought; but he didn't do that and he never wrote. I did call him again: and this time he acted busy, mumbled something, and that was the last of him and me. Well, a person sees a lot in a lifetime and I'm only twenty. I guess I'll have my share of queer happenings. But none like him, and you know what I mean."

He was taken in by a family named McGann and in less than a year from the time he had left Hungary he had murdered the mother and father and raped the daughter, then fourteen, but did not kill her. Through an accident, the younger son, Matthew, was allowed to escape unharmed by the killer.

Joe Tapir had been living altogether less than three months in their home when he brought down doom on the McGann family.

Matthew, the boy, then nine, had slipped on the ice that afternoon on Darraugh Street, and in the confusion and pain of his broken bones had been among strangers in the Montefiore Hospital where his leg was being set when Joe Tapir was about his grisly business. Matthew had been injured less than two blocks away from the hospital and had been discovered on the sidewalk by a porter coming to work.

The phone at the McGanns' rang all night as hospital personnel tried to find someone to come to take Matthew home after his bones had been set. He remembered crying all night, more concerned that there was no answer to the phone at his house than his broken ankle. His sister, Paula, had lain in a coma after Joe Tapir raped her and left her for dead with her throat cut, and it was she who finally staggered as night fell into the street to tell of Tapir's crime.

Matthew, not knowing anything of what had happened, tried to escape the doctors and nurses and run from the hospital the few blocks to the street where he lived, but once outside, his legs unsteady, he was unnerved—he sensed catastrophe. The darkness of his first night without a family and the feeling that something dreadful lay in the fog that had settled on the slush and black streets came at him from every side. It was not that he was in an unfamiliar place. He knew the streets. He knew the hospital. He walked here every day. But there was something new on the air that night: not just that he couldn't walk properly, his first injury, or the first that he could remember. He was a cautious boy and had never broken any bones or hurt himself or had fevers; and that night he ached strangely in his forehead and he could not stop sweating. In the cold air he alternately felt as if he were going to die of cold or ignite with the heat inside himself. He shivered and could not control the trembling in his arms and legs. He sat on a curb on the street leading up to where he lived and hoped his mother would come along or his father or sister Paula or Joe Tapir from Hungary who lived with them all.

He did not care for the feeling in the shaking of his jaw and his eyes that would not focus the touch of the overwhelming call to newness, the bitter inability to think that things would soon be right, that the night with its streetlights were like people watching, not him, but something and old things were over, terrible new things beginning. But streetcars still ran, their bells assuring people they were there and going somewhere and Matthew knew a short block away people were eating in the Tottles Restaurant.

No longer fighting the streets, even the short walk to his house—the night was too uncertain and he felt small and helpless in it—he staggered back into the brightly lit hospital. He tossed all night, crying in his sleep, the first of many times where nameless ideas and darkness alarmed him and closed off sleep.

He was not taken home directly the next morning.

Father Farrell, the priest at St. Agnes, came for him and drove him the few blocks to the church. They were both silent in the car. The priest patted his hand and asked, "How is your leg?"

Matthew said, "Okay, but my mother's going to worry."

The priest nodded his head.

"Be strong," he said. "Your mother and father would want you to be strong."

"I'm scared, Father."

"Yes, sure, scared, your leg is broken. It's scary."

"No, it's something else. How come it's you they sent to get me?"

"Me, as well as anyone. I'm pleased to be with you, any help I can be."

Matthew began to tremble again when Father Farrell said, "We can pray together."

"I want to go home," Matthew said. "Father, I want to go home."

St. Agnes's Church is an old building, rebuilt in 1909, always there for the neighborhood, beyond time for children. It might have been there a week after the Crucifixion, Easters from the time of St. Paul, long time, rolling with mystery and death and baptisms and marriages and joys and Matthew was frightened. A broken leg was no occasion to be brought to the home of all answers to suffering.

Inside his warm office, Father Farrell helped Matthew into a chair and did not sit behind a desk. He motioned to a nun who had walked in and said, "You know Matthew McGann, don't you, Sister?"

"I do indeed. How's your sister? She's a lovely girl."

Father Farrell quickly stood and spoke softly to the nun, and she said, "I'll bring you a cup of chocolate, Matthew. I'm sorry." Her face was the color of the white in her wimple.

Father Farrell took Matthew's hand. "In the course of the world, in its treacheries and sorrows, your mother and father have been taken."

"Taken, how taken?"

"It's not clear yet. I just spoke to Captain Carr at Number Four. He says it was a murder."

"Murder, my mother and father? Murder."

Matthew began to make a sound that occurred to him was

like something an animal makes, a howl and a sob. Sister and Father Farrell held him. He fell from the chair and would have run but with his broken leg he remained writhing on the floor until the nun and priest helped him to his feet.

Father Farrell said, "To speak to you now of Heaven will be a sorry consolation, and it's not my intention to ever make of a blessed reward a substitute for love on this earth. There's still love in Oakland, Matthew. Your mother and father died loving you and that's not an emotion that death can change. And you loved them, and that's as real now as it was yesterday this time and will be true thirty years from now. Heaven's one thing, much to be desired, this love is another, equally to be desired. Your sister's been hurt but she loves and you and she will survive this. I think your mother and father are with us now while you love them. They are somewhere where you can tell them of your love, and I believe they will hear you. I'm a grown man, Matthew, and an hour from now I will speak to them and tomorrow too. I'm not a fool. I don't think I'll be talking to myself. I think they will hear me. And they'll show the both of us an extraordinary mercy, they and God will help us to allow our hearts to heal. They'll help you with the pain of their absence. Even, after awhile, you and Paula, I know she will live, you and she will try to find forgiveness for the person who did this to us."

Matthew, bewildered, went to live with an aunt about ten blocks away.

He never again lived in the house on Darraugh. His aunt, his father's sister, and his uncle were kind. It was not easy for them. They could not help shielding him, and, still, they were careful not to leave him oversheltered. Somewhere he knew a decision had been made to have him live as normal a life as possible. And

that was not there in the facts about himself, even when he suc-
ceeded in persuading everyone, Father Farrell, his aunt Maeve,
his uncle Jeffrey, later his sister and her husband, that he was just
as fine as could be, if not happy then not brooding. But of course
it was not so.

Everything connected with the murder took on an importance to Matthew that he concealed from everyone: no friend
ever heard a word of it, no member of the family ever suspected it.

Streets leading up to the event, around it, after it, held a mysterious meaning to him that he could not explain. Where he had
fallen and broken his leg was sacred, like the place a saint had
been stabbed with a holy sword or an unearthly light had once
appeared. Here, he thought, looking at the exact spot, was where
I was and was not murdered because of it. And there where the
trolley makes its way out to East Liberty is where another trolley
last year—then it was two years ago and then five—rode with
no one hearing my call for help. He measured things by the
murder; he counted his feelings from before and after it had
happened.

A cry in the night, a scream on television! Was it the sound
that was the last utterance of his mother? Eisenhower became to
Matthew, whatever else he was, the president of the United
States when his mother and father had been killed.

Nothing in the smell of flowers, the coming of winter, the
rattle in a window in the wind, the face of a clock at certain
hours did not speak directly to him of his loss and terror.

For years he came back to look at the house where Tapir had
murdered his mother and father, never going inside, walking
around it, trying to feel Tapir, to smell him, remember him,
capture him, and imprison him in memory. He stood silently

watching the place. Other people, not knowing him, lived there, another family. He was sure they knew little of the details of the house. A story too terrible not to be told; but the details became muffled, the exact events at the house changed, probably now unrecognizable even to Matthew, who dwelt on every moment of the time. He stared first at the front stairs, imagining who had walked there. He circled the house. There were old things there in the small yard he knew had been there the fateful twilight, but he did not remember them from childhood. A broken path from the garage to the back porch, weeds there in the crevices— had the weeds, those same weeds, been there the night it happened? He came to the house mostly as the day was closing, trying to see it as it was the day it happened. But nothing brought them—and Tapir—closer.

He hardly could make out in his mind Joe Tapir's face or his body. He had lived with them so briefly and came and went quickly.

Matthew remembered mostly his father and mother, she about the house, inhabiting rooms even when she wasn't in them, her feel to cushions and the plush old sofas, pictures on the wall, stains in the kitchen from steam where she had once cooked. Then he remembered his father, the man taking the family on annual vacations to Atlantic City and the boy to baseball games at Forbes Field, each pitch explained, given meaning, every ball game important and the two of them, father and son smart enough to attend double headers, two games for the price of one for those smart enough to know a bargain. Forbes Field was about twelve blocks away, and Matthew remembered the slow walks there after Mass: he was young enough that his father held his hand, and he remembered that. They talked of lofty things, Pirates' chances for the year, the opposing teams—so many times the Chicago Cubs that the Chicago team stayed in his mind to the degree that he thought perhaps it had been only one memorable Sunday that the Pirates beat the Cubs twice and that had filled in all the other Sundays of his youth. His father, an electrician with a good and steady lifetime job repairing wiring and installing outlets at the Grant Building downtown, had assured Matthew the boy would do even better. College was the ticket for his sister Paula and Matthew when they were ready.

Matthew had dreaded the thought of his mother and father ever dying. He had gone to funerals of people the family knew from St. Agnes. He had put out of his thoughts the idea of them ever dying. Shadowy, quick, and self-assured, sleeves rolled, there came then Joe Tapir to live with the McGanns, and the end of all of life was given a new meaning to Matthew, not the ceremony at St. Agnes and the talk of the long, virtuous life of the deceased. Now he knew the close to everything was on the morning air, given breath with each dawn but still bearable in its incompletion by sunlight or even the cloudiest days. Only at night did the unmeaning take its final shape, which was to be always no form at all, a stab in the dark outside the light from a lamp post, a person with no sound or movement waiting around a corner or standing remotely draped by a closet curtain in a dark room waiting his chance to cut goodness to pieces.

He slept with a light on, his aunt permitted it, and he seldom went out at night, remembering the first night of dashing from the hospital in the darkness and later knowing there was no place to run. All was gone.

His sister took Matthew to live with her some years later when she married, and she and her husband and Matthew spent hours, not every night but often enough, talking about what they would like to do to Joe Tapir if he was ever found. They spoke of hurting him, stabbing him, at other times praying for him and pleading with him to ask God for forgiveness for what he had done to them. They tried to find out who he really was from the Hungarian Catholic Mission that had sponsored his welcome to the United States. But little was on record about him. He had been admitted under the American policy of special visas for what were then called "freedom fighters." He had been in Hungary at the time of the revolution, but what part he played there in the chaotic days was apparently never to be known. It was suggested by many people who had succumbed to the feeling of participation in the destruction of one of the great evils of the twentieth century that Joe Tapir might have been an escaped maniac who had managed to forge papers and come to America in a diabolical ruse. Other people said he had probably returned to Hungary and, wanted even there, had blended back into the native population. His English was poor. He could not be anywhere in the United States without standing out for his limited ability to speak the way people did in Pittsburgh or Detroit.

It was said further by people discussing the subject at the Ancient Order of Hibernians that Joe Tapir might not have been his name at all, and that he may well have been an unrepentant communist sent to America by his masters to sow confusion in the minds of well-meaning people.

Outside of Matthew's hearing—people did not talk about the subject within earshot of him as if he had done something discreditable and was somehow linked to the hatred of Joe Tapir and his terrible deeds—it was said that perhaps the devil, as had been stated many times, had taken human form once again. It was surmised so senseless was the butchery that the devil, understanding that consternation, panic, and meaninglessness were his major weapons, had come to Pittsburgh in the form of Joe Tapir.

"It makes sense, you know," Dickie Trent said some years after the event. "If the devil took hold of one of us a person could say, 'Well, poor Mahoney was always soft in the head but never homicidal. Charge it up to simple lunacy,' the devil making no point except crazy people do crazy things."

"Then again," Pal Mahoney said, not at all daunted by the allusion to himself as a lunatic, "if it was Dickie Trent who went on a rampage, no plausible explanation, people could say, 'Given the family and the boy's inherent disposition to deceit and fraud, you'd have to guess it was as inevitable as sunshine following the rain he'd one day run amok to show us what's behind that smirking choirboy exterior.' No devil in it at all, no confusion on the homicide."

"I think," Cleet said, "if the devil was to walk in the door this minute not one of you would recognize him. Your business with him so on the hour, regular, lost in easy morals to make your ordinary killer of ten cry at your righteousness covering the billy goat. I tell you, Mahoney, if pride is the sin it's cracked up to be, you and the Jesuits who deranged you are on the train going south."

At that moment, Matthew McGann walked through the door at the Irish Club, and Corny Sullivan spotting him first made a gesture indicating sudden silence with his hand sawing the air, and Cleet, who knew him best, called, "Matthew, over here, my boy, Mahoney's in full flower of listening to himself talk, good for a laugh every time."

Chairs were rearranged for Matthew, but no one expected him to speak. He seldom added anything to a conversation, but he always listened attentively, his eyes following the speaker.

He said, "Any score in the Pirates game yet?" but no one thought his mind was on a baseball game that night or any night.

His mind was on Tapir, and one day, at football practice, he thought he saw him. It was a wind-swept afternoon and the stands were empty except for one man who sat on an upper bench. The team at Schenley High was running and blocking, quarterbacks passing to runners putting together diagrams, when Matthew, a tackle, looked up and noticed the shirt, the haircut, the small beard on the man, familiar and still strange. People seldom watched the team practice. Matthew tried to forget the man but could not.

When he saw the man stand and start toward the end of the benches, Matthew could not contain himself further. In uniform, he ran after the man into the parking lot. Hearing the sound of Matthew's cleats on the asphalt, the man turned quickly, a friendly expression on his face.

"Matthew," he said.

"I know you," Matthew said, taking his arm.

"Sure you do."

"Joe Tapir!"

"Matthew, it's Jack Boyle, Harry's uncle. I was at your house when you were a kid."

"What are you doing here? I mean, out watching me practice?"

"Not you, Matthew, little Davie Devitt, my sister's son. I did see you out there, looking good, but it was Davie I came out for, figuring there'd be some hitting. But you know, this is nothing."

"Jack Boyle? I don't remember you."

"Well, you remember Harry?"

"Harry Boyle, sure."

"You were five, maybe six. I used to come by with Harry when we lived up on Darraugh. You were a nice little boy, grew up to be a husky. Harry's in the army."

"Yeah, I remember Harry, but I don't remember you. But you look familiar."

"It was a terrible thing, Matthew. We think about you all the time. You don't know how happy it made me to see you out here, playing football. Getting on with life."

"Yeah, I'm sorry, Jack, I don't know what I was thinking."

"I have one of them faces, Matthew, you know. People think they know me all the time."

"I'm sorry, Jack."

"You're in my thoughts, kid, you and the rest. They were great people."

Boyle turned and walked away quickly, embarrassed at the subject, too near the center of the tragedy, Matthew thought, for what his feelings were about all of it. And who could blame him? It was nothing to think about too long, Matthew thought, unless you're to become like me.

The wind was raw on his face when he ran back to the practice field.

Hardly knowing what was happening to her brother, Paula took Matthew on a vacation to a small farm outside Somerset, about thirty miles away, ten years after the events on Darraugh Street. It was only she and Matthew. Her husband stayed to work in Pittsburgh. It was the thing to do, he thought, if what had to be dealt with was all that anyone saw in looking at him, a boy, capable of laughing, sometimes moody, but not too distant from other people or carrying on his forehead his circling formulations.

She thought to encourage Matthew to see something of the world away from the frightening things that clung to all of them. Sky broad and blue, cattle in their innocence slow and lost to themselves, the wind in high grass blowing from a great distance, it comforted her; and its easy long days and nights, a time of natural wonders, simple, seemed to her a fine medicine for them both. They stayed with a farmer in his main house, and in the day they drank milk and ate home-baked bread and walked and talked. They removed their shoes and socks and sat by a creek, cooling themselves.

"This is the best summer of my life," Paula said. "The country lets me loose of thoughts."

"I think of the time before Joe Tapir," Matthew said, "all of it as my happiest time. Nothing after can be as happy as then, all of us—well, at our best and finished, what we were meant to be. Then he came along and nothing was ever really happy again. Now we are unfinished."

"I understand that feeling, but doesn't the water on our feet feel cool? Isn't the sun good the way it makes us squint?"

She knew he was not making things better for her, it was not at all like him to lie, when he said, "Yes, this is good, Paula, it's happy, and it's good. But it's not the happiest I've ever been. I can't think of a happiness greater than the time, all of it, before Joe Tapir came."

"Can't you think of him like a storm? Bad luck. A building collapsing on mother and father."

"No. I think there was a meaning to him. Maybe there's a meaning to a fire that kills people, and maybe the same for a building collapsing. But he's a person, and I'm religious, Paula, and I think he made choices. To come to us, to kill mother and father. And God knew it, so I wonder what was God's purpose."

"You know that's something you'll never know."

He stood and did not put his shoes and socks on again. He held them in one hand and reached down to help Paula stand with the other hand. "Not knowing what God had in mind, never, you're right, gives me only one other thing to think about," he said. "What was Joe Tapir's purpose?"

"You mean why did he do it. He—"

"No, I mean his purpose in our lives, not what he thought he was doing. Maybe he had no thoughts about it, just did it, and wondered himself why he did it. Maybe he did it in one place or another and it had become something ordinary with him and not to be thought of. I'm not thinking of him in that way, I'm thinking of us. Please, I don't want to talk about it anymore. I love this place, I love this farm, the quiet hum of things, the smell of hay and grass. Let's not talk about what happened to us anymore today."

They did not talk about it seriously perhaps ever again.

After a few days in the country, Matthew woke one morning to think he was somewhere he should not be. He walked out to a barn and inhaled the smell of chickens, roosters, cows, hay in the distance, grass not yet burned with summer's heat and felt wrong. It seemed to him that the country, being out of Pittsburgh, was a half place. He had nothing here; it was not a place with its soft hills and cattle and fences and still air that was anything but a disruption to his thoughts. He could not after awhile even think of where he was. It was enough he was not in a place where Joe Tapir might be: never out here, too implausible, too otherworldly to expect to see him in a field, wading in a stream. There was a place he would inevitably be, but here on the farm was not anywhere connected to him.

It had been a mistake to come; he was abandoning his slain mother and father and that terrible night, once more absent when he should have been present. Standing in a hot morning sun, he shuddered. It felt sickening and peculiar to leave his parents and their pain and their house somehow behind him, as if he had moved forward. The farm was beautiful and his sister's love was real, but it was a trap. It made of him two people, one who was here and one back in Pittsburgh, the one there as unhappy as ever but more whole. Here he was less than himself as he was coming to know what he was all about because there was no beginning or end to himself that did not include the chance perhaps to reach and touch Joe Tapir, not really, but to feel as if it could happen. It could not feel like that in rural sunlight and the innocent buzz of houseflies and leaves shivering in quick wind.

He packed his suitcase quickly and without saying good-bye to anyone left the farm. He caught a bus on the highway back to Pittsburgh. He did not ever want to betray what he held dear, in all its complications, by seeming to close the door on it, to put it into memory as if remembering was a storage closet never to be visited, where the hurt and anguish might be gone but with it the goodness before Joe Tapir too.

Right after high school, Matthew took a job in a supermarket, bagging groceries and helping customers cart the food to their cars. He liked the work, and he enjoyed the other employees and the customers he spent his days with. The pay was not good, but he did not care. No one in the supermarket knew who he was, and that had become over time not unusual. Years had passed, and there were terrible and unnatural murders, new ones in the paper every day, and he was not remembered in the rush of other things that happened to people.

As he was hanging up his apron to leave one night when the supermarket was closing, the lights already off, he became aware of a stir in the front of the store.

Two men waving pistols stood at the front door and shouted things to the employees in the store. The first thing he thought was, It's not Joe Tapir, and he felt cursed that the murderer was in his mind though the men in the front with guns could kill someone now while he watched. He knew them to be not much older than he was. The men raged at the people in the front of the store. They did not seem aware or care that Matthew and another bagboy stood near a time clock the distance across the store from them and were watching. They did not look to the back of the store.

One fired his gun in the air and it struck the ceiling, the noise loud.

They loaded paper bags with money, and the second robber fired his gun into an aisle with canned goods. Food flew from the bullet. The two men shouted they would kill everyone if anyone moved. They would be waiting outside with guns trained on the door to see who dared follow them. "Count to twenty!" the one said. "Count to twenty before you make a move or you're dead."

No one moved as the men ran out the front door. Matthew did not move with the others when the place began to stir with activity. Women were crying and men were making themselves busy with cleaning the store and cursing to each other but not in front of the women. Many of the men said what they would have done to the punks if they had not had guns. The police came and took notations on the two criminals. Everyone had a story to tell, but Matthew told only what he had heard, hardly what he had seen. The descriptions of the men were plentiful. The thieves had done little to conceal themselves. "This is going to give me bad dreams for a year," a woman said to Matthew, and he wondered if that was true. No one had been hurt; the criminals had not seemed to want to hurt anyone.

Matthew was pleased to take a mop and clean up the floor where the canned goods had been cast in all directions by the bullets. People gathered around each other, some of the women wept, and Matthew was consoling with the rest, putting his arm around a cashier named Gladys.

"They could have killed us all," she said, the same thing many of the other employees said.

Matthew agreed, but he did not believe it. He did not think after Joe Tapir a gunman would kill him: somehow that was not the way it was, the game to be played out. He knew he was different. He would not die by accident. That would have made Tapir part of a larger accident, and that was unthinkable.

In the store, for days people spoke of nothing else, eagerly going downtown to the police station to identify possible suspects. Matthew did not know if the men were ever captured. Their fate did not interest him. He did not care if they went to prison. The truth was that he had not been very concerned even as the two thieves cursed and fired their pistols. It did not seem personally worrisome to him. What could they do, what could anyone do to him with guns or knives that was worse than what Joe Tapir had already done?

He felt, even as he heard the gunfire, that it was not directed at him. It was almost as though Joe Tapir's conduct had led Matthew into a special world, a fate, where his future was as peculiar as Tapir's had been. It could not be that Joe Tapir came, murdered, and went as mysteriously in one portion of his life as he had in all the others. Closing the doors to terror and uncertainty that Joe Tapir had opened would make it all normal.

How could anything with the monster in it be normal?

Plunging a knife into people and killing them! He woke at night, scenes and blood in his mind, and was thankful he was frightened. He welcomed the shivers. The sweat that lay on him cold and constant was comfortable. Otherwise, what had happened would make sense as it made its way into his dreams and life and became part of ordinary things.

When he was old enough, Matthew acquired a chauffeur's license and went to work for the Yellow Cab Company. He drove mostly in the daylight, not caring for the city after dark, but still, being out at night in his cab was not the same as being on the sidewalk. There he felt the presence of an unseen accumulation of enemies in doorways or watching him from passing automobiles. He did not know their names. He never saw their faces in his mind. They were hardly people. They were part of a huge wave of uncertainty, he thought, that would catch him and whirl him into nothingness again, more complete even than what had happened the night Joe Tapir had announced his bloody presence. He did not marry. He left his sister's house: Joe Tapir rang in the stairwells and a telephone's signal, a creaking board, there among his survivors through the years like a bell marking hours or days.

It was enough that inside himself the murderer never left his thoughts for longer than a day, but hearing his brother-in-law and sister speak of him constantly as if the talk of Joe Tapir was never to end became finally too much. He was their most familiar subject; he became easy to them as talk. Frozen, they watched the ruin of innocence unfold before them and knew in their bones justice was somewhere else, not here, maybe nowhere. They could not, in their realization that the darkness held no mercy, stop the dagger thrust in the dark that says I am, Matthew thought, and, you kind fools, you are feathers in the wind. Once he came unannounced even in laughter, he was a fever in the blood, a deadly disease not to be taken lightly.

Moving into two rooms on Dunseith, Matthew avoided his sister and her children and their house. All had been colored by the man who had come so swiftly and departed in equal haste. Life altered, life destroyed. But where had he gone?

After driving a cab for four years, Matthew admitted to himself what he was doing.

No matter the business at hand, the destination of the fare in the cab, he was cruising the city and watching the faces outside his cab and the people riding with him for Joe Tapir. He drove a taxicab to search for the murderer of his mother and father. He had come to think that as accidentally as Tapir had leaped into his life he would, so strangely, come again. As he drove, he looked into faces, measuring years there and expressions: ten thousand faces of passengers in his cab, watching them, waiting. He had come once: why not believe he would come again?

Matthew often drove his cab to a small platform at the top of Mount Washington where he could look down on the city. Leaning on his elbows, he studied the confluence of the three rivers as they became the Ohio River. It all seemed purposeful to him, but he was certain he would never know the purpose. Somewhere in the city with its chimneys and red brick houses and leaning wooden buildings on hillsides there could be his man, even today: hidden in Pittsburgh, and why not? Who but the McGann family remnants wondered about him fifteen years later?

When he talked to his sister and her husband he knew they worried about him.

Now that they had children they only spoke of Tapir when

the children were not present. Matthew did not stay long on his visits. Women did not interest him. He was, in truth, not very interested in himself. It was Joe Tapir's meaning his life had become. That he could arrive, leave his message, and then vanish not to be remembered, not as a person, his crimes good deeds for all anyone cared. Father Farrell cared, but Matthew did not enjoy meeting the priest's look even when nothing was said. He knew what the priest wanted. And he knew it could never be there: he could never forgive Joe Tapir for pulling aside the curtain and in swift strokes of his blade teaching Matthew truths better left unlearned. Perhaps it ran in families: that ability to appear in others' lives for fleeting unhappy moments, never to return except as a bitter reminder of the cruelty that could cut loose in ordinary places, among familiar people, on days or years not noteworthy for anything else.

When he was twenty-nine, Matthew took his first vacation since he and Paula had gone together to the farm outside of Somerset.

"I think it's just the thing to do," Paula said. "It'll do you good."

Atlantic City where they had gone before Joe Tapir came: a place of sweetness and lost boyhood, it was just the thing to do as he approached thirty, Paula said.

"Remember the times we had in Atlantic City?" she asked, taking Matthew's hand.

"How could I forget?"

Cotton candy and hot dogs on the boardwalk and the smell of suntan oil and the salt off the ocean and the wood under their feet giving off oldness and ocean and sounds as people walked there, and to see again those faces in promenade coming at him as he had when he was a boy. Nowhere could he remember seeing so many faces, moving toward him, stepping aside, talking, chewing, yawning, smiling, laughing, frowning against sun in their faces. He had the dim but persistent feeling that in all those faces surely one would be Joe Tapir. But why there in Atlantic City? Because Matthew would be there. And why at the very time Matthew was there? Because he had come to Matthew before at random—others in Oakland had wanted to take him in but by persistence of good will and fortune the McGanns had received him and were consequently murdered and he and Matthew, if any of it meant anything, were bound to meet again. He had dreamed it for years in his taxicab, a last thought before he fell asleep at night. Atlantic City, with all the stream of faces, seemed after awhile to be exactly where Matthew and Joe Tapir would be together, the same chance that had thrown them together when he was nine would connect them again on the old boardwalk.

He took a room off the boardwalk in a decaying, cheap hotel after the bus ride down from Pittsburgh and dressed himself to meet Tapir. He wore his shirt out over his trousers, looking, he thought, like a tourist, and combed his hair neatly. He wore well-worn shoes, knowing he would walk a great deal in the week he had allowed himself. Almost lost in memories of his mother and father and Paula, he wandered nostalgically down to where the Steel Pier had been, the old convention hall, the end of the boardwalk where the ocean came in with a mighty roar. He lost his sense of emergency: he did not stare into faces. If he was correct, Joe Tapir would be here, unhurried and unaware of Matthew. He would be startled to be discovered, he would lie. But Matthew would know him.

He took from his wallet the yellowed newspaper clipping of Joe Tapir's picture, a small insert in a larger photograph of what the story had called "The House of Murder." He placed the very unclear picture by a lamp in his hotel room, feeling free. Not that he needed the photograph: he knew his man.

For two days he saw a number of men who could be Tapir, but he did not stare long. The eyes were not steady enough, the coloring was different. As he ate dinner in a small restaurant on Atlantic Avenue one night he felt Joe Tapir very close.

He came back to the restaurant the next day and saw inside from the sidewalk a scene he knew he would one day encounter: Joe Tapir inside the restaurant, dressed in a policeman's uniform, carrying a cup of coffee, looking out at Matthew, not aware of who stood on the sidewalk. He was talking to the waitress at the cash register and had apparently drawn his coffee himself from a machine at the front of the restaurant, and, as Matthew watched, he turned and went to sit in a booth in the rear, his back to the door at the entrance. He could not be observed from the front of the restaurant.

Matthew took from his shin the long knife he had strapped there. Since childhood he had carried it, waiting for this moment.

He walked quickly into the restaurant and sat in the booth facing the policeman.

"Joe?"

"Yeah, who're you?"

"Joe Tapir?"

"Joseph Fox, who are you?"

Matthew reached across the table and put his knife to the man's throat. "Give me your gun," he said, "and I won't kill you."

"Who the hell are you?"

Matthew pushed the long knife into the man's throat. "Give me your gun."

"Take it easy, take it easy. I'm not Joe Tapir."

Matthew took the gun and put it in his shirt.

"We're almost even today, Joe."

"Partner, you have the wrong man."

"Joe, it's been a long time."

"Don't do nothing crazy, okay? Let me reach in my pocket and show you my identification, my driver's license."

He took out cards and pushed them toward Matthew.

"That's supposed to fool me? They all say Joseph Fox, is that supposed to fool me?"

"Okay, listen to me: I was born in New Jersey, Asbury Park, and I went to high school there. I was on the swimming team. That lady behind the counter, the waitress, is my ex-wife, she and I went to high school together. Okay? I'm in here talking to her because there's a mix-up. She asked people to our daughter's wedding two weeks from now I told her were poison. Ask her. They go, I'm not going. Ask her. Ask about high school."

Matthew leaned out of the booth and called, "Waitress!"

The importance of the slow moment that occurred while he waited fell on him. If the man was lying, as Joe Tapir would, the truth would soon settle in on the counter, the linoleum floor, among the scents of food. He would find himself across a table from the enemy.

"Steady," he said. "Steady, Joe."

The other man said, "Relax, just relax."

The woman walked back toward the booth. She wore a pink uniform and a small, tidy apron. She dried her hands as she came closer. Matthew could see in her quick glance at him and the

other man a long-time association with the policeman, some affection, mostly studied indifference. "I'm telling Joe here he
looks like a friend of mine," Matthew said, "and he says can't be.
He says you knew him since you were young."

She looked from one of them to the other. "What is this?"
she asked.

"Answer him," the man said. "Tell him the truth. Don't
change nothing."

"Who is he?"

"Just answer."

She answered quickly, certainly. The man had indicated to her
the importance of the question to him. "Since high school," she
said. "We've known each other since high school. I used to date
his brother but I married him. I was never good on choices."

Matthew slid from the booth.

"I'm sorry," he said to the woman. "I'm sorry," he said to Joe
Fox. "It's a mistake, like it happens sometimes, a mistake."

He started to walk out quickly but turned. "I'm going to put
your gun on the street outside. I'm sorry, I'm not doing so hot."

"Wait a minute. You can't—"

Matthew placed the gun on the sidewalk and ran down Atlantic in the late afternoon, shadows long on the street. It was not
an easy athletic dash toward a goal of any kind; it was painful,
his breathing wrong, places on the sidewalk becoming too large
and then not being there. He was running in a dream landscape,
himself hardly there and what there was of him wrong. He was
not sure of his exact destination, but he knew where he wanted
to go. He knew only one place he might complete his search: if
not there, where? Once more up to the boardwalk, he thought,
one last time in the salt air and suntan oil perhaps to discover
him, but it was, as twilight fell, not a sensible idea anymore.

Joe Tapir would not be there. But he ran toward the ocean anyhow. He crossed the boardwalk. He avoided bumping anyone but ran fast. He did not feel pursued but called somewhere, a summons from a long time ago. People were leaving the beach, carrying picnic baskets down the narrow side streets. He ran into the street to avoid bumping into anyone. He caught his breath on the boardwalk, streaks of orange in the far sky as the day ended.

On the beach a small girl walked toward the water as Matthew watched her. There were people near her, but none seemed to be with the child. She walked slowly into the surf. "Stop!" Matthew called and ran down the steps to the sand. He ran toward the child. When he was about ten feet from her an older woman walked up briskly to the girl and took the child by the hand and turned briefly to Matthew. "She does this all the time," the woman said.

Dressed fully on the beach, shoes sandy, Matthew said, "You have to be careful, lady. A wave could take her."

The woman said nothing, turning away.

"You have to be careful," Matthew called.

The woman walked away from him faster. Matthew stood watching her and the little girl, hearing the ocean's sounds as it came and went on the shore. Without removing his shoes he walked into the water, knowing that in minutes there would be an end to Joe Tapir. Whatever waited after the water in his lungs, the suffocation, the end of the dread in the murderer would be soon. He swam out, thinking he would swim until he was exhausted and then let the ocean take him and Joe Tapir in his mind. The water was warm and the afternoon was disappearing from the sky. His swimming seemed ordinary, no particular purpose to it. There had not been many people in the water and as he saw the shore recede he was alone. The feeling was not frightening. The water carried him and he felt reassured that he had water and sky and something to say about the matters that plagued him. But as he became more tired he knew he did not want to die: did, of course, to end it with the monster, but chose to live because he did not care to add to Tapir's score of victims.

He was not swimming out to die, he realized. He sought recovery in the water. He floated and bobbed and moved about, no longer moving farther from the shore. He had, for the moment on the sand, not known what to do; now, he knew that he would not kill himself. Even this small triumph, his death, was too large to accord the man. He had thought he had been brought here to the water's edge in a good cause, and perhaps there was a solution and an ending to the meaning of Joe Tapir in sand and deep, endless and rolling Atlantic Ocean. He swallowed salty water and spit it out. He took a deep breath and removed his shoes in the water.

He felt his clothes billow around him. Letting the ocean carry him, Matthew drifted back toward the shore. The overhead sky had become darker, but the air was clear. He paddled slowly, sure of the sand and the firmness under his feet. He breathed hard. He lay without moving on the wet, packed sand. He stood slowly, shoeless, and walked inland.

He sat on the dry sand, wet and feeling the warmth of the sand, attracting little attention. People passing him, walking toward the boardwalk, did not ask what he thought he was doing, jumping fully clothed into the water. Perhaps he had his reasons.

He stood and stretched, aching, studying the ocean and the boardwalk behind him, the deepening sky and the vanishing horizon.

It is himself Matthew is looking for, the boy who could not

grow up after he had entered the doors to oblivion that waited for someone like himself buried in ultimate loss. Tapir had stopped being a man, an exile from Hungary, if he ever had been one. Joe Tapir, he thinks, was a ruined roadside that fell away in a hard rain and could plunge Matthew in his taxicab into a ravine. He was a sudden undercurrent that could pull him from the boardwalk in Atlantic City and send him to a watery death in the ocean. Lately, Matthew had come to think there was no Tapir and perhaps never had been—he had dreamed the man and his arrival and departure. Twilight once more announced on a gray Atlantic City day that with night the search was over.

He took off his wet shirt and rubbed his hair with it. The sound was of living, cloth on scalp and somewhere laughter on the beach and people walking toward the boardwalk, holding the hands of their children. It was all normal, even Tapir, or it was all nightmare, even the innocent children, their parents, the ocean going nowhere. All that seemed certain was that he could not die. The memory of Tapir would die with him. He was a witness to Tapir's crime, perhaps soon the only one. By the hour and then years the man's crimes diminished. Soon there would be no one to remember them; and when that happened it would be as if Tapir had never come to live under the same roof as the McGanns. He would if he were gone regret the absence of the pursuit and hunt. Brought to his doorstep by Tapir, he had come to understand better than most the terrors in darkened staircases and who finally it was tarrying, breath indrawn for silence, in monstrous alcoves on familiar landings. Tapir had been a messenger, a priest of the lesson in life most atrocious and true: there was not a whole lot of sense to who paid and who did not. When you turned in a certain direction there were the winds that tore apart with no great sense to them farms and huge buildings, oceans reaching up to clutch the shore back to themselves and a noise that would deafen people everywhere if they stopped to listen. Somewhere behind what looked like everyday life there was fire. Ice could on the minute fall from the sky. The ground was always cracking, and there were mists and fogs and a blackness of caves and there was plenty of news everywhere that was the condition of things as truly as sunlight and love and a god coming to redeem every human, bird, and blossom. But the darkness had its town criers. And that was who Tapir was, the man who had caused Bibles to be written and tears to be shed over the unthinkable. He realized that Joe Tapir might not ever be found. No one looked for him except Matthew. Tapir would exist only in the despair left in himself against the rage tormenting forever a boy of nine.

Once back on the boardwalk, the lights of the big hotels caught his eyes, bright and beginning night in their fashion. He returned to his hotel room and changed to dry clothes. He strolled outdoors, anticipating dinner, and later he would walk the boardwalk for the rest of the evening, looking into faces. Drink a beer, mumble at Heaven in the dark skies over Atlantic City, ask a policeman for handcuffs for the crime he would commit himself if able, there was to be no justice in any of it. He did not think he would ever think again to kill himself over the man's crimes. He would continue the honor he placed on his family by never spending an hour without seeing the murderer's face and imagining the last minutes of his mother and father and Paula's terror.

Something had occurred to him in the command to drown himself that he had missed in his years of connection to Joe Tapir. Not Matthew McGann, or anyone else, had ever discovered how to live in a world where evil prowled breathless beside us, reached to seize us by the moment with never a cause a victim could understand, only an effect. He had been summoned to emptiness because there was nothing else for him to fill in the time and space where life was. Weep or wail or howl with anguish, there was no conduct on earth for how to act.

He heard behind him as he walked on the boardwalk the sound of footsteps, running feet, and knew without turning it was the policeman he had recently accosted in the restaurant. "Say there, stop!" the policeman called, but Matthew ran. The cop shouted, "Stop him! Stop him!" But Matthew turned at a flight of wooden stairs and ran down them onto a side street. He ran into a Laundromat, and a woman standing at a washing machine. She said nothing, watching him as he tried to catch his breath. He waited. He heard no sounds of people chasing him. He nodded at the woman. She stood still, fearing him. "It's not me to be afraid of," he said. "It's the things I know."

He walked slowly out to the boardwalk. He knew himself to be safe there. No one expected a man leisurely walking in the night air in the crowds of people. He fell into step with two other men, and they were hardly aware of him, the three of them looking like people who might be together. His pursuers were looking elsewhere. A last stroll like just another person and then good-bye.

Content he was beyond capture, he thought, there was no philosophy at all, seeing the meaning of things clear under a low, dark sky, no way to live with the knowledge as it enfolded him like a mean vine choking a plant to death.

Someone should know.

On the boardwalk the first person he saw was a man in white shirtsleeves standing in front of a keno parlor, an electronic version of bingo, with slot machines to be pressed to keep count of the winning numbers. The night air lay thick on the beach and curled around the lights from the keno in a soft haze that muffled shadows and even sound. There was a stillness for a moment, and the man in the white shirt turned, startled to observe Matthew, who was moving too fast for the occasion. The man was after all standing still, not going anywhere, not threatening to run.

Matthew took the man by the sleeve, an older man—maybe he worked in the place. "Listen," he said, "you have to be careful. You have to be real careful. Even though it might not do any good at all you still have to be careful."

EIGHT

A Guest on Good Friday

HUGH MURPHY had been married eighteen and a half weeks on Good Friday and with his bride, happily pregnant, had taken the first floor in a large old house in a section of Pittsburgh called Point Breeze. It was a little distance from Oakland and the government housing project where Hugh had lived with his sister and widowed mother until he went into the marine corps. Returning home after his injuries in Korea, with Maura, his new wife, Hugh wanted a fresh start.

He had no quarrel with Oakland or his friends and times there, but the three-room apartment in Point Breeze was the first place he had lived that was not in an apartment building. Maura's father, with plenty of cash and only two daughters, had offered to help with a better place, but Hugh and Maura wanted to live only where they could afford the rent.

Hugh, in his new apartment, had the electricity calculated in the rent, heat included, the use of the front porch, and, best, a small, toy-like backyard, what someone raised as Murphy had been—in a communal collection of flat rectangular buildings with concrete patios and bolted-down wooden benches in front of entrance doors—would consider a lawn. He and Maura sat there on weekends in striped lawn chairs, another sign of changing times, red and yellow and aluminum, something of the world of the future in it. Nightly, he folded the chairs and put them inside the kitchen. Someone else might leave them out on the small back porch, but not Murphy. He was not going to tempt anyone to steal a four-dollar chair. He knew he amused Maura with his frugal and cautious ways, but he knew too she loved him because he appreciated small things.

He and Maura were happy. They paid sixty-five dollars a month rent, including everything except the telephone, which cost three dollars and sixty-five cents a month, plus tax, long distance extra of course, but Hugh had made only two long distance calls in his life, one to his mother from San Francisco after he returned from Korea, the other to Maura on the same occasion, and never expected to make another.

He was working, a fair job in bookkeeping in an importing business in the Grant Building, and Maura was a receptionist for a dentist, doing well on their own with no help from her family (his was an impossibility), and from where he sat in Point Breeze, a baby on the way, good neighborhood without all the screaming and rocks thrown in the streets, things seemed as promising as they could be to Murphy. He planned to look into accounting courses at Duquesne, take advantage of his veteran's benefits from his time with the marines, and then the Friday afternoon before Easter Wee Clarity was there knocking at the door to the porch leading to the street.

From his front window, standing to one side of the curtains from the five and ten, Murphy could see who was on the porch at the front door and he saw Wee Clarity, known the length of Oakland as the atheist, but outside at the curb the small truck with what looked like a mountain of rolled carpeting in the bed and hanging over the sides. There hardly seemed a time in the last half of the twentieth century, Hugh was to think, when the accompaniments to doing better in the world in taste and well-being had not been wall-to-wall carpeting or the refrigerator with a freezer. Today the bell on the front door did not ring with urgency but made a three-note appeal, and wood paneling began to cover everything in 1950 like a natural growth infesting the inhabitable world. In later years, Murphy thought he had been there at the inception of the frenzy in the carpeting fashion, but of course he had not. His encounter had been dramatic, but there had been wall-to-wall carpets perhaps for years before Wee Clarity arrived in the small truck in the street in front of his house.

Hugh opened the front door and said, "Ho, there, Wee, what brings you to my door this beautiful Friday afternoon?" He did not invite him in; Wee made his wishes known. He would walk in if it pleased him. And, brushing past Murphy, Wee said, "It's not a beautiful afternoon, Hugh, but you're right about it being Friday. Fifty percent's not bad. Look up to the sky and you'll see there's rain."

Hugh stepped slowly out to the porch and to the front step. Slowly, with deliberation, he looked up at the sky, north, east, and then he walked back to the front foyer where Wee stood.

"You're right," he said. "I detect clouds that could amount to rain. It was very quick of you, Wee, to note there might be rain ahead in what seems to the unpracticed eye like a beautiful day." He was, in his elaborate consideration of everything natural, supernatural, nonsensical, or apparent, mocking Wee Clarity's tendency to fiddle with every statement of word, fact, or being and deduce after considerable speculation there was no God.

"Any jackass could see it was going to rain," Wee said. "But I'm not here to argue with you."

"Are you here for any reason with that mountain of rags in that truck that would make sense to me or anyone else?"

"Come down here," Wee said and walked out to the front porch and down the stairs to the truck, waiting for Hugh, who lingered. "Come on," he said. "Come on, Hughie, it's going to rain. You said so yourself."

At the truck he patted the rolled-up carpeting. "I bought this for a song," he said. "There was a sale, an estate sale this morning down on Fifth near here—that's why I come to you, knowing you lived in the neighborhood and rain was in the sky—and I bought what you see for a song. What you see cost someone thousands, twenty thousand maybe, and I got the lot for a hundred dollars. I figure we split it up and I take half and you give me thirty dollars or so and I give you half."

"Wee, I don't want any of this carpeting. If it was carpeting worth a million and you were to offer me half for thirty dollars I don't want it. There's no place for it here. And you know damned well if you're telling me about an estate sale, you picked it up in a rag shop for ten dollars and asking me thirty is going to make you twenty richer from the start. So while I still think it's a beautiful day, please go. Maura's out shopping and she's pregnant and gets a little shaky sometimes, and seeing you, nothing personal, will set her off. I know this carpeting can do it. There's something about this stuff rolled up like that, like you have bodies in there, that makes me nervous. I don't want to handle it, I don't want to touch it. Do you get my point? It's carpeting rolled like that, smelling like old hay, that's not appetizing, do you know what I mean? I mean, Wee, it's Good Friday and fooling with you on carpeting that might be stolen isn't my idea of being reverential. Even if you did pay for it, I don't like thinking about money deals on Good Friday."

"I can't say that I understand you, Hugh. I find carpeting civilizing. I guess you'd like to be walking on mud floors if you had your choice. Does this religion you speak of forbid floors looking good with carpeting from the estate of a millionaire down on Fifth? I have the papers for the sale in the truck. I didn't steal it either. It belongs to my cousin, Egan, and he'd be here this minute helping me, but he threw his back out kneeling and falling over with ecstasy at St. Paul's Cathedral this morning at Mass. There's a riddle for you. Why'd the Lord want Egan to break his ass on Good Friday?"

"Probably, Wee, to keep him from associating with you."

"It's your choice, Hugh. God likes mud floors or rich carpeting. What's your position on the subject?"

"My choice is not to stand out here with you. It looks like rain."

"Who's asking you to stand in the rain?"

Hugh turned and said, "Well, I'll be seeing you around. Let me know how you do selling your carpet. Looks like a good buy."

"I'm not here to sell you carpeting; that was a favor to let you in on a good thing. I'm here to use your backyard, before it rains, to lay it out on your lawn. I heard you speak at the Irish Club two weeks ago about the fine lawn you had, you were talking to Mahoney and that dumb kid, what's his name, Larson, speaking of the pleasures of your backyard, and I was passing your table and overheard your good fortune about living out here in this lovely neighborhood. And then making this excellent purchase down on Fifth, in the same neighborhood, and remembering your backyard, I came right over. I'll give you scraps, enough for a nine-by-twelve by the look of the size of it, no charge, nothing at all to it. Just friendship. I'd like to see you with a millionaire's fine carpet in your living room, to go with the beautiful backyard."

"There's rocks in the backyard, it's muddy, there's ruts. It's small, too crowded to turn around. There's the neighbors on all sides, they're fussy, Wee. Lot of old folks with bad hearts and diabetes, terrible for their physical and mental conditions if they see you rolling out carpet in the backyard. Fact, there's a man who's a Mason lives on the other side of me who'll think worse of Catholics if he sees you playing around with the carpet. No, it's a bad idea. No carpets in the backyard. For no reason at all you can provide me!"

"Hughie, it's going to rain, and we're wasting time. You just tell that Mason I don't believe in that God monkey business anymore than he does. He'll be giving me a secret handshake in ten minutes and having me to dinner."

When Maura came home from shopping at the small grocery store two blocks away from where she and Hugh lived, she found her husband grimy with dirt from the carpet and with Wee Clarity, who to protect the carpet had taken off his shoes after it was unrolled but, wary of danger to his feet, still wore socks. Hugh sat on the front porch in a rage.

"Who is that in the backyard dancing around in his stocking feet on that diseased old carpet?" she asked. "Are you buying old carpeting for this place?"

"It's a guy I know I'm letting use the backyard to cut up the carpeting."

"Hugh, the neighbors are going to think you're crazy. Who is that man?"

"His name is Wee Clarity. I've known him for years, grew up with him."

"Is he a midget?"

"No, he's just short. He looks like a midget in his stocking feet jumping around on the carpeting, trying to smooth out the wrinkles before he cuts it into proportions for his apartment."

"Hugh, it's Good Friday."

"Maura, I know it's Good Friday, and I know Sunday is Easter. Okay?"

"You don't care what the neighbors are going to think? These people are observing Good Friday. Is your friend Jewish or something?"

"No, he's an atheist."

"Who is he? Where do you know him from?"

"He's a guy from the old neighborhood. Just a guy. I grew up with him."

Maura said she was going to visit her sister and if Wee Clarity or any of his carpeting was still on the premises at six o'clock, she'd keep on driving when she passed the house, and he could spend Easter with his atheistical friend. Maura was tall and slender, a victory of a rare sort for Hugh. She had been much desired as wife and companion in Oakland, but before Hugh went to Korea she had told him she'd wait for him. If he still wanted her, they'd be married when he came home. Wanted her! He believed in the bitterly cold days on the peninsula, before he received shrapnel in his right forearm that troubled him only on damp days, she was what brought him through: not just the days of recuperation in the hospital but the months of ground fighting near Chosen when there was only the thought of home—and Maura—to bring him through.

"Look, I'm stuck," he said. "I don't even like this guy very much. Nobody does, but what harm can he do for a couple of hours out there? It looks like rain. He'll buzz off. Don't go."

But she took the car and left, after standing for a long time at the door to the backyard and observing Wee. He waved at her. "Mrs. Murphy," he called, "I'm putting aside a fine scrap of this carpeting for you and Murphy. Come see it."

Her father owned several prime buildings in the heart of Oakland and was a part owner of the warehouse across the street from the Montefiore Hospital. She had grown up well to do, and people, particularly cynics at the Ancient Order of Hibernians, Division No. 9, had said the marriage would fail because of the social and economic differences. But it flourished by overseas mail during the time Hugh was in Korea and was now well along in eighteen and a half happy weeks. It would survive Wee Clarity, but it was true that Hugh did not like, felt apprehensive at, her rich girl's march, away from her husband and the house they inhabited.

"Look, Wee," he said. "I'm giving you an hour. It's four o'clock. You're gone at five."

"Regretting your better instincts already. Well, I'll hurry along."

Wee had brought crudely drawn floor plans of his apartment and after he laid out the carpeting he walked around it, measuring with a yardstick. He briskly made chalk marks. Then with his socked foot he erased the marks and made others. He drew lines and stood back with his eyes closed imagining alcoves and corners. Standing on the carpeting, eyes closed, it began to rain, very softly, the mildest of April showers, not hard but thick.

"Okay," Hugh said. "Truck time. I'll help you load up this disaster."

"Only to your back porch, maybe a little into the kitchen till this is over. It's a shower. You don't have to help me. You've done enough. I'll just tug it down there myself."

The owner of the house, Andy Baggs, came at that moment out to the backyard. He lived on the second and third floors with his wife and a son named Andy Jr. "Say, Hugh," he said. "I've been watching that short guy jumping around out there. Dragging that old carpet across it is going to kill whatever grass I had planned on coming up this summer. Now I know I told you that you had the use of the backyard, you and Maura are great kids, but I never planned you'd be doing commercial things out there. Cutting up carpet remnants."

"Andy, it's a friend of mine, not a good friend, a guy I know, and the carpet's for his own use."

"I don't want any of it in my house, okay? And the truth is I don't want that queer little guy jumping around out in the backyard. Don't he see it's raining?"

"He's trying to move the carpet back here under the roof."

"Won't work: that's a lot of carpet. Where'd he get that much rubbish?"

"It's a long story."

"It's not stolen, is it?"

"No, I don't think so. He says he has a receipt."

"Is he sort of a dummy?"

"No, he's just short."

"Why's he walking around on toes on the carpet? Leaping around, you know, like he was celebrating Maypole Day."

"He doesn't want to wrinkle it or dirty it. That's why he's wearing socks."

Andy looked at Hugh. Andy had a white mustache and he and his brothers and brothers-in-law drank beer and argued religion on Saturday nights. Hugh enjoyed listening to them, falling asleep as if to calm music rather than serious questions about the Virgin Birth. "Things will work out fine," Hugh said but knew that the question between them was not of the carpet and Wee Clarity but of what sort of people the landlord had rented his first floor to that such a dance could occur in Point Breeze on Good Friday.

Reluctantly, Hugh joined Wee in the tugging at the carpet to bring it in under the small porch roof. "Watch it there, Hugh," Wee said, "you'll ruin it, dragging it like that."

"How can anyone ruin a rag like this?"

"Rag! You should have seen the home it came from. People don't know carpets, but that's why it's me with the bargain and others buying dregs of used mattresses and pieces of cast-off old overcoats and bragging they have Orientals and Persians. And it's me with this masterpiece, one of a kind, made for a millionaire."

"I say let it rot in the rain."

"I'd rather it be you rot in the rain. Hugh, you don't have a sense of beauty, you never had."

The rug lay partly exposed to the rain; a portion was curled in on itself to fit into the open kitchen door. Hugh became more pleased, watching the rain from the eaves come down hard on the carpet, soaking it black, that Maura was not home. This was something not to be seen by anyone; this was an event in its complications and bad-to-worse rhythms not to be dreamed of once the peculiar moments with rain, a carpet, and Wee had passed. Undaunted, Wee took the sharp tool he had been using and began to cut the carpet into smaller pieces in the kitchen. Laying it out on a chair, partly on a table, he ripped away at it.

"Are you mad?" Hugh asked. "Get this out of the kitchen."

"I'm making it workable. I'm putting it into smaller pieces so that when it stops raining I can just trot out there and put a few finishing touches on it and then be gone from your charity."

"It's still raining out there."

"I'm aware of that."

"The ground is soaked."

"That's what happens every time, Hugh."

"You'll get the carpet wet you lay it out there on the grass, even if it stops raining, and that doesn't seem likely."

"Hugh, you're not following your own logic. You're not watching me. I have this beauty practically whipped. See, it's down to four pieces now; from that big carpet I cut it into four pieces. Now it's a pull here and a tear there and I'm done. No need at all to go out of doors into the rain, lay my carpet out on the soggy grass, just a little tuck here and there and I'm done."

Maura returned at seven o'clock but did not drive past the house.

She stood at the door to the kitchen and said, "Hugh, I want to talk to you."

"Mrs. Murphy," Wee said. "It looks like I'm going to have a piece of this carpeting big enough for your living room left over. You ought to see it when it catches the light from lamps. This kitchen light doesn't do it justice."

In the corridor outside the kitchen, Maura said to Hugh, "Do you realize what that carpet's going to do to our kitchen? We'll have to burn everything in that kitchen to get rid of the fibers and dirt you and your friend left there. Hugh, I think you are making a very big mistake, choosing your atheist over your baby and me."

"Maura, it's not like that."

"How is it like?"

"Please, I'll tell him to leave."

"This minute."

"This minute. Of course."

When they came back in the kitchen, Wee was on the wall phone there. He was laughing. He had tears in his eyes. He was apparently listening to someone on the other end. He said, "*Deus non existe,* Father!" and hung up. He turned to Hugh. "That was my cousin, Brian, the priest. I call him every Good Friday. In my pleasure with this little beauty I almost forgot to call him this year."

"You call your cousin a priest and say something in Latin to him?" Maura asked.

"There is no God. I say it to him every Easter season, mostly on Good Friday. Sometimes I call Christmas. You ought to hear him. Jesus, he gets mad!"

Maura said, "Hugh."

Hugh said, "Get this stuff out of the kitchen this minute."

"To where? It's raining outside. My carpet will get soaked."

"I'm going to drag it out if you don't."

Wee said, "All right, if that's what you want. If that's what you want, Hugh, Mrs. Murphy. I'll get it out of the kitchen."

He tugged at the carpeting, laid it out under the small roof of the porch in front of the kitchen door, stepping out in the rain to look up at the sky. An early evening quiet had fallen on the backyard. The rain persisted but even more gently. Bushes heavy with water dripped slowly. Sighing to himself, Wee began to pull the carpet in the rain back into the yard.

Maura went to the small window over the kitchen and said to Hugh, "What's he doing?"

"He's putting it on the ground in the backyard again."

"Hugh!"

Standing in the kitchen doorway, Hugh called to Wee. "Wee, listen, I don't want that carpeting in the backyard. I want it off the premises."

In a rain that fell down his forehead, into his eyes, down his nose, Wee called back, "Hugh, I'd be no further ahead. I still have no place to lay out this beauty. Give me an hour."

Maura said, "No. Tell him no."

Hugh called, "No. Get it out of here this minute."

Dripping rain onto the linoleum, Wee came back into the kitchen. He took off his wet socks. "A lot of good these are doing me." He put the wet socks in his pocket. He wiped at his face with his wet shirt. His eyes were red with water. He blinked them. "Well, Hugh, Mrs. Murphy, I'll be back as soon as it stops raining."

"It's not you," Maura said, "it's the carpeting. We don't want the carpeting."

"I'm practical," Wee said. "It gets me into trouble, I don't let things bother me. Was from a kid. I don't worry about heaven or hell like most people. It's show me, bud! There's not much to be done with that carpeting except to leave it. I'll be back the minute it stops raining, finish up, and leave you a beautiful piece."

"Wee, I'm going to haul that trash away."

"Honest to God," Wee said, "I'd like to see that. It'll take them an hour to put it away and the truck rental and first getting someone to do it. Be reasonable, the minute it stops raining I'll be here, making short work of it. It's been a pleasure meeting you, Mrs. Murphy. Hugh was right, this is a fine neighborhood."

Neither Hugh nor Maura knew exactly when Wee returned, only that sometime during the night it had stopped raining. And under a clear, bright moon, in their backyard, a spectacle for anyone who was abroad at that late hour (it might have been two in the morning), Wee was out on his carpet, doing an odd prance in his stockinged feet, a pirouette, a spin to avoid a gathering at a fold on his rug, a twirl to put down a place of hesitant flatness, and then a leap and spin to catch a slipping end, thrusting his cutting tool to cut off a flapping piece of the carpet. The moon shone on his large balding head and down his shoulders and his short arms as he spun about on the carpet. Hugh laughed to himself.

"I never saw such a sight in my life," Maura said. "Why do you put up with him? I don't see anything but a man dancing like he was drunk in the moonlight on a Good Friday night. Is he mocking God or something?"

"I guess there's more than meets the eye in Wee out there in the yard."

"Not believing is not believing, Hugh."

"But it leaves room, you see, for believing other things."

Hugh watched the figure in the silvery movements, bowing under the moon and swooping. "His father used to be a butcher," Hugh said, "coming home bloody in his shirt up Darraugh Street and caked on his shoes where we lived as boys and people moving away from the look and smell of him, little like Wee, small man walking nowhere quick. And his mother was nuts, nuts like a runaway train, no two sentences connected, and he had a brother who left town about fifteen, a year before the father vanished. Cleaned out the register of the pool room where he was supposed to be sweeping up. And there was a sister, went crazy as the rest of the family, walnuts, cashews, almonds, reading all night, passing on to Wee that this was God's fault and that was God's misdeeds. Till Wee came to recite it, chapter and verse like the things we learned at St. Agnes, but the reverse as he preached it. God did this in India, should have done this in China, dropped an atom bomb on Japan, caused the dust bowl in Oklahoma, and was holding up a cure for cancer, the sister knew it for a fact. Took over when all the others had died and been evaporated and run to the Allegheny River with hopelessness, she raised Wee in the government housing project where we all lived. We all knew the facts on the family, but we didn't know what he knew living it. And being who we were, too dumb to know better, I guess, the years then, we found a little excuse for him, the mother, the sister, the ideas. He's out there making things right with people none of us knew existed. Getting forgiveness, you know, from the darkness. I see the butcher in my mind slipping and sliding, making his way up Darraugh in the ice and snow and moving about two inches every five minutes."

Maura said, "Let him dance, there's no harm in it really."

The carpet itself lay lifeless and still, wet and dark, and on it in the rug's spiritless gloom Wee danced his dervish ballet to keep it in order as Maura and Hugh stood at their kitchen window.

PART TWO

Unnatural Expectations

NINE

The Chorus Girl

THE SMELLS of the roasted peanuts at Donohue's Arcade on Diamond and ground coffee, the scent of rain on the coats of people pushing through the revolving doors of the Pittsburgher Hotel overpowered Brendan with waves of longing, love, and music in which he swam on the sidewalk before the Casino Burlesque Theater. The organ at the roller rink three blocks down on Diamond played "I'll Be Seeing You," and he felt giddy and loose with expectation and heat: all music was only for him today, a woman beyond anything he had dreamed, sidewalks of heat and promise, not in the future, but his forty-eight hours ago and now. Never had he dreamed the acts of sex and lovemaking could be so complete, and when it was over he had understood with Loretta, at last, what people talked about when they spoke of it, a simple enough thing (he had been married for four years), but he had never understood the mystery until two nights ago with a stranger. Had he wings he would have soared in yellows and orange above the crowded street in high glossy flight.

A young man pleased by his opportunities, a widowed mother fairly well off, and a successful tour of duty in war zones during World War II, Brendan Brake tended to make much of his good fortune. He had tried to calm in himself the rising sense of great things around the corner, but it had been no good, even with a loving wife, a handsome war bride, respect from the local boys, those who had gone to war and those who had stayed in Oakland, and a steady job with a chance to buy in on the business. The lack of a child between himself and Signe, a problem of her tubes, had been the sad part of his life. But, given what he thought of as his blessed state, life turned beautifully, like a caterpillar into a butterfly, into what he would have wished for, had he known of such things.

On the sidewalk on Diamond, savoring his moment, he was greeted by three of the old boys from Oakland, Kerry O'Toole, Jimmy Steele, and Dickie Trent. They were prowling Diamond Street in search of the occasional adventure there with a prostitute or a pick-up shopping in one of the stores, and, failing all the rest, most frequently, a visit to the Casino to see almost naked women dancing.

"Hey, Brendan, your wife let you have a little longer leash today?" Jimmy asked.

They and Brendan were all in their middle twenties, Brendan the only one married.

"I'm my own man," Brendan said.

"Long as the missus agrees," Kerry said. Kerry and Brendan had been pals since the first grade at St. Agnes. They had drifted apart when Brendan had volunteered for the army and Kerry had been found to have inner ear problems. They had not resumed friendship when Brendan returned and married Signe. Brendan had thought himself since boyhood different from the best of them, a man marked for adventure, big in sex and world things; but lately, until his recent incredible awakening, he had thought he was no farther ahead than any of them who had not been to Europe and stayed in Oakland, hoping to run into something there, or went to the whorehouses in Homestead or the North Side.

"You going in here?" Dickie asked, pointing to the theater entrance. "I'd think better of a boy used to be on the altar at St. Agnes."

"I may and I may not. My mother likes the sweet ham and fresh corn over there at Donohue's and I was looking at these posters. That's not a crime now, is it?"

The posters were eight feet tall and the women in them looked out on Diamond Street with gazes that could have meant anything: lust, gluttony, envy, or boredom. But they were women, and their look was a challenge, whatever their expressions meant.

"Come around," Kerry said. "There's nobody going to bite you at the Irish Club. You've been missed. Corny said just Friday you gave the place a spirit of uplift, he couldn't put no more than ten beers away in a night without your virtuous presence on the premises."

"Yeah, I think about it, but something comes up, and I go somewhere else."

They all three shook hands with Brendan, and he crossed Diamond, walking toward Donohue's Market and Cafeteria. Inside, he walked through the aisles for about five minutes, then returned to Diamond. He walked quickly back to the Casino Theater.

Brendan paid his dollar at the front window and went inside, enchanted. He could not have felt more in possession of himself and the theater had he been the owner of the place, the band conductor, the choreographer, maybe something higher, even spiritual on this fine day, so right was it. He sat bathed in the pale blue light from the stage: girls walked around in slow poses, half smiling, sequins capturing the flash of the white baby spot. He was not sure at first as he watched the girls in their promenade which was Loretta, the one he had held for two hours and swore to her in moments of release and bond he would love her forever. The room had been, according to the agreement, completely dark, and he had said no more than, "I'm over here."

It had been the tall girl with the long dark hair, no other, the other girls on stage too short, hair not long enough, thinner or heavier. He would know her bust anywhere, the hips parading with the low-slung skirt trailing the stage floor with seductive twirls and sweeps.

The contract between Loretta and his wife, Signe, had been made with his permission; but he had not met the young woman outside the bedroom. He had not been part of the discussions.

Loretta and Signe had agreed for the sum of ten thousand dollars, the amount Brendan made annually in 1948, five thousand down and the rest after the baby was born, that Loretta would have sex with him—no preliminaries beyond those necessary, no conversations that could lead to unimaginable emotional difficulties, the woman's name not revealed to him—and then when and if a baby came it belonged to Signe and Brendan, theirs to keep, the child belonging to them at least half by blood.

Brendan had met Signe in Norway shortly after the war, and she wanted children but could not bear them. She had assured Brendan the practice she had worked out with the girl, of impeccable reputation, was common in the Scandinavian countries.

Loretta worked nights on stage at the Casino Burlesque, sort of a chorus girl, never taking off all her clothes completely, just tall and standing on a pedestal with her thighs bare and sequins in the musical numbers, smiling as if she had secrets, a "show-girl." Occasionally she promenaded around the stage in high heels, swaying to the beat of the music.

One of the girl's brothers, Signe had determined, escorted her to the theater and she was picked up by her father at eleven fifteen after the last show. Her character seemed excellent. Her respectability, her warmth in the bed with him had caused a revolution to run through Brendan's veins. He wanted after that first night to leave Signe and marry Loretta.

Since the night with her he had not eaten or slept, daydreaming like a boy; he cannot get their night of lovemaking out of his mind. He thinks as he watches the young woman on stage he will rush down the aisle, leap over the footlights, and before the audience in the dark seize her, throw himself on her, resume where they left off two days ago.

In the dark Brendan understands everything about the girl, himself, and Signe: there are things around him waiting to be observed, strange things. He knows wherever he looks and once was puzzled he will now know the truth hidden from him in ordinary things.

Signe had counted on his inexperience for the agreement to work. It was true, as Signe knew, he had only his wife as a point of reference for what sex was about; but a man with Loretta learned fast, like lightning illuminating the night where he lay with the showgirl. It was not that she was accomplished, knew games like a prostitute, but was as natural and giving, offering him easy warmth, depth, and even humor. She was quick and oddly comical even in the dark room, laughing to herself and at him: it had not been studied or bound by anything except in what happened of itself. Never before had Brendan lost himself in another person, and he knew, he knew it, she had lost herself in him.

Signe, for her part, he thought, imagined the liaison would be harmless—Brendan will hardly know good from bad in the sex matter; she herself, Brendan understands now, thinks it's all the same anyhow. But an awful passion flares in Brendan's mind.

Seeing Loretta as she moves with slow silken movements on the stage, he silently prays she will not conceive after their first time, that it will take two, oh, Lord, three, maybe ten times with her before she becomes pregnant.

He is, as he watches her hips and shoulders, wild with his thoughts of having possessed her. He has closed the circle on owning her completely, no mystery now of anonymity or distance. He has found her phone number in Signe's purse where he has rummaged for some clue to who the woman was who ignited him with all the knowledge the world could ever hold. Her name and number and address are there and with them the name of the theater. He is now not the outsider to the agreement, he thinks.

Only he, he thinks, applauding wildly the conclusion to "Orchids in the Moonlight" to which the women have been dancing, of the three of them, knows everything. It is Brendan who knows how badly he wants Loretta forever, damn the bargain, and the other two will learn.

Knowing, though, that he had achieved what he has felt missing in himself since boyhood, he did not find a picture before him on how to proceed: where to start making his romance with Loretta permanent, what to offer, pledge, promise with all his heart to reach the woman he knew was behind the artless enchantress of his magical night. He would begin with the love he felt in the dark room. He could hope for no better moments than the recent time of his life, experienced once more in her breathing, the touch of her. What words, never his strongest gift, did one use to notify at that swooning time a woman, who while not a prostitute came close, that she was more than the love of his life; what transpired for him was the lofty ecstasies of religion and rebirth.

To say simply: "I love you."

To hear: "Are you crazy? This is a business deal."

To say: "I am here today more than I was before, I am not the same man."

To hear: "Are you crazy? This is a business deal."

He decided that the bedroom with its passion and powers over him was not the place to begin: winning her was not a question of controlling her body. *This is a business deal. Are you crazy?* Finding her at being herself was to locate her oddly at places where it was not the sex between them that would break the bonds of distance. To win her he had to start elsewhere, where people walked up a street, drank a milkshake, knelt in church, or sat in a movie theater with the light from Bette Davis and Glen Ford on the screen bathing the audience and forming one creature of them. Leaving her after the second night, as dizzying as the first, he thought on the sidewalk before the Carlton Hotel in East Liberty, Now was the time to watch together sunlight on flowers.

The roasted peanuts at Donohue's Arcade on Diamond spoke to him of longing and music in rhythms he had never dreamed he would know, the daily acts of waiting for the show to begin on the sidewalk before the Casino Burlesque Theater became visits to a holy shrine. When the organ at the roller rink played "This Love of Mine," he wanted to accost soldiers and sailors on the sidewalk, people hurrying somewhere with their heads down, women with shopping bags, and say, "I am in the center of all this now." The expectation in him hourly was for an entire life stretching before him, beckoning, to be lived: nothing stirred on the streets that did not become part of his passion. He sat in the theater nightly a victim of the pale blue light from the curtains and spotlights on the stage: sequins and thighs forever.

After three weeks, it became apparent to Signe that this experiment in producing a child was going in odd directions.

"Brendan," she asked after he returned home from one of his three times' weekly visits with Loretta at the hotel, "is everything well with you?"

They had agreed not to discuss the specifics of what happened with the young woman: only that it transpired. He had no sex at all with Signe in the time.

"Yes," he said. "How should it go?"

"You are not yourself."

"This is a peculiar thing: it leaves me feeling strange."

"Do you think we should stop?"

"No, no, why would you say that? Then all this time would be wasted."

She looked at him, he knew, when she thought she was not being observed herself. He dutifully returned home from his meetings with Loretta, as had been agreed, at ten o'clock. And Loretta, it was understood, told her family she worked in the concession stand at the theater, earning an extra twelve dollars a night, money Brendan gave her each time, and money for the cab home.

Saturdays, Brendan slipped away to the theater to watch her on stage. Tuesday, a night he was not supposed to meet her, Brendan went to the theater to sit absorbed in the blue lights and the music, thinking if he listened he could hear her footsteps on the stage as she slithered about, in love with those sounds too. One night, emboldened finally, he went backstage and was not stopped by anyone. He wanted to stand close to her—as people do, not enclosed in love's embrace—and at a distance of five feet, she looked up at him and looked away. He smiled quickly, and she turned to see if she knew him, so familiar was his sudden appraisal of her. But again, she looked away.

To his astonishment, she reached to take the hand of a young man standing near the wings with her. Brendan had not seen the man; he and Loretta did not seem to be together until the sudden, intimate movement. It was a gesture of support she asked for, a quick moment of exchange of touches, and then she was gone into a dressing room. Brendan blinked his eyes at the young man. Who was he that he did in public what Brendan could never do with a woman he possessed sexually three times a week and loved?

"Hey, pal," someone said to Brendan, whose ears were ringing, "you looking for something?"

Brendan made a friendly movement of salute with his hand and turned to follow the young man who had touched Loretta. As he walked a few feet behind him, Brendan became aware the man was not as young as he had seemed. In a tweed sport coat and an open-collared white shirt he seemed youthful, but as Brendan observed him he saw that the man was perhaps in his forties. That would make him twice Loretta's age, and Brendan didn't like it. There were any number of sinister people who prowled around the edges of the girls on stage at the Casino, and

Loretta in her innocence was no match for a man like this who knew his way around the darkest corners of burlesque theaters and Diamond Street. Brendan, circling in his mind that brief quick exchange of trust and need between the stranger and Loretta, did not sleep that night. At a quarter after four he went to sit in the living room, and when Signe awoke and joined him, she asked, "Are you okay?"

"Please go to bed," he said.

"Brendan," she said, "this isn't working out."

"Please go to bed."

By daylight, he called in sick to the awning installation company where he worked and about ten in the morning took a streetcar down to Diamond Street. The first rush of customers at Donohue's and at the crates of fruits and vegetables had started, the ground steamy with the water from the food displayed on the sidewalk. The organ at the Diamond Rink mocked him as it played "Always."

The long street of excitement and heat had become menacing; there were things Brendan did not know, and in the easy association of nude dancers, older prostitutes on the street, and the men who freely moved among such women lay mysteries he was sure he would never understand. Loretta was the second woman he had had sex with, and the first, Signe, had been no training ground at all.

He waited for Loretta on the sidewalk.

She was left off at the curb by her father shortly before six. Moving quickly from the drugstore next door to the Casino, Brendan stepped in front of her. "You know me," he said. "I'm Brendan."

"Brendan?"

"Brendan Brake."

She stood looking at him, young by the light on Diamond Street, not as imposing as the woman on the stage—somewhere between the fantasy woman of the East Liberty hotel and the showgirl. "You're not supposed to do this," she said. "It's not the agreement."

"I love you."

"Stop that: it's not true. You don't know me."

"I know all I care to know. I want you to be the mother of our child, I mean for us to raise him. My wife and I are finished—it's not you. We weren't meant for each other. We weren't married in the Church."

"I don't want any part of this. This wasn't the deal."

"What's so bad about me? You know you and I have a great time together. Admit it."

He heard the organ from far away. People walked around them on the sidewalk. They would not to a stranger's eye appear to be quarreling, two people talking before darkness settled in and the lights on Diamond Street shone more brightly with night.

He was not sure of her response. She looked at him with surprise and said nothing. Later, trying to understand her, he would think she may have meant with her startled look, the two of them standing in front of the huge theatrical posters of half-naked women rising out of furs that ringed their shoulders and elegant necks like magical cloaks, Mister, I always have a great time in bed, it doesn't need you!

She could not stop him in the following weeks from talking to her of themselves in the Carlton Hotel room where they made love. He was pleased with himself. They talked in what he thought of as the kind of conversations that lovers have. Now after knowing the depths of all that there was finally to her as she kissed and caressed him, he thought he had found the way to fumble and hold hands like high school sweethearts. He had seen it and not known it would ever be for him when he watched young men and women in Schenley Park. He had found a way to spread his coat on the grass so they could sit as strangers beginning something. This awkwardness between them was good, it was the way lovers start.

Signe told him that Loretta had called to say she was pregnant. "Now," Signe said, "there's no need to see her again—I'll take care of everything now."

"No," Brendan said, "I'll talk to her one more time. It can't end like that. For her respect for herself."

"You shouldn't see her alone again. I'll go with you."

"No."

"I don't like this."

"We shouldn't have started this."

"What are you saying?" she asked, but he had stood from the chair in the dining room where he was sitting and left their apartment.

Two days later, he thought, waiting in the street, Loretta would not come, standing near the Carlton Hotel, a Wednesday. She had avoided him at the theater and not answered his messages left for her at the ticket booth. He had written "Same time, Brendan." He stood in the light from a bar two doors down from the hotel. Ordinarily, he registered at the front desk and she came up to join him. Her knock at the door, gentle but insistent, as much not to be alone in the corridor of the seedy old hotel as to join him, was a treasured memory. He could not bear being in the hotel room without her, waiting, telephoning her somewhere, pacing the small room, and returning to his apartment, to resume conspiring again. At eight thirty, he saw her walking quickly in the street as he stood at the bar entrance.

"Did you register?"

"No, I'd like to, but it's up to you."

"Yes."

And together they walked to the front desk and he registered as Mr. and Mrs. Brendan Brake. He felt grown-up: she had moved him from boyhood to a lover of a beautiful woman. His wife, sermons at St. Agnes, general talk in the barrooms had not prepared him to be lost in the joy of it.

"This is our child," he said when they were together in the room.

"I know that," she said slowly, by the soft light of the room's one table lamp, removing her clothes. He had never, bound by their absurd agreement for darkness and no conversation, seen her take off each garment, stop and smile at him, reach to touch him, smile.

"Loretta."

He saw her in the next few weeks all outside the agreement. They met at the Carlton.

Leaving him one night in April, she said, "The game's too much for me, Brendan. I'm twenty now, and the family knows I have a boyfriend but I can't tell them because it's you. I can't bring you home. I'm ready to explain the kid—what can they do, kill me?—but it would be nice to have it all legal."

They stood on the corner of Highland and Penn where she caught her cab. It was windy even for that famous corner of wild wind in all seasons.

"Then I'll marry you."

"We've been through that."

"No, we haven't. I'll divorce Signe."

"And what about the five thousand I'm supposed to get for the baby?"

"I'll give you the five thousand—is that what's on your mind?"

"No, it's three times that. I need fifteen thousand altogether. Either that or I lose the baby."

"What do you mean, lose? You're not saying abortion?"

"It's still early enough, but I'd just as soon give you and Signe the baby and find the ten thousand more myself. I need it desperately."

"Loretta, do you love me?"

"I guess so, Brendan, but what's that question at a time like this?"

"What's the purpose of the other ten thousand?"

"Don't ask me if you're not serious about me."

"What's it about?"

"My mother needs an operation, it's awful. There's nobody she's told except me, it's her eyes. My father can't take it, not having the money, my brothers don't make it in a year between them."

He knew the story was of yesterday's fish, but it was only money. And maybe she did love him, and what was it she would do with the money if not give it to her mother? It was harmless if she exaggerated or even lied. She would know his love soon. She wouldn't lie when she saw his adoration for her. The money, if it was to go to a brother's gambling debt or furniture for a niece, was a small investment to make in a large, bright future. He told her not to worry about the money, he'd get it. She said,

"You will?" and he said, "This is only money between us. I'd do anything for you."

"I guess you know I'd do the same for you."

He held her close on the street corner and kissed her. It did not matter now who saw them or what Signe might think: he was to be a father, a husband, a lover forever.

The first six months of marriage to Loretta were like the nights at the Carlton, but now ripe with the promise of the baby. In December the baby, a girl, was born, and because Brendan was hurting financially—the ten thousand he had borrowed from his mother under the pretext of buying into the awning business lay like a rock on his soul—Loretta returned to working at the Casino Theater. Every night she would dress and apply makeup, and Brendan would drive her there. Sometimes there would be a rehearsal after the last show, called seemingly on the choreographer's whim, and he would pace uncertainly in their apartment, waiting for her call. After the last show when she called, he packed the baby into his old Chevy and drove down to Diamond Street to bring her home.

By days he worked at installing the awnings and returned home tired. She had dinner with him and left. In the first winter of their marriage, when the awning installation business was slow, Brendan did not leave the house all day. When she came home, they spoke of little at night, mostly the baby. She seemed always tired. The two nights a week when she did not work, she was picked up by her brother and spent most of the day at her family's house in Greenfield, taking the baby with her. Brendan went there a few times to give her a ride home, but her family were a silent lot. They watched him as if they thought he had eyes for the silverware. Caught between an incomplete marriage to her, she thinking of something else most of the time, not him obviously, and no particular place to be, Brendan felt left out.

She was no longer the ardent companion of the nights of love-making at the Carlton and the early months of their marriage. Occasionally he found her at the telephone, and she hung up too quickly when he saw her.

"Who was that?" he asked.

At first she pretended not to be on the phone at all. Then she said a name, "Myrt from work" or "Roy, my brother."

"Yeah?" he said, trying to convey to her that he did not trust her, not now, not the story about her mother and the ten thousand. But she just left the room quickly and became busy as if she had not played games with the telephone or noted his suspicion.

Once he said, "Funny how many times that guy needs you all to dance till one in the morning."

She said, "It's not my show. Better that way than have us come in on an off-day."

No fool, he thought, he left the baby with his mother one night and went down to the Casino Theater early. Backstage he saw Loretta again with the odd Diamond Street bird, the same seedy man he had seen her clasp hands with before they were married: by the look of him a local numbers bookie, a hanger-on at the theater, maybe a grocery clerk or a bartender in one of the places on Diamond. This time she quickly on parting took the man's face in her hands and kissed him on the lips. Brendan began to move toward them out of the shadows under the steps in the basement where the dressing rooms were but thought better of it. He knew he and Loretta were through; it was all about learning what truth was to be known now. He hurried home and was not surprised when she called late and said there had been a rehearsal.

He picked her up, the baby in its seat in the back, and they drove home in silence. He studied her face. Nothing there to speak of where she had been. How much easier life would be if other people's faces told us who they were or what they did with their lives! Then again, he thought, our faces would tell too: not at all to be desired except for the lunatics or the born liars whose faces would show nothing, the deceivers believing their own stories. Others keep their secrets, we keep ours, best all around. Brendan had no quarrel with that department of men and women and people generally, but why was there never to be peace in the long warfare with what we dreamed ought to be and what was?

A man's wife carrying on, held and loving it with another man, and Brendan Brake supposed to be in the center of things, not even an uninvited guest at the mischief.

When she started coming home late three nights a week he knew his concerns over the baby and their marriage and his strange inertia had ended, as if to have spoken to her of it would have made it more real than it was.

He smacked her in the face on the sidewalk in front of the Casino Theater where he usually picked her up, she sliding into the passenger side of the car.

"Have you lost your mind?" she asked, stepping back, holding her cheek.

It was a cold night in January. He had not worked in six weeks. Diamond Street was empty at two in the morning. The winds off the river blew newspapers down the street. Somewhere, Brendan heard the soft murmur of voices, probably drunks in a store doorway, burrowed in for the night.

He took her by the collar of her coat and shook her, and she said, "You lost your mind? Is that it? You lost your mind?"

"Have you lost yours?" he asked and struck her with his open palm again.

"I'll have you arrested."

"You'll be dead before then. I may kill you."

On the way home he explained to her how he had given up everything for her, lied to his mother, and dissolved a marriage to a good person. He explained how he loved their baby. Groping for words, he tried to let her hear how much she had meant to him. How he had trusted her. "And what was the ten thousand extra for?" he asked. "The bummer in the old sport coat? Don't lie, Loretta, I seen you. I had you followed." He would have, but there was barely enough money to get by on for necessities without paying private detectives. But he had seen her himself, and it wasn't information for a divorce he was gathering.

"Was it the bummer's gambling debts or his old mother losing her eyesight you took my money for?" he asked.

She cried a good deal over the next few days but went to work anyhow, the money from the Casino vital and there being a chance she'd lose the job if she called in sick too often. She swore she would never see the man again, if that was what Brendan wanted; it was not a romance. She had known him since childhood. He was a friend of the family. She called him, in fact, nothing but "Uncle Frankie." Yes, she had kissed him on the lips—it was impulsive. She was falling apart, she had nowhere to turn. Pressures were everywhere, work, her mother and father, here at home with her husband and kid. She loved Brendan, she loved the baby, she was going to practice her dancing and singing. She would work her way up in entertainment. Uncle Frankie knew people. He was a friend of her father's. "Ask him," she said. "Ask anyone!"

The question was, Why did she want to stay? And that was not a question with an answer Brendan would ever know. Maybe she did not know it herself. But stay she did: probably, he thought, until something better came along. As spring broke he laughed and was happy and sad at the same time, knowing he'd be soon back to work and an idea occurring to him. There were people stayed married a hundred and seven years waiting for something better to knock at the front door.

Alone with his daughter in March, he rocked her cradle and sang some old songs to her as she fell asleep. As he sat waiting for Loretta's call, he decided that he was really waiting for a recurrence of a feeling he had lost: back to where to find it? He would have wanted to return to that ecstatic moment when he first held her or when he sat in the audience in the Casino Theater and realized the height of his achievement.

Between the real woman who was this moment somewhere outside of his feelings for her and the woman in his troubled future he held on his mind to the one shadow of Loretta that stayed easy and good: on stage in artificial light, her hips swaying to music of every melody he had ever loved, and the long skirt in blue sequins like a wedding gown calling him with folds and sweeps. He had in music and dance believed that things possibly could go storybook right with a woman. He had heard airplanes bombing farmhouses and seen roads with people hurrying somewhere no better but thought he was somehow safe.

He called Signe in California and said, "I've done you a wrong. I'm not asking forgiveness, I just want you to know what my mental state is about you right this minute."

She said nothing but waited a few seconds, thinking of what she'd heard, and hung up.

It was once dreams of perfection that lay in the half-naked girls on the stage at the Casino Burlesque and all that they and the music promised. And before that it was raucous boys five in an old Ford going to some section of the city where whores dwelled. But at the beginning it was talk among them, whispers actually on the street corners of Oakland and eyes rolling, unbelievable forecasts of a future. And even if things were not like in the movies the sun came up the next day and there was no permanent loss. Not at all like life, he thought, where things began in innocence, blundered into confusion, and with him, twenty-five years old, became wounds like something in a war of bombs and shrapnel to be carried to the grave.

Loretta called and said he could come pick her up. He listened for what might lie in her voice but found nothing there. Maybe tonight was a time when she truly had been at rehearsal.

"Loretta," he said, "I could kill you like changing socks. What you've done to us, to me."

"I'm tired, Brendan," she said. "I'm tired. Why is it you loved me and wanted me and were ready to throw over your wife when I wasn't nothing to you, a body in a bed and you didn't know my name? You saw me on a stage and nothing more and said you needed me by your side forever. And now you know me and you want to kill me? Why is that?"

He had loved places of naked women and costumes sparkling as if precious stones were everywhere; and then it had been a fever in him that there were women to be had in beds of satin sheets if a youth had the price of admission. But there was more to it. Putting on his jacket against the March winds, he thought, You know, there's something in what she says.

TEN

Alias Eleanor Roosevelt

ALONE, New Keenen felt watched, noticed.

Meps Young came up on his right side and said, "Hucka-hucka, New, McCannon's in bad shape, very bad. Saca-saca."

Meps mostly spoke a language of his own, fearing silence. Sometimes when other people spoke he mumbled, "Saca-saca," to keep what seemed to him a conversation going, other times he said, "Hucka-hucka," in answer to a question. Mostly he threw syllables of senselessness into things he said, changing his inflections in rhythms that began to make sense when someone had known Meps for years. New had gone to grade school with him at St. Agnes. A prostitute who had once been a neighborhood girl told New on a trolley going out to East Liberty one day that Meps, a frequent customer, sometimes said nothing at all in an hour but hucka-hucka, saca-saca, lucka-lucka, and other nonsense words.

"McCannon's been in bad shape since he came home from the war," New said. "That was fifteen years ago, and people who knew him said he was in worse shape before he went to war. The war made him more sane. That's what people who knew him said. I didn't know him. But I know he's in bad shape ever since I knew him."

The night was warm for November, weather wildly changing daily.

"McCannon said you were a true friend and he's sorry things came between you. I've known him, lucka-lucka, all my life, and he's in worse shape I've ever known him."

"Yeah," New said, beginning to drift away from the corner of Oakland and Forbes. "That's too bad." He seemed to himself to be acting like someone very upset but accidentally moving as if called to go somewhere else.

When he was six feet away Meps said, "Might be his death."

"Yeah," New said. "Well, we all got to go sometime. You see him before he dies tell him New Keenen sends his best."

"Old lady he lives with, rents, you know, nothing personal, old lady's going to kill him. Mrs. Murphy. It's an emergency."

"How's an old lady going to kill McCannon? He's not in that bad a shape; he walks, he talks. Even running slow, maybe even walking slow, he can get away from an old lady. Tell him you see him I said walk fast she comes to get him."

"Stepson, saca-saca, big guy, he gets involved in something not his business and tears off McCannon's head and he's gone. Stepson is like an animal, he lives to kill. You ever see an animal lives to kill? The stepson is an animal like that, and he loves his mother, Mrs. Murphy, raised him like her own. He'd kill somebody he loved for her, lucka-lucka, for his mother, and there's nothing says he even likes Davey McCannon."

"Tell him hide behind a tree, the stepson will never find him."

"No, guy's just big, not stupid. He'll see McCannon behind the tree. Do him more harm for trying to hide. He'll take it an insult to his mother McCannon climbs a fence or hides behind a tree."

New was now in the middle of the street. "Well, maybe tell him to dig a hole in the ground, and if that makes the big guy angry, tell himself he put up a fight for being such a well-known weasel-bastard. I say, though, dodge the old lady and the step-son. Be somewhere else when they come around."

"He can't dodge them, New, he lives there. He lives in the house."

New said, "And he's past due on the rent."

"New, you should have been, hucka-hucka, in the mind-reading business. That's part of his problem with the old lady."

"No, it ain't, it's the whole problem. People get mad other people don't pay the rent. Not paying the rent supersedes any other problem. We moved a few times ourselves when I was a kid because people didn't get tolerant about skipping rent."

"Not to kill somebody. Anybody try to kill anybody in your family when the question of rent come up?"

"Might have happened like that."

"Them was violent times, these are peaceful times, except for the Chinese and the Russians. People don't go around trying to kill people in Oakland about rent superseding all other prob-lems. New, that's Davey sitting across the street in Ryan Moody's Buick. We were all three driving up the street and Davey Mc-Cannon was saying it might be his last ride up Forbes when he saw you out the window of the Buick. He says God dropped New Keenen into my life the minute I needed him most. Sucka-lacka, he's the finest human being in Oakland and when you need him he's there for you. He says you'd dive into a machine gun nest for your friends."

"Meps," New said, "I haven't spoken to Davey McCannon for more than three years. Nothing personal. I'm not running into a machine gun nest for him. I'm not turning my head to look at the Buick where he's sitting with Ryan Moody. I didn't look like it when we started this conversation, but I remember now I have somewhere to go."

"Where? I'll go with you, and we'll talk. You just wave to Davey and Ryan we're walking."

"No, thanks, it's somewhere I have to go alone."

"You know if you're in trouble McCannon would be the first to help you out, rent, guy trying to kill you, things like that."

"I know that," New said. "Tell him I appreciate all the help he'd give me I don't need at present."

"Where can I find you in an emergency?"

"I thought you said this was an emergency right now?"

"Yeah, it is, I'm glad I found you. Davey said it was a miracle you here on the corner."

Meps came from a family well off in financial terms, a big house farther out Forbes toward Squirrel Hill, the father in some business that kept Meps in a new Ford every three years, enough money for good, fashionable clothes that made him seem a half a hundred higher up the IQ ladder than he was, new ties, tailor-made jackets. But the answer was in his mother. She had a tendency to abandon Meps and his sister twice a year ever since he had been a boy; it was apparent, given the ferocious example of his battling parents, marriage was not for him. In his middle thirties he made a career out of bringing people with problems together with other people, not necessarily anyone who could solve the problem, only someone to share the predicament with

Meps, who was generous and sympathetic, and the person who was in the quandary in the first place and did not care who helped him, given his precarious state.

Sometimes Meps wanted no more than to discuss the third party's problem, feeling somehow talking about a dilemma even fifty miles away from where it was centered would help to solve it. When he had no current problems to worry over, nobody personal at peril, he talked about communists or the bad management of the Pittsburgh Pirates.

Walking away to a place no more substantial than had been his vacant situation before Meps talked to him, New did not wave at the Buick across Forbes. He crossed Oakland Avenue, heading east. He could be going to the University Grill or he could be going to the public library; he was, in fact, going nowhere, more or less walking now with no more purpose than he had while he was standing still.

"I'll tell McCannon I spoke to you about his problem and you said you were going to do what you could," Meps called.

"That's it exactly," New called back. "I'll do what I can, but tell McCannon my advice is to take a train to Cleveland. Get off between stations to shake the big stepson."

The truth was that the feeling between New and Davey McCannon was not friendly, not even presently unfriendly, but cold, dead. Meps did not know the facts. New did not intend to talk to Davey McCannon ever. It was not the money.

It had started with a discussion at the Irish Club late, very late, one night about Winston Churchill's mother and father. McCannon had said they were both Americans. New had stated Churchill's mother was American but his father was British. McCannon did not like the British. He said he liked Churchill just fine, but his mother and father were American. Then, he said, the reason New was confused—the hour was one lost between darkness and dawn and maybe no one there was as logical at three in the morning as they had been at eight the evening earlier—was that Franklin Roosevelt's mother was British. New had said, "Davey, that's ridiculous." And McCannon said he had twenty dollars that said it was New that was ridiculous. But no one at the table could say with certainty who was right or wrong in the argument, and the subject was taken to the bartender, Paul Kerry. Kerry was a student of World War II, but he had already gone home and Mouse Carr, who was filling in at the bar at that late hour, could not be counted on to know, having started with white wine and worked his way to brandy, whether his own mother or father was British.

But old Christy Lynch, who seldom spoke, never drank but sat for hours listening, chose at that moment to declare, "Churchill's mother was American, Roosevelt's mother and father were American, and you're all jackals." But it was too late for the bet.

McCannon, with his dubious twenty, had vanished, and he and New did not speak when they saw each other. It was now into years, the bad feeling.

New, having not a lot on his mind as winter approached, holding a job mixing cement and eating cement twenty-four hours a day, on the job paid for it, after work the cement in his throat and eyes a bonus, all the emergency he could handle, did not think about McCannon or his problem. McCannon always had at his fingertips a pressing problem or two—nothing, it was true, like tasting cement from working with it all day. McCannon hardly ever held a job. He had arrived at his forties with no profession, no record of steady work, no family except a sister in Cleveland and a host of problems with landladies, people he had borrowed money from, certain physical ailments that took him to the veterans' hospital once a week, and a seventy percent disability from the military service. He said he couldn't find work for the thirty percent of his health that was sound so he lived a hundred percent unemployed.

Mixing cement was good for the back; it could strengthen it if the constant bending did not cause a disc to rupture or a hamstring to go out. But other than that, New would be happy when cold weather came and work slowed. He liked rainy days, no money for building big back muscles to become a cement mixer for a career, but cold beer, feet up, rain on a roof somewhere, maybe a movie in the afternoon, a double feature. He was nagged, though, by the thought that time was passing, no jobs but they did not turn out temporary, no women but ones paid for at the moment, no hold on much except the idea something might happen to him one day.

Two days later, rainy November days when New was feeling good about things, no money made but no work either, Davey McCannon himself came up on him fast where New was sitting at the bar at the Cozy Tavern in Oakland. "New," he said, "I'm not going to pretend this is an accidental encounter. I'm looking for you. I need you."

"I know all about it."

"You going to invite me to sit?"

"That's up to you. I don't own this bar."

The retreat into New's investigation of himself had started because he had come to think he was too hard on other people. Davey was a good place to investigate the fruits of his soul-searching. Davey, historically, was someone to be difficult with, if not to avoid altogether. Avoiding Davey was hardly an intentional act, a quick movement to evade being spattered by mud as a clumsy bus passed in the street.

A respectful attention to Davey would demonstrate to New's satisfaction that he had rounded a corner in his desire to be easier on other people and in the bargain himself.

He had come to realize he acted disagreeably to other people and enjoyed it; not able to concentrate on school, he had quit Duquesne in his freshman year a long time ago, almost twenty years now, and come to consider most other people intruders. He seemed to need no one else but the people he thought he knew well in his daily rounds and he was not always good with them.

He was annoyed at the way other people looked and spoke. He was bothered by what they did with their lives, genuinely no damned concern of his. Lately he had been asking himself, after some dumb hiding away and piece of surliness, "Why did I say that!"

He could not pretend with himself that his leaping from people brought him pleasure. It did not exactly bring problems either, only a sense that there was something out of line. If truly he did not care if the rest of the world went to hell all on its own, why bother to be rude?

He said to Davey McCannon, "How have you been? Don't see you around much."

"That was a misunderstanding a few years ago," Davey said. "The God's truth was I didn't have the twenty to pay the bet and I rushed out to borrow it from Phil, the news kid on the corner of Atwood and Forbes, and when I came back you were gone. It was an embarrassment all around. Phil wasn't there. I came back to apologize. I'll do it now. Friend to all your family, I'm sorry for the misunderstanding."

The family he spoke of was New's brother, Kenny, who had fallen into the Allegheny River from a bridge he was painting. He had broken his neck and was hospitalized for a long time and then a longer time unable to move in a bed at the Keenen home on Darraugh Street. Davey had faithfully visited him, bringing him magazines and candy bars. One of New Keenen's early memories after the war when Davey came home a mess was him reading comic books and *True Detective* magazine to him as his brother lay staring up at the ceiling.

New's mother and father had followed Davey around the house, suspicious that wherever he sat a stain might appear or that he would lean somewhere and cause discoloration of wallpaper or a painting in a corridor, the generally disheveled look of him, clothes too large, shoes flopping like a circus clown's. Then, he always stayed for dinner. He was not particularly welcome, not the lack of funds to feed another mouth the problem—by war's end old Keenen held a steady job driving for Sears Roebuck—but the general dirtiness of his shirt collars, ragged seams at his pants legs, filthy handkerchiefs he extracted from his rear pocket to mop his brow or Kenny's forehead that were enough to turn a host's stomach. Nowhere else to be, Davey did good works at the Keenen house where the eldest son lay in a state of between here and there, but both of them prisoners: Kenny Keenen encased in a plaster cast, head to foot, and Davey there because mostly no one else would tolerate his shabby presence.

Still, he was with poor Kenny often when no one else was, no estimating his peculiar reasons.

"Okay, you're forgiven," New said. "It wasn't that big a deal. You could have just stood around at the Irish Club that night and said you were short the twenty but Roosevelt had an American mother and father."

"I was alias Mrs. Roosevelt myself most of my life, New. A person like me tried to walk in her shoes. I tried to do good for common people like yourself, like your brother. I meant no disrespect for the family saying they were British. It was a misunderstanding from beginning to end. And now I need a little favor from you."

"Why me in particular?"

"You know the circumstances. Meps Young told me he told you."

"You want me to fight a homicidal stepson?"

"No, no, hell no, there's not going to be a fight. I need a strong guy and someone I can count on. Two things aren't always in the same person."

"My back is weak, and you can't count on me."

"How's this Saturday? Are you working this Saturday?"

"This Saturday is fine. I'm not working this Saturday. But are you going to tell me what you want?"

"Help me move. That's not so complicated. Just carry a thing or two."

"Don't sound unreasonable."

"Two, three. Five blocks."

"You're moving a few minutes away?"

"Sure, where would I move? Down the street."

"I'll see you where?"

"Out on the corner near the Briar Bowl."

"Okay, out on the corner."

"Five o'clock."

"Five o'clock! The sun's not up yet. You're moving out in the middle of the night."

"It's no crime committed. I don't want to wake the neighbors, nice lady, Mrs. Murphy, she rent me the two rooms."

"Why are you moving?"

"I ask you questions you ever need a favor? Just tell me the favor and I do it. I never in my life asked a person needing help but one question: What more can I do, what you need, pal?"

New had no happy picture of himself, a friend to Davey.

Davey was by trade a petty thief. He lifted sunglasses—his trademark, he wore them proudly, various pairs until someone admired them and then he gave them away and stole another pair—socks, can openers, boxes of rubber bands, anything not nailed down. In one quick swoop he made things his own once belonged to someone else. And running with his type, even if Davey was the last of a certain kind, gave New the feeling he was no better than a scuffler himself. Scuffle a living in six jobs a year or on the fly with other people's property, hustling friends and strangers alike, hot watches, stolen sweaters, stories of misery to claim loans or affection, misrepresenting, getting by, proud to be getting by as if the world owed them a living, a dream of marrying rich, a soft spot with the county. Gambling. An inheritance. A stranger leaving them a sizable amount because of the liking they took to the style of the scuffler. It scared New that he was always one step short of descending to lifting sunglasses and probably not as good at it as Davey McCannon who never got caught. But, like a born scuffler, he shared the dreams of coming into better things through Lady Luck.

There might still, though, be time to take fortune in his own hands. Plenty of guys made something of themselves in night school, accounting, bank jobs, anywhere but a diet of cement on sunny days. He was not too old to reenter Duquesne College.

New was on the corner at five in the morning Saturday. "This has the feel of something illegal," he said to Davey.

Davey wore dark glasses on the still nighttime street.

"You really think I'd get you into something illegal? You're a solid guy. That's why I asked you. You want a cup of coffee?"

"No, I had some."

"Well, I'd like one. My check don't come in till Friday."

New bought him a cup of coffee at Scotty's Diner and Davey ordered three doughnuts, putting two carefully into a napkin. "I love these doughnuts here. I'm going to save these for later."

They walked down Forbes toward Coltart where Davey roomed.

There had been snow on the air and as they walked bright quick flakes tumbled around them; part of the snow was mixed with a fine rain. "This cancel plans?" New asked.

"What?"

"The snow, maybe rain?"

"It rains all the time, New. Pirates play in the rain all the time, monsoons. Ships sail in typhoons. Airplanes go through thunderstorms. You and me walking on Forbes in a light rain is nothing."

On the corner of Coltart and Forbes stood a group of men, odd in number at that dark hour of the morning. "They let out the worst ones from the nuthouses and jails early this morning," New said softly, then recognizing the men he said, "I got the feeling them ghostly figures has something to do with you."

There stood old O. C. Gedunsky, the freelance politician, generally a Democrat but knowing enough Republicans to render help when the Republicans frequently captured the governorship.

Cheerful, a kind word for everyone, man, woman, and child, but because of his age and general disposition against lifting, hauling, pushing, shoving, carrying, or being around places where such things were occurring not a man to enlist on a blustery November moving day or for that matter one in the brightest sunshine. Gedunsky wore a raincoat, suit, and tie, dressed for a conference with a bail bondsman at City Hall. Probably old when God was an altar boy, he held little promise of aid to Davey. And with him was Brick Conlon, dressed well enough for action, two sweatshirts piled on for cold and arms like tree trunks, but the tough younger brother of Ace Conlon, a famous loser in every street fight he ever waged, the younger usually tried to help the percentages in the family win-loss column, however irregular the occasion for a fight. New never saw the young man but that he felt insulted by someone and leaped to battle.

With them on the corner was Fat Teddy Ormsby, who often had his arm in a sling or walked with a cane. He had fallen, he said, or been pushed down a flight of stairs. His health was never good. Sometimes he said he was recovering from very severe surgery. He had large blue eyes and an expression, round, unchanging, and puzzled, that made him seem frequently on the edge of retreating in alarm.

"This isn't going to work," New said. "I never saw such misfits by the dawn's early light. How did you get these guys out here this morning?"

"You ever hear of money? I offered them fifty dollars, all but Meps and Gedunsky. Since they said they weren't going to be here the whole morning they'd come to help for nothing."

"This is like the Last Judgment," New said. "The whole section for the poor and down at heart showed up in a body."

Meps, natty in a fresh, expensive raincoat, double-breasted

with epaulets and brass buttons, waved at New. "Reinforcements, man," he said. "I'm leaving now. Good you come, New."

He turned quickly and walked up Forbes in the direction of the Briar Bowl, where Davey and New had just been. "Wait a minute, Meps," New called. "We ain't started."

Walking fast, Meps called back, "I'd be in the way."

New stood on the corner with young Conlon, Gedunsky, Davey, and Fat Teddy Ormsby, who was eating a Clark bar. As they stood watching Meps walk away, a stout man, perhaps in his fifties, with fair blond hair came running down Forbes. "I'm glad the moving didn't start without me," he called. "Someone bring the beer?"

New did not know the newcomer well, but he recognized him by sight. There was always a question at the Irish Club about when in the day the man, Harry Halbert, started drinking. New could testify now. He was ready at five fifteen in the morning; he was present and thirsty.

"Davey," New said, "you don't have fifty dollars to pay Teddy and Harry. And how come you didn't offer me any money?"

"You're here as a friend, the other two I already owe money. I'll just owe them some more."

At about that moment O. C. Gedunsky nodded pleasantly, said something, and walked up Forbes. "Where's he going?" New asked.

"Well, he did say," Davey said, "he wasn't going to be here except for the morning."

"But it's not five thirty."

"New, you ask a lot of questions."

"Men," Harry Halbert said, "I know where there's a certain bar they start getting ready for opening about now and the bartender is a personal friend. Someone give me a fiver and I'll come back with two six-packs, some pretzels and potato chips to get us going."

No one moved, and New put his hand into his pocket for a five. It was too early to drink for him; but the thought of moving Davey's things without Harry being present was a good one. He handed Harry the five. "Five I owe you, road buddy," Davey said. "You're a peach."

"Where's the truck? You have a car or something?"

"Ryan Moody said he'd be here, but between you and me he's not too reliable."

"How much is to go? We going to carry stuff up the sidewalk in the snow?"

"Just down to Bates."

"Bates is a long street."

"We could stop at Lasek's for some hard-boiled eggs we go down there," Teddy said.

With the small army in retreat from good sense, New walked down Coltart.

Light began to appear in the sky over his shoulder and the day was going to be dark. Just as well, New thought, deeds like this done best mostly under gloomy and camouflaging skies.

Davey lived, or had lived, in two rooms in the cellar of Mrs. Murphy's house. He had his own key to the front door and a special key to the rear door. But in the confusion of the morning, searching himself, he could find neither. He shrugged his shoulders and said, "Nothing to it but to kick in that little window down there. Thank God, there's no screen or bars, we'll be able to be in and out without waking anyone." Swiftly, young Conlon kicked in the window that sat at street level.

The noise sounded like an alarm at the Mellon Bank the day bank robbers might strike.

"Jesus," New said, "Brick, you got a foot could bust into steel vaults. Davey, Mrs. Murphy locked you out and you're breaking in. She changed the locks on you. She's holding your stuff till you pay her back rent."

"Son, the questions you ask! By the time I answer all your doubts we could be halfway to my new home without a crazy old lady and a stepson who wants to play baseball, my head being the ball. She's a geriatric case, I've not had time to tell you. She hallucinates. She dreams up money I owe her. She says she's quit the Church because the pope ain't a woman. You have anymore questions?"

"Yes," Teddy said. "I have a question. How do you expect me to get through that little window? I'm big in the shoulders."

"I was thinking New would just slip in and hand stuff out to us."

Brick said, "I'll climb in there. Let that old lady try to stop me."

"Wait a minute, Davey," New said. "You ain't planning on entering your own basement?"

"You lost your mind, kid? You think that woman in there ain't capable of notifying the United States government that an ex-soldier collecting a seventy percent disability is going to be doing gymnastics at her downstairs window? There might be a government spy watching us this minute or the old lady herself going to take a Polaroid of me dancing into that window. New, I can't do it. It's not smart. There's nothing illegal here, that's my property in there. But I act like Vera Zorina in the last act of *Swan Lake* and I'm out on the street for good. Good-bye, pension."

"How do I know what to hand out?" New asked.

"There's not that much there. I just want the electric fan and the boxes I have things. There's the little carpet near the bed, the lamp with the lady holding a basket of fruit on her head, plaster, get the picture of me in uniform—I'd die she tries to keep that—the toaster, the hot plate, the heating pad, and the electric blanket. And the books on the shelves, the paperback books, some of them took me through the war. There's a little bookcase, it was my mother's. Try to poke it through the window."

New avoided getting cut as he wiggled into the window, landing on a floor with linoleum.

"Any trouble, New," Brick said, "you call out. I'm here to keep the peace."

He found a light switch in the dark apartment and flipped it, but there was no light. "She turned off your electricity," New said. "I can't see in here."

"Grab what you can. She didn't turn off the electricity. She took the light bulbs, it's an old trick of hers to make me miserable. New, listen, before anything, find the two pair of shoes by the bed. They've got holes cut out for my bunions. I'm dead without them shoes, I'm a corpse."

New passed out the shoes and began methodically to hand things out the window.

It was not a warm day, a November sharpness to it, but he soon was wet with sweat. He realized it was nerves, not heat. He worked desperately, anxious to get back out on the sidewalk. Once there, he would desert the moving party. Let Davey call a cab to make three trips, let him stir Ryan Moody, let him do anything but count on New Keenen. He threw angrily six scruffy ties out the window.

Outside on the sidewalk, New heard sounds.

A woman's voice. "Whoever is in there is subject to arrest,"

Mrs. Murphy said. "Mr. McCannon, tell the thief to step out here and leave my premises or it's the police called on an intruder. I'm not playing games with you, Davey."

"Nothing to worry about," New called. "I'm just going to leave by this back door. Don't call the police. I'm leaving, Mrs. Murphy."

Mrs. Murphy shouted at Davey, "Mr. McCannon, return that electric fan to this house. Everything in that basement apartment legally belongs to me, but it's okay if you take your junk and leave. Worthless trash. But not that fan!"

"It was a gift."

"It was a loan to a paying boarder."

"Here's my friend," Davey said. "New Keenen. Just helping me out, Mrs. Murphy, no harm intended. He's just doing a good deed."

"He needn't do good deeds on my property."

Brick Conlon said, "Why don't you just vanish another ten minutes, lady, and we'll be gone."

"I'll call my son."

"No," New said, "we're leaving, the fan's yours."

"You're damned right," Mrs. Murphy said.

"I don't like a woman cursing," Brick said.

"Let's go," New said. "Leave the fan."

"That's my fan."

New lifted the small fan. "Here, Mrs. Murphy," he said. "It's your fan, keep it."

"Legally, I'm entitled to everything here. You broke in."

She was a small woman but her rage gave her bulk and size. Particularly, she glared at Brick Conlon. New understood the look. She and Ace's younger brother had found each other.

"Mrs. Murphy," New said, "take everything."

"Not everything! My picture, my shoes, my ties."

"Let's go," New said and started up Coltart. He turned and said, "Brick, there's something I want to ask you." Conlon detached himself and New put his arm around his shoulder. "I've seen your brother Ace walk away from situations like this a thousand times. Let me buy you breakfast. The old lady is trying to put something into her life."

"I don't like language like that from a woman."

"Who does? That's why we're better than she is."

"Old bitch."

"Let me buy you breakfast."

"Wait!" Davey called. "I can't leave my things on the sidewalk. New, take these ties, they're from me to you."

New left Davey and Teddy and Mrs. Murphy on the sidewalk and took Brick Conlon for breakfast to the Sun Drug. He was thankful that the stepson had not arrived. He was filled with gratitude that the whole day still lay ahead for him, the Cozy, a movie. He could fill his mind with nothing. There was no decision he was going to make, not to consider going into the Briar Bowl for a pack of Chesterfields or down Oakland to the Irish Club, the hour early. The chill weather made him think of the pleasures of sleep and all that he could put together if he let himself break out of the hold of being too easily satisfied with things done in old ways.

But later that night, standing once more on the sidewalk, now in front of Gammon's Restaurant on Forbes, New felt himself again in the presence of Davey McCannon. The streets were wet with melted snow and the lights of the drugstore and the restaurant fell across Forbes, lighting the snowflakes as they spun and fell and turned to water.

"Fat Teddy helped me finish," Davey said. "Harry come and

we went down to my new place and drank beer. I wish you'd been there. I appreciate you trying to help even though you pulled out on me. No harm done between friends." In the lights from the restaurant behind him Davey looked very old. "It became a matter of principle between Mrs. Murphy and me. I left her a toaster and that was it, that and the fan you give up early."

"Davey, I have somewhere to be."

"You know, New, if there was a fire and you and anybody you had a connection to was trapped there, even a dog, I'd run in to save you or the dog, a cat, a chipmunk foaming at the mouth if it was something close to you. It wouldn't matter."

"I guess I know that."

"The past is bygones."

"Not exactly."

"Hard feelings to me about I ran from a bet?"

"No, the past before that, where I knew you for a guy who had bad luck, losing your health after they shot at you in the army and ruined your nerves."

"Yeah, I was never right after that, but the point I'm making is that I'll be there for you. Maybe I'm in six pieces, but the parts go to war for you, New." The face of a thousand tricks, veins and dissipations, cons and deceits, the eyes popped as Davey removed his sunglasses to look directly into New's face.

"That ain't it, Davey, and you know it. The point is I'm never going to be in bad enough shape to ever need you, better off dead, as I see it, but my trouble is that I'll be there for you if you get trapped in a fire or jump off a bridge and drag me with you."

Davey said, "It don't matter what you do or don't do for me: you're still my kid, I look out for you."

New stepped back. It was impossible not to run from such a

man with all his false promises, even hide behind a tree to escape him as if he were a moose ready to trample a person. But I'm not running, New thought. Whatever his devious purposes, New remembered his steady voice reading to his brother by the hour while Kenny in frustration wept silent tears of anguish, never to walk right again, never really to be happy again. But that wasn't Davey's fault.

New felt the burden, that he would be there soon again with a forlorn band on the sidewalk to serve misfit dreams and ambitions, failing himself at the simplest things in his own life but there for Davey McCannon to the last bitter caper. "New?" Davey asked, beginning something else, and New turned away from his fake-o friend, nowhere to be except in the round of daily problems other mutts and freaks put together for themselves. Davey put on his sunglasses to study him as he walked away.

"Babe, you need anything?" Davey called. "Ever!"

ELEVEN

The Death of the Quarterback

SHE HAD BEEN BORN on the same day as Helen Keller, the famous blind and mute woman who had made much of herself in a world that did not welcome her either. The eldest daughter, it fell on Opal to bear the burdens of making decisions for a family of two brothers and three sisters, a mother too weak to know her own mind, and a father who lacked ambition. Someone not knowing the special qualities of Opal would think there was nothing unusual about her, she thought, seeing no hidden power that could aid her in elevating her brothers and sisters and raising her mother and father from their humble aspirations. As a child, though, she knew from the beginning that if she did not seize the sword and hold off the family's enemies no one would. There was a map in her mind. She saw clearly, without having been there, the territory to follow that would take them all out of the sorry condition they had allowed themselves to inhabit through not knowing what she knew.

She would fight anyone in the name of her family and make for all of them a world better for her being there. She knew there was a road that certain people followed, and she had seen the Connell family was not aware of it. They took things the way they came: she knew that education, sobriety, piety, thrift, and trusting in each other could save them. Endowed at birth with an uncanny love of her brothers and sisters running in her veins, not there by half in her weak mother or father, a solitary sort of miracle that could never be explained or even commented on by herself, just known and witnessed by Opal, she observed her steadfastness and bravery as if it were a quality possessed by explorers in a children's book, a gift to a stranger, not her.

It was a hard world, and she had chosen not to yield to it, not for herself or anyone else in the family.

Her only friends were Rog and George, her twin brothers, and her sisters, Margie, Berry, and Bliss. It was she, whatever their given names, who had renamed them all, at an appropriate time calling them nothing but what she had chosen and insisting that they call themselves and be known to the others by the name she knew to be best. Left to her mother's devices there would have been Frankies and Bernards and Marys and Mary Catherines: no way to enter life as if a person were trying to sneak in with someone else's driver's license.

No particular man appeared on her horizon until Willis Shook, and she knew, as did everyone else, that he was the chosen man to be her husband. He lingered, following her schedule as if he knew it in advance, church, a movie, a long walk around Oakland, touching the cathedral, the Mellon Institute, the

Carnegie Museum. And while she did not care for these places particularly, she felt that a promenade there was appropriate for two people, neither very young and planning marriage. Willis was an upholsterer at Allegheny Bedding and Sofa on the North Side and thirty-eight years old and Opal was thirty-six, and though she said she already had a family and saw no need for another, it was known she strongly endorsed marriage and someone as sober and industrious as Willis was would probably be exactly her choice for a husband, if she had wished for an eternal union.

There was, however, no discussion of children between them: Willis had been an only child and not happy and Opal felt she was too old to bear children. Of connubial relations, she confided in her one friend, Beatrice Walsh, that neither she nor Willis cared very much for that in its specifics. "It is not the point of marriage at our age," she said. "We help each other in good times and bad. We've saved fifteen thousand dollars and more in our first five years of marriage."

She tended her brothers and sisters while they lived at home, not allowed drinking of anything strong, even at weddings or wakes, no loud arguments, no clothing that reflected badly on the Connell family. On his days off Willis wore a white shirt and tie, as did Opal's brothers, and when women began to wear pants, called later slacks, during World War II, the Connell sisters were the last to take up the fashion. When in due course Mother Connell died, hardly breaking stride, sad for her wasted life but knowing life must go on, Opal stepped into being mother and sister and Willis's wife.

"The family would have gone to Hell without you," her friend Beatrice Walsh, who had never married, told her.

"Not so," Opal said. "We are very strong people. We do not go to Hell easily, Beatrice."

Beatrice lived with her aged mother and weekly doted on news of the Connells, stories from their work, their families as they married, reminiscences of their early days, the tribulations of Willis Shook with inept and lazy upholsterers and salesmen at the firm where he worked. In exhaustive detail Opal related to Beatrice about nine every morning on the telephone the events of the past twenty-four hours, and once a week, after Sunday Mass, she met with Beatrice for two hours and summarized what they had talked about earlier. The truth was Willis seldom came up in their more serious conversations: it was her sisters and brothers, their marriages as they aged, their near fatal errors of judgment, saved at the last minute by Opal, her father and his stubbornness—he continued to drink outside the house, often coming home at night and going straight to bed before she could confront him when she lived at home, and later when she had left for marriage and her own home on Bates Street, five blocks away, eluding her sisters who might bring her an accurate report. She was kept busy after awhile in a correspondence with her brothers and sisters: they each in turn left Pittsburgh, moved away to disreputable places like Los Angeles, Toronto, Philadelphia, or Detroit, puzzling her. What could there be in these places that there was not in Oakland? Here were museums, movie theaters, the same television programs people watched coast to coast, and certainly the sort of jobs they took elsewhere.

A person did not have to go to Philadelphia to work in a factory or Los Angeles to sell insurance. She suspected it was their husbands or wives who coerced them. Not really knowing her, not understanding that she was the soul of the Connell family, they dashed away—she was no fool—to avoid her.

One of the twins, Rog, was twice divorced, and Opal had it out with him when he returned to Pittsburgh on one of his periodic visits. He brought with him, in the style of the sixties, a young woman with whom he was obviously "shacking up," as people used to say. Not under the family roof, of course: he knew better than that, but their sordid relationship was clear to her.

"Do you think," Willis asked, "it's really your place to talk to Rog about such things?"

"I do not," she said. "I do not meddle in people's lives. It's a conversation with the woman I'm going to have."

And she did.

After an hour into their visit to her house, the day being fine and cool, Opal invited the young woman to stroll with her around the neighborhood. She said to Rog, "We'll get to know each other."

Rog had said he was going to marry the young woman.

Opal wasted no time in acquainting the young woman with the truth of things. "Do you understand anything about our family at all?" she asked. "My father was a humble millworker all his life. He would not have raised the children to be who we are if I hadn't stepped in. We are not millionaires, but Willis and I are quite well off, better than you think—you see how our house is furnished, probably better than any house on Bates. And Willis is just an upholsterer: he's not a rich man either. But we have accountants in our family, salesmen, my sisters are married to hard-working executives in some of the biggest companies in America. You've heard of Alcoa, one of the girls' husbands works there and another husband works in Las Vegas managing a bar and grill that turns over a million dollars a year in business. Now, I'm going to ask you, Daisy, if you hear of our accomplishments, are you going to be able to live with them? Are you going to take them personally—as a reflection on your lack of success?"

"What are you talking about?"

"Never mind that high horse: you have no education and you have no profession. Are you going to be able to handle that you are in a family with degrees in finance and years of solid experience in the business world? Roger went to the Robert Morris School of Business for two years; he could have gone to Harvard, but women ruined him. Are you going to continue his downfall, or will you help him rise?"

"I don't understand what you're asking me."

"Well, it's plain enough: Rog has no parents to talk to you so I'm taking it on myself to tell you about us. Friendly, in a family spirit: will you help your husband or will your jealousy about us blind you to how well we've done?"

"I'm not jealous of you. I don't know any of you. Until just now, I had hardly thought of you. Rog said you were impossible, but I wasn't marrying you. The others seem okay."

"Okay, that's it: we're just okay. Well, maybe to you. But I assure you others find us better than that."

"You're a horrible woman."

"To tell you of our family accomplishments makes me horrible?"

"No, to put me down."

"Put you down? I don't know you, and you don't know us. I am welcoming you to the family. You act your part, respect what we've accomplished despite our humble beginnings, and you'll find I'm your best friend. You'll be one of us."

"Please, Opal, let's stop talking. I'm confused, I'm not sure of my direction on this street. I want to go back to your house. I don't want to talk to you."

"You will have to talk to me one day. Rog is a fine man, but he's weak, like his father. You'll come to me for help and I'll be there—if you want me. If not, go on your own. But you've been served notice on who the Connells are: don't say you haven't been warned. We are unusual people."

"Oh, God, I haven't enough money on me for a cab, and I'm lost."

The young woman turned in one direction, then another.

"Follow me," Opal said and strode on ahead of her.

At Opal's house Daisy, the young woman, was red-faced, in tears. Rog comforted her, but she would not be seated. Willis tried to intervene and Rog pushed him, and Opal was appalled at Rog's crude shove at her husband. "It's come to this," she said, and Rog said, "I'm never coming back to Pittsburgh. I'm never talking to you again. What did you say to Daisy?"

Opal shrugged. "Is bragging about our family a crime now?"

When they left, Willis put his arm around Opal. "What was it about?" he asked.

"I'd say again tomorrow, it was nothing," Opal said. "I'd say it if God woke me from the dead a thousand years from now. It is the truth and God knows it."

Over the years through catastrophes, births, deaths—Father Connell died in his sleep—and Opal reciting daily to Beatrice the disorders of her life and her triumphs, she gave her experiences an importance as each new turn in the Connell history was discussed and made larger through Opal's victories, like a modern Helen Keller. She held her family together; without her they would have long lost track of each other, maybe even of themselves without her to remind them of the strength that lay in them. She knew she might be boring to some people—lately her hearing was failing and she talked through other people's conversations, seemingly lost in what she herself was saying but not caring that she interrupted anyone. What had anyone to say that could compete with her knowledge of the world? *She and Willis had a hundred and six thousand dollars in U.S. savings bonds.*

The value of the lives of the members of the Connell family, she decided, depended on her interest. Her life with Willis was perhaps shallow but dignified and good—she once woke at midnight, thinking she was an embryo somehow not born yet—and the value of her life was magnified as Connells fell into trouble and were repeatedly saved by Opal's advice. She never, on principle, ever gave any of her brothers or sisters money. She had provided sums for the funerals of her mother and father, while the others had hung back, and it was a lesson to her. Money was the way to lose them. They needed a beacon, not a banker. "They don't need me for a banker," she proudly told Beatrice when the idea occurred to her. "I'll ruin their characters. But you know very well should they need me—even for money— I'll be there."

The deep mysterious need never occurred: she was never asked for money, she long forgot that she had once said she saved her money because one day her brothers or sisters might need financial help. Rog had not spoken to her for twelve years, still apparently married to the foolish young woman who harbored such animosities toward people obviously superior to her.

Thomas Kincaid, her sister Berry's husband, died in a car crash on the Pennsylvania Turnpike, a seeming suicide, alone in the night, running his Buick into a concrete piling; and Opal summoned the family to attend his funeral and only they and the man's one daughter, the child of another marriage, under the influence of alcohol that very afternoon, were there of Kincaid's family. The Connells were in assembly at the Philadelphia funeral home a mighty army: Opal loved every fiber of their bones when she looked at all of them, even Rog, who still would not speak to her.

Celebrating all their lives by comforting the poor, addled daughter, Opal felt her strength in all its strange power: she felt God. Without her, there would have been only the young woman hardly able to find the reception room for her father. Scarcely knowing Berry's husband—she had met him only at the wedding and knew by the melancholy cast to his eyes, his habit of wiping at his mouth when there was nothing there, that she had encountered a soul who would one day fail her sister and the family.

There was little she could do; she was no more than a woman who loved her family.

Kincaid's torment had triumphed: she was never sure what had caused him to kill himself, perhaps the daughter or something he could not name himself, but she had tried to speak to Berry about his unnatural moodiness, and Opal knew that, for whatever it was worth, he had died better for being in the company of Connells, doomed perhaps but better for his association with them.

She could have written a book on people who had lived and died, richer, more complete, sailing above themselves, for having joined her family. Where would Willis be without her, and the rest? Even Willis, as close as they had become over the years, plotting their retirement and maintaining the house on Bates and putting away money for a rainy day, did not understood her concern for her family. And Beatrice? Where would she be without Opal's strong right arm to hold off adversity?

Once, seeking to enlist Willis, she had tried to explain to him how the care and future of her hapless family had fallen, all unwillingly, on her, and he had stood up from where he was sitting and, unsmiling, retreated to their small back porch. It was strange of him; he was polite. He always listened. Now she imagined that there would be times, even her husband growing frail with her need for strength, there would be many tribulations she would have to face alone. She closed her eyes with tears: Beatrice Walsh would one day die, and then? Opal Connell Shook could face whatever the future held, silent, keeping to herself entirely if it had to be that way. She saw that her burden and gift could not be explained even to Willis, perhaps not to Beatrice.

Her love for her family had taken its price. She knew she did not love her husband in the ordinary sense of the word, wife to husband, although Willis Shook had very little of that kind of love in himself and no sense as she had of an extraordinary mission. Taking home with her sister Marg her infant son from the hospital, she realized when she held him that she probably loved every Connell ever born and to be born as profoundly as any mother could. Still, she knew that the full force of her love was denied to the baby as it was to her husband and to any single person in her family because it was the idea that she would not let all of them sink that drove her. It could be called love, she thought, but more than that: to not let these people fail was her destiny.

She tried to explain it to Willis or Beatrice, what caused her at night not to sleep with the excitement of it, but the words were hard to come by and too inexact. As each of the Connells packed their suitcases to leave Oakland forever, except for the occasional marriage or funeral, she yearned to ask, "Do you know what I have tried to do for my family? Do you think I live an easy life, none of you with the sense to worry and all of it falling on me? I live for all of you and I don't draw a breath of my own. I suffer for my family, I'm suffering for you at this minute. As you leave us, remember my sacrifice. I have no one but my family. I raised you all by myself. I had no one. Forgive me if I failed."

She would have thrown herself before the moving vans, stood in the church against the priests in the wedding ceremonies, anything to stop the departures from a place where she could save them all as she had from the beginning, but each of her brothers and sisters left, causing her terrible pains in her chest and nightmares of them being lost on lonely roads. They abandoned her as if she had just been an older sister by accident. Some never wrote and humbly she had to find their addresses from someone else in the family. Each Christmas was an agony, who would call and who would not.

She never complained except to Willis or Beatrice at the injustice of having a mission in life that would make her seem obtrusive and domineering and not concerned with anyone else's feelings. If she had her way, no shaking her fist at God here, she would have chosen to have a mother and father like herself, a sister or brother strong as she was—and let someone else take all the misunderstanding heaped on a woman who had been thrust into directing a family lost without her.

Not that anyone after awhile sought her counsel, the brothers and sisters ignoring her, sometimes seemingly perversely doing the opposite, and paying for it, but she persisted. When they did listen in these later years, or pretended to, she wondered whether it was the rumor of her money that caused them to play-act at taking her seriously. She lived frugally; she purchased nothing that was not absolutely necessary, knowing great calamities could fall on any of the Connells at any time and money had to be there for them, and she considered herself better off than anyone she knew. Perhaps they said among themselves she had never worked and had had all that marriage seemed to offer and now seemed content without the struggle for money or the continuing love of her husband of many years. Looking at Willis across the room as they sat with the familiar shadows of an autumn evening falling on Bates Street, she thought, as she often did, that he had been part of her destiny too, like the family she had worked to save. Sometimes she thought he understood how much she had given up for her family: she refused to go on vacations, she bought clothing that fit only the barest need. Around the house she wore no shoes except sometimes a pair of Willis's old shoes, no need to spend money when his shoes were perfectly good and no one was there to see her anyhow and a pair of the heavyweight socks he wore daily, having to stand on his feet for long hours. Soon he would retire from his longtime upholsterer's job, now white-haired and no longer ruddy in complexion, and observing him in the twilight, she crossed the room and kissed him on the forehead. He sat upright, startled, and she moved away quickly too. She had not realized she would astonish her husband by kissing him unexpectedly.

"I didn't mean to startle you," she said. "I suppose you were deep in thought."

"Yes, yes, I was."

It was the middle of October, and by the end of October, one day returning home from a visit to the Carnegie Library, she found Willis unmistakably gone from her life—except as an unanswered mystery that she considered hourly, an enigma that would be with her till her death, a few fumbling telephone calls and an empty chair, his lamp throwing illumination where he would never sit again. To her horror, of the two hundred and thirty thousand dollars they had amassed in U.S. savings bonds in a safe deposit box at the Mellon Bank in Oakland, he took exactly half, one hundred and fifteen thousand dollars. A lawyer sent her a letter that her husband had stated she could keep the house—they had no car—and if she wished a divorce that was fine with him.

She spoke only to Beatrice of Willis's betrayal—and the others in the family, those she still heard from, understood her wife's sorrow and, she liked to believe, respected her for her fortitude. In the months following Willis's departure, she tried to hold up for her brothers and sisters, even phoning Rog, on the telephone sometimes for hours, the first and last to attend funerals of those close to them, prompting them with heartfelt letters to leave some brute not worthy of them and preparing lines for them to deliver to their erring children and nieces and nephews. Rog refused to take her call. The others, it was not easy to determine, did seem to be listening, but no one agreed enthusiastically with her in her judgments.

"Why did Willis leave?" Beatrice asked finally, the night she moved in with Opal in the house on Bates.

"He was a tired old man: he just ran away, no sense to it. I don't think for a long time he realized and maybe he did and that hurt him that we're something better than people who work with their hands. He was only a workingman. I must have pained him terribly with our family."

Instead of a family, she had tales brought to her on the telephone, held her breath, even moaned slightly, then like a loyal, ever true fountain poured forth her sympathy. As her savings accumulated again, she remained among her roses and lilacs, a thousand familiar scents on the air, old faces she had known a lifetime, but sometimes, alone at night, she wept for all of them, roses and garden and brothers and sisters. She missed each of the absent family and even, slightly, Willis. Beatrice was no great comfort: she had not the same devotion to her as she had to the lost, wandering clan. Would they ever reassemble in this world or the next? She told Father Farrell at St. Agnes of her numbness at the terrible emptiness that descended on her, and he nodded. Thinking she spoke of the humble upholsterer, Willis Shook, he said, "Think of the fine years you and he spent together. They're solid in memory and they'll never let you down."

She had not long to grieve.

There appeared on her doorstep one morning in June a young man, tall and fleshy, loose, blond, and with a fair complexion: she knew him even after peering at him for no more than thirty seconds. He was a Connell.

"I know you," she said. "You're familiar to me."

"Aunt Opal," he said.

"You're—?"

"Your brother Roger's son."

"Come in, come in," she said, knowing the age of miracles hadn't passed even yet in Oakland.

The boy wasn't a mirror image of Roger, not now or even remotely as he had once been, but he was close enough. "Bless you for remembering your family," she said.

The boy who was fifteen had come by bus not exactly to see her but Willis. He wanted to be an upholsterer and it seemed that Uncle Willis was a place to start. But, in keeping with his jovial good nature, he was not distraught that Willis was not there. He laughed and shrugged his shoulders and drank tea with Opal and Beatrice and let himself be persuaded he would stay over the weekend. He liked ice cream and she bought it by the gallon for him and he and Beatrice and Opal ate it all every night. He was a comical boy who did imitations of Elvis Presley and Groucho Marx and he had his serious moments. She would see him sitting on the back porch looking at the light from the setting sun falling behind her bushes and she would feel good, not caring to disturb his pensive moods. He seemed to her altogether too original to have done well in school and that was why he dropped out. Sometimes quick wit like the boy's and intelligence could be a handicap in some schools. And to his credit, he told Opal he would never discuss his mother, Daisy, with her. She was, he said, the source of all his problems: enough said.

"He knows what you want to hear," Beatrice said. "And he says it."

"Don't talk nonsense. I say only the best things about his mother. Such nonsense."

Walking down Robinson Street from St. Agnes with Opal on Easter Sunday, he said, "Aunt Opal, the way I read this family— I never got along with my father and we never talked about things and my mother is a closed book—but this family is like a football team. It has one quarterback, and that's you. The rest are running around like chickens who had their heads chopped off, except you and me. You call the signals for all of them, like the quarterback, do you follow the game?"

"Of course, I do. Yes, it's a good thought, and very accurate. I'm flattered, K.C."

"Okay, without you to put things together and people like me to follow the plays, none of the rest even know the name of the game, there's no Connell family."

"I can't believe you're only fifteen."

A week later he bought her a poster of Joe Namath, the quarterback for the New York Jets, and she was to treasure it for the rest of her life, but in the third month of the young man's stay Beatrice moved out, saying she did not trust K.C. Probably jealous, Opal thought, she had no nephew like the boy.

K.C. stayed with Opal for eight months, and he was not able to find a job in that time in Pittsburgh; only fifteen, he could get no work permit. But one day he announced he had a friend in Canada who had a job in an upholstering plant in Montreal and Opal accompanied him to the bus stop, taking a taxicab downtown.

She gave him a hundred dollars and bought his ticket and reassured him he could always come back to Pittsburgh, plenty of furniture stores here. He kissed her on the cheek and said, "I'll never forget you, Aunt Opal."

Even after she discovered he had, like her husband, stolen certain U.S. savings bonds, she remembered herself as the quarterback. She kept the bonds, a few not in the safe deposit box, in a space in the kitchen table, between the leaves of the table, which were never expanded. She could not imagine how he had discovered them, but she knew it was he. He took only one third of what was there in a large envelope. She had kept the bonds out of the Mellon Bank, thinking should the safe deposit box be looted again, she would not be destitute. The sum he took was considerable; but she had no one to leave the money anyhow. The bonds were at face value ten thousand dollars and she made no attempt to notify the bank or call the police. "No, no," she told Beatrice, "let him think of it as a loan, I'm sure he sees it that way. And if I make a fuss he'll never come back. Beatrice, I think K.C. understands me. That's a precious gift in this world, to be understood."

Beatrice moved back in but found Opal more illogical with each passing day. She continuously called her brothers and sisters and hardly remembered they had hung up on her the day before. And every day she left the house briskly at nine o'clock, took a trolley in the direction of downtown, and did not return till evening. Beatrice tried to speak to her of her routines, the calling and the streetcars, but Opal looked at her vaguely.

With each dawn Opal thought the beginning of the last chapter was starting, it having dawned on her, her brothers and sisters had once left Pittsburgh by train or airplane or bus, and they would, when it happened inevitably, return by a public conveyance. She had only to go downtown to the railroad station where she had once gone to see off her brothers going to fight in two wars and wait: sooner or later, in ones and twos, sheepishly or boldly, each to his or her nature, they would return to acknowledge her love and sacrifice.

Where the station had once stood there now was a new building that housed T-shirt stores and restaurants in the shell of the railroad station, flower stores and souvenir shops with painted wooden turtles and snowmen under glass with bits of paper like snow in the tiny domes. There was a drugstore and booths where a person could take her own photograph, and Opal was bewildered at first at where she should wait until the family arrived, but, after awhile, she realized her brothers and sisters would come from behind the back of the stores, walk out toward her between the rows of T-shirts and paper flowers, and greet her where she walked and waited in the aisle of the building. She listened for the sound of trains but heard none. She saw luggage stores but no one carrying suitcases as in the old days. Daily she worked at the mystery, knowing they would all return home by the railroad station and that she would be waiting, the details not clear to her.

At the end of the summer, as twilight was leaving the sky and night was settling in, the telephone rang, and Opal, knowing by the light in the sky and the urgent ringing that this was the night it would commence, ran to the phone.

"Yes," she said, breathless with the joy of anticipation.

"Opal Shook?"

"Yes. Berry?"

"Mrs. Shook, I'm with the Superior Paint Contractors, we're doing some work in your neighborhood, and we wondered whether you'd be interested in our twenty percent off special for homeowners doing their exteriors."

"Berry," she said, "thank God you called. Tell me where you are. I'll come and get you. You must tell me everything, everything."

TWELVE

Say Something to Miss Kathleen Lacey

THINGS WERE supposed to happen to a soldier on furlough, Mackie McCafferty in particular, a young man marked for getting things going, exactly like this: a woman a little older, maybe ten years but still all there at about thirty, and himself a ready nineteen. He let his army combat boots carry him, sort of tell his story that he needed space for his shoes and the swagger that came with being his kind of man. He knew the man he was; he had with enough time, and given a break, now the goods to make himself become a proven fact to who he was in the world. His uniform brass polished, creases cut sharp as knives in his pants, and the boots to do their own walk telling the story of watch-out-he's-here, a strut maybe not too modest, but who was judging?

Once nobody's hero, young McCafferty, an only son of a

widow, had marched with those boots through basic training into a fine nine-to-five U.S. Army job at the motor pool at Fort Meade, a few hours from his hometown. He liked fixing cars, grease on his hands, plunging into the motors of three-quarters and Jeeps and bringing them back to life. He had high ambitions that had nothing to do with fixing motors, but he knew no matter where his destiny took him he would always be the kind of guy who liked grease on his hands, lying under a car and letting it tell him things by ticks, low sounds, and groans. Later, when he settled down, it would be a clean-hands job for a living but never giving up monkeying with carburetors. All there now, in the army, the best of times. Doing his two years to get the GI Bill after World War II, but not so far away by bus that he was not forgotten on the same old streets of Pittsburgh, not giving his mother a stroke with being in a foreign country with bad water and thieves and renegade enemy soldiers in the night. He kept his hand in things, handy for weekends with the old boys, reading for college, and now Miss Kathleen Lacey, something good now and maybe forever in good memory of when he had been nineteen and ready and able.

She lived in a house next door to a car agency on Forbes in Squirrel Hill and the Chevrolet salesmen and mechanics seemed to know her. It was the time between Christmas and New Year's Eve, cold and lights still up in houses and on telephone poles and the city around him damp and big and black. The red and green lights in the car agency blinked slowly in the late night, the street wet with rain but no snow or ice. A long slow wind blew down Forbes, coming from somewhere cold and making indoors, any interior out of the dark and deep frosty air, a place to seek for shelter, any place but on the sidewalks home. The trolleys on Forbes seemed in a rush to be elsewhere. Walking her to her door, having asked her to dance earlier that night at the Ancient Order of Hibernians, Division No. 9, he observed the friendly greetings she received from men at the car agency.

The place was open late. Men hurried indoors from the lot in front. It was past midnight and all the lights inside, behind the Christmas lights, were still on. Inside, Mackie could see groups of men talking to each other, the day after Christmas nowhere particular to go, no buyers for Chevrolets but better than being alone. Mackie McCafferty of the United States Army had a warm place to be.

He had scooped her about eight at the Irish Club, and she said she had to be home, she had a kid. Okay, that was no trouble. She said she was divorced; so Mackie was not going into unexplored territory with her, a kid, and learning about life from living with a man to whom she had been married, and it was 1946!

She knew what to expect, why he was there. She had introduced herself as they danced as *Miss* Kathleen Lacey: it was only when they stood on the sidewalk in front of the Irish Club and she asked Mackie if he'd ever been married and he said, "No," that she said, "I made the mistake once."

Mackie did not have a car. Sitting on the trolley out to Squirrel Hill, she kissed him passionately. The trolley was mostly empty of passengers. When Mackie looked up the few people in the streetcar were not observing him. She had been married five years and divorced now three. She told him he would never know loneliness like hers. She had been more lonely married than she was now, but she still wanted a man.

Mackie had never heard such direct talk.

Maybe it was the army uniform, here for the minute, see you later, kid. She wouldn't expect a longtime romance with him.

He was in the army, almost a year and a half to go: it was foolish to make plans with someone liable to be on his way to Germany. She knew the score. He was in town five days, take it or leave it. She had been at the Irish Club with two other women from work and peeled off with him after they danced. He told her he was twenty-nine and she was vague about her age but he guessed altogether she was at thirty. That was not outside his range: between nineteen and thirty, Mackie in his army outfit was man enough for anything to come from a woman who openly admitted she was lonely. That meant one thing where Mackie Mc-Cafferty was from: it was a statement understood all over the world.

"You know a lot of guys in that car dealership," he said while she unlocked the front door to her house. It stood by itself on Forbes, probably marked for demolition one of these days. Forbes had few houses in this neighborhood. Large houses, some with apartments, fronted on Forbes, and there were apartments over many of the stores; but even these places were being taken by dentists and foot doctors, small real estate companies and accountants.

"They're good guys," she said. "I can call on them for anything. I get a rate on my car. I need advice on borrowing or something fixed, there's always a guy handy."

"You go out with them?"

"Just friendly."

He stepped into a living room directly from the porch. "The guys waving at you," he asked, "are they some of the just friendlies?"

"Jesus, Mackie, you remind me of my husband. Sit down, I'll get you a beer."

She kissed him long and hard, leaning over him. Some of her

powder had melted and her lipstick tasted stale, but none of that mattered. He was not here at her place for the romance of a lifetime. This was what it was, and if it went well four more days and then a Christmas card from her and he would decide how much past that if he ever saw her again at the Irish Club.

In one corner of the room, on a small table, there stood a small Christmas tree, no taller than two feet, more like a branch than a tree. It had perhaps five lights on it, but remarkably it had no base. Someone had attached a wire to the top of the tree and bent the wire so that it ran up the wall and was coupled with a curtain rod. It was a death-defying contraption, Mackie thought, not a Christmas tree. Bumping any part of it or disturbing the drape where the tree was held by the wire could bring the tiny stunted tree down into the room. He studied the wire as it ran up the wall to the rod. It was held in place by a clamp. A lot of care had gone into keeping the tree upright. Its lights glowed in the darkened room, a queer and disturbing imitation of festivity, and Mackie turned away from the sight when he heard her footsteps approach.

She came back with the beer already poured in a glass.

She said, "Kieran's awake."

"Can I see him?" Mackie asked.

She looked at him a long time. "Here he is," she said. "Kieran, say hello to Mackie McCafferty."

He was almost as tall as Mackie but thicker. He was about thirteen years old, maybe younger a year or a year older. His handshake was soft like a little kid's. He did not take his large brown eyes from Mack. "The army all right," he said. "You're a soldier, huh? A major?"

"No, I'm nothing. I'm up for corporal. I'm a private first class now."

"Yeah, that's right, corporal: guess that's pretty good. Can I have a beer with Mackie, Mom?"

"No, you don't drink beer. He's big but he's twelve. He's only twelve years old."

"Yeah, big kid. You'll be playing for the Steelers soon."

"Why can't I have a beer?"

"Because I said so."

"You make me feel like a baby."

"Well, you are Momma's little baby. He's my pride and joy, Mackie. He's all I got. My mother and daddy separated a long time ago, and I haven't heard from either in more than five years. So it's Kieran and me, right, kid?"

"Yeah, Mom, sure, but why can't I have a beer?"

"Because I said so."

Mackie drank a beer with Kathleen Lacey and Kieran, but he found it hard to swallow. The truth was the boy was like a man, but a big sad man, a man stuck for a while being a kid. Heavy and maybe sorrowful with guys coming to see his mother and liking the guys but knowing, probably crazy kid's thoughts about what went on, and not sure of how to act. He stared at Mackie. And Mackie could not taste the beer or down it easily with the kid watching every move. The talk was of nothing, Christmas already over, a new year coming, and Kieran off school and nothing to do. Mackie, listening to himself, was ready to run into the cold night air. His neck was stiff.

From far off he heard Kathleen say, "It would be great if you could go downtown with Kieran and look at the windows set up for the holiday and the after Christmas sales in the stores and the people. I can't: I feel like a rotten mother. We work on Sundays over the holidays, and Kieran doesn't get to see anything. He's too young to go downtown himself."

"I'm not," he said. "A lot of kids my age go downtown by themselves."

"Not my kid. I'm not raising a street boy."

Mackie sat in a large silence and then he said, "A couple of hours won't hurt." He made his voice strong. "I'll meet you down in Oakland at Forbes and Atwood, where the Gammon's is. Two o'clock tomorrow."

"Are you sure it's okay?" Kathleen asked.

Mackie nodded and the boy kissed her on the cheek and left.

Kathleen seized Mackie and kissed him hard when they were alone. He pushed her back on the couch and slid his hand up her leg, feeling her stockings and then bare thigh. "Wait a minute, wait a minute," she said, and sat up.

"What's the matter?" Mackie asked while Kathleen lit a cigarette. "What's wrong?"

"Nothing's wrong, there's nothing wrong."

"Did I do something wrong?"

"I said there's nothing wrong," she said.

He said, "Do you want me to go?"

"Did I say that?"

"Well, what goes?"

"What is this? Blitzkrieg? Who do you think I am? Mackie, I'm not what you think. I'm sorry. You seem like a nice guy."

"So?"

"So why are you spoiling everything?"

"How am I spoiling everything?"

"By trying to get everything at once. What do you think I am?"

"I didn't mean anything by it."

"Well, slow down."

"I'm in the army, I'm not around all the time."

"Look, I have a kid to raise, I have to be careful."

"Like how? What's a kid have to do with it?"

"Okay, what's the army got to do with it?"

She lunged forward and put her cigarette into an ashtray. She kissed him hard again, holding him pinned down and kissing his neck and cheek and running her hands through his hair. He held her, not sure of what to do next. "I go for you," she said. "Mackie, I go for you."

"Me too," he said, unsure. He knew there was something he should say to her, about herself or himself, the boy, the evening, the world, but no words came.

They kissed for an hour on the couch and every time he went to touch her legs or rear or bust she moved away, not angrily, but quickly and certainly. Occasionally, when she had not been able to elude him, she said, "Mackie!" But then she seized him and kissed him again wildly.

He stood to leave at close to two in the morning, and she said, "Damn it, this Christmas work, but they give us overtime. I'll be up in a few hours."

He put on his army cap.

"Aren't you cold in just that jacket?"

"No, I'm okay."

"Mackie, you really made Kieran happy."

When he said nothing, she said, "It's still on, isn't it?" Her voice was cold, and he did not like it. He had thought five seconds earlier, The hell with this, I'm never going to see her again, the voice, the tone of it, was like something said to an enemy of a lifetime. It was damned bad-tempered to a guy who deserved better.

"Sure, I said I would, didn't I?"

"Kieran really likes you, I could tell."

She kissed him again at the door. "Oh, lover," she said, "you're great."

"So are you."

"Kieran needs a man like you around, Mackie. He really likes you."

Thinking of that big dumb kid, Mack changed his mind and was at Gammon's Restaurant at two the next afternoon. He had planned and had been only able to fall asleep when he decided he was not going to show up at the appointed place. Maybe the kid would forget; maybe Kathleen would change her mind about the afternoon and not let the boy come. Maybe a brick would fall off a high building and kill him. This was old-time bad luck but he knew the boy would be there on the corner.

"Hi, Mackie. You looked better in that Ike jacket."

"I'm wearing this overcoat because it's cold, do you mind?"

"Mackie, you're funny, honestly you're funny, the way you say 'Do you mind?'"

"I'm freezing my nuts off, Kieran, okay? I'm not trying to say funny things."

The boy was still laughing when the two of them boarded the trolley downtown.

Despite himself, Mackie felt a comfort with the kid, waves of affection as he watched the boy in his earmuffs and plaid scarf knotted obviously at his mother's urgent pleas to avoid a sore throat. He was like the kid brother he never had.

Mackie told him army stories, about creep-guys in the barracks, imitating a southern accent, describing the lousy food in basic, dried fish with a water-thin gravy made of tomatoes to put on the fish. Kieran laughed and became sad, laughed again. "Really?" he asked. "That really happen? What did you do, Mackie?"

The ride was over quickly and they were downtown in a procession of people moving in and out of stores on Fifth, around to Market, down Penn. Kieran wore a leather jacket and kept his gloved hands inside the side pockets. He shambled along with Mackie, never keeping up but not falling too far behind. He was the sort of large boy who casually bumped into Mackie as the two of them walked, causing Mackie often to side-step colliding with him. When Mackie pointed out something the boy was always intently looking somewhere else. He seemed asleep. He said, "Hey" and "Huh?" often.

Mackie bought him a milkshake and a ham sandwich in Donohue's.

"You're lucky to have a fine mother like you do," Mackie said as they sat at a cluttered table.

"She's all right."

Mackie did not know what to say to the boy: he did not seem to know about anything at all.

"Nice scarf," Mackie said.

"One of mom's boyfriends."

"It's very sharp."

"It's an old one of his."

"Not a gift."

"No, he left it when he moved out. Al."

"How long did he live with you and your mother?"

"Not so long."

"A year?"

"Mort was the one lived with us a long time. He used to be in the army. He gave me a Swiss knife, but I lost it. Maybe it was stolen, but I remember I didn't have it one day."

"How long did Mort live with you and your mother?"

"Two years, maybe five."

"Do you want anything else to eat?"

"Another sandwich?"

Mackie gave Kieran a dollar and waited till the boy returned from the cafeteria line. He watched the boy eat the sandwich. He felt a small pain over his right eye. It was probably the cold, and he thought of the army barracks at Fort Meade. It would be overheated. Soldiers would be lying in their bunks in stockinged feet. The room would be filled with smoke. A radio would be playing hillbilly music. Mackie marveled at the things that seemed like home in the cold time between Christmas and the new year.

He and the boy did not talk beyond a few words on the trolley back to Oakland and Squirrel Hill. A man across the aisle from them ate a hard-boiled egg and the egg spilled over into his small beard. Once Mackie poked the boy and pointed to the man eating the egg.

The boy asked, "What?"

Mackie said softly, "Him eating the egg."

"Who?"

"The man, the man with the egg in his beard."

Looking, Kieran seemed to see nothing across the aisle. He stopped looking for the man and then he looked past the man out the window. "Yeah," he said, faking that he saw what Mackie meant outside the trolley. The man across the aisle smiled and wiped egg from his beard.

In Oakland Kieran said, "Mom said to ask you for dinner. To tell you you're welcome if you want to ride back out to Squirrel Hill with me. She'll be home in a couple of hours. We could watch television together until she comes home from work."

"Kieran, who put up that Christmas tree in your living room?"

"Guy named Dom next door at the car place. You coming to watch television with me?"

"No, I'll pass. I have a few things to do," Mackie said, knowing he was going to have to duck the Irish Club for the next few days in case Kathleen showed up there and maybe skip it on the next visit or two home. "Tell your mother I'll call," he said, a lie to the boy sticking in his throat.

As he pulled the signal on the trolley before the stop on Atwood he felt like a truck of enormous size, large and commanding in his overcoat, brushing people on both sides of the trolley aisle as he stepped out from the seats.

The boy said nothing, watching him like a curious dog, not able to make sense of the departure.

Mackie turned. "Kieran," he said, "you're really a nice kid."

Kieran nodded, and before he started down the aisle in his boots and overcoat, Mackie said, "I like you, kid, you're okay."

McCafferty's face burned with the heat on the streetcar and the sudden strong emotion he felt. The overcoat was a furnace and he left it unbuttoned as he strode toward the front of the car.

Outside the air rang with cold but touched him immediately with the bustle and rare urgency of the freedom on the streets after the trolley and Mackie knew he would forget about Miss Kathleen Lacey soon.

A young woman stepped toward him on the corner and said, "I thought that was you, Mackie McCafferty."

He said, "That's me."

"I'm Louise's sister, she graduated with you."

"You're not Maura: no, you're not. Maura's still wearing diapers."

"Stop it, Mackie. I knew it was you when you got off the streetcar. I stopped what I was doing, I was on my way downtown. I said, 'That handsome soldier is Mackie McCafferty. It can't be anyone else.' Louise is married now."

"Yeah, how old are you? No kidding. Be serious."

"I'm seventeen."

"How about a cup of coffee with me. We could go into Gammon's here."

"Sure, Mackie. Louise used to have a crush on you, now it's my turn."

She was wearing a pale camel's hair overcoat and the cold did not make her face look pinched or red. Her eyes were bright. He took her elbow. "Maura," he said, "I remember you when you were this big."

He put his gloved hand down to where it was two feet off the ground, then took her elbow again, the day overflowing, high spirits back.

Feeling a traitor, he accepted an invitation to dinner with Maura and her family. Her brother, Joe Kerrigan, was there with his wife and two daughters, and Maura's father opened a bottle of white wine and toasted Mackie. It was good, noisy, familiar, and full to bursting with a lot of things Mackie had forgotten about being with people he knew well. Sunday morning he went to Mass at St. Agnes with Maura and her family, his mother attending with her sister Anne, who walked with a cane and occasionally leaned on her. Afterward, both families drove down to Isaly's on the Boulevard and had sandwiches, ice cream, and milkshakes.

Mackie knew this was probably a moment he lived in a kind future, somewhere after the army. But that night he took the streetcar out to Squirrel Hill, not anxious to let the largeness of himself as an army hero fade so quickly from his walk and talk.

He knocked on the door and Kathleen opened it. "Well, stranger," she said. "I thought the wolf ate Little Red Riding Hood."

The tiny Christmas tree was still in place, and in the dining room by an overhead light Mackie taught Kieran card games at the dining room table. The boy hardly understood the rules of card games but Kathleen sat at the table as if she witnessed things too important to be interrupted. She seldom spoke, looking from her son to Mackie, smiling, bringing out beer and pouring it into a glass.

"Can I have a beer?" Kieran asked.

"You sure can," she said, and Mackie knew this was a night for the history books between the mother and son.

"You mean I can?"

"Why not? Nothing's going to happen while Mackie's here: he'll take care of us."

When Kieran had gone to his room for the night, again Mackie and Kathleen wrestled on the couch in the sparse light of the Christmas tree. Finally he sat up and said, "I don't get it."

"What?"

"Why you fight me off."

"I'm not fighting you off."

"I think you like me. "

"Mackie, I love you, there's a big difference."

"Okay, you love me, but you jump six feet when I get too close."

"Jesus, Mackie, how close do you want to get? Do you think I kiss strangers like I'm kissing you?"

"But it stops there!"

"So! What do you think I am? Take your time, it's all yours, the right time and place."

"You have a date set?"

"That's up to you."

They rolled around for another half hour, she moving quickly away from him when his hands became too insistent, and once she jumped to her feet and moved across the room to light a cigarette. After each rebuff she kissed him until his teeth hurt. She clutched at him but pinning him in the arms and legs. Occasionally, when he tried to protest, she put her finger to his lips gently. "Not now," she whispered. "Don't speak now, this isn't the time."

A long time later, about midnight, he said, trying not to seem eager to recover himself by rushing into the outdoors, "Well, I go back to camp day after tomorrow."

He stood vacant, feeling she was shutting off his hearing and sight: he felt lost and numb.

"You'll be back, Buster. You know what's waiting for you."

"Yeah," he said, and she held him for a long time in the doorway, and he left, knowing he would never see her again and feeling uneasy, as if he had failed her somehow and not she him. What was there to examine in their foolish performances the two times they were together? He had no excuses for himself, and he forgave her too. Maybe the leaping at unwelcome touches and vaulting for cigarettes was a time-proven act, rehearsed to perfection by practice with every car salesman in Squirrel Hill and an army of men disguised as bad lighting from a Christmas tree held together by a wire present every time she was alone with a man on her couch. He would think of it no further, getting off the trolley at Oakland Avenue and walking happily alone down to the Irish Club, without her as a promise in the future of clean hands and a good job and maybe a girl like Maura. Miss Kathleen Lacey was not there for him any further in Pittsburgh as a guarantee of good times for the hero but not a puzzle to worry over either.

In the next two days he had left on his pass before he returned to camp, she receded in his mind, soon to be barely there. She was not, in her hot, cluttered living room, very clear in his mind even at that time he was with her, shadowy and grasping, coiling in on him and then in seconds losing her hold. But he had regretted it, even as he sat in a booth in the restaurant with Maura Kerrigan as in the best of the old high school days, that he was doomed never to forget her big, dumb kid, his scarf and his pale, large, soft hands that would never know how a man gripped another man's hand in salutation or farewell. Never know a father. Hardly come up for air about anything at all except what his lonely mother, too clumsy to trap even a dope like young McCafferty, told him.

THIRTEEN

Hello, Good-bye

THE WORLD of the future, Donnie thought, is sitting here all about me: sun-baked and rosy, plants looking like someone wiped them clean of fingerprints, Florida, heat so bad a person is cold all the time in air-conditioning. But I'm your tired and poor, he thought, and if no place else wants me, Orion College here I am.

In an exuberant burst of good feeling for a Catholic president, Irish at that, Donnie had first enrolled in the Peace Corps. He was prepared to serve where sent. Positive, he thought, that he would return with malaria from wherever but teach in the spirit of the times grateful islanders to put up strong poles to insure their roofs did not fly away during tropical winds. If John Kennedy was president, then his man Donnie Cunningham could go anywhere on the planet for him. But he broke his ankle the very week he was accepted, and righteousness, or a "right livelihood," as the Buddhists called it, had then to be put aside momentarily.

His leg in a cast, but the recent thirst for respectability still throbbing in Donnie like a new strain of undiagnosed virus, he had that very week received the letter accepting him as an instructor at Orion College on the outskirts of Orion, Florida.

The mood of monastic public service, a call to greatness from his friend in the White House, had lain on him all the long bus ride down to Florida. Briskly and feeling destiny as the skies changed to a deeper blue, he still walked with a cane.

Orion, in what appeared to be a jocular, or at least impulsive, decision, had opened after two years of preparation the Conservatory of the New Era School of Undergraduate Studies in the College of General Humanities and Arts and Sciences. In this two-year beginning body of higher education the disciplines would be merged. Using television, the school would double its enrollment, perhaps triple it: change was in the jasmine-scented air, progress shone from the giant television screen with eminences lecturing freshmen on Beethoven and diagraming sentences on blackboards. Real musicians would play real pianos. Scholars would bolt or in lovely, languid movements waltz daily from English to astronomy, if such was their interest, and come up with a course called astro-English. Students would no longer be shackled to traditional ways of taking essay tests, studying, observing the world. They would be liberated from dismal facts, now as useless as Lou Gehrig's batting average in his final year of play or the number of years Winston Churchill was out of power.

Donnie sat bathed in sweat from his run from the Orlando bus for the first convocation at Orion, his suitcase rubbing against his thighs.

He had never taught anywhere. After Pitt, he had applied to three hundred and seventy-two colleges in the continental United States, Alaska, and Hawaii. He had only a bachelor's in history. He had applied to colleges in Australia, Nigeria, and Saudi Arabia, the sultanate of Kuwait, and the People's Republic of China. He had two replies in the bitter spring of 1959, one from a two-year school in Montana, the other from Orion.

He accepted the offer from Orion, the low salary, the peculiarly worded letter making no promises about tenure or rank, the evasive reply on his duties. But he had his reasons.

Donnie had never been away from home. He knew every brick in Oakland; he knew who lived in every apartment, in every government housing building in the apartment complex where he had been born in Pittsburgh. If Terrace Village Two was known for short-time wanderers, nomads up from West Virginia, tenants fresh from jail or the madhouse, the population there now shifting to college students who could live cheaply all the way through med school and then on to orthopedic practice in the best parts of Pittsburgh, he was a boy whose only roots were in the soulless brick buildings. He had been born there, gone to school at St. Agnes at the foot of Robinson, three blocks away, then a half mile to Schenley High. His eldest brother, Kiley, had joined the air force when Donnie was a child, a card at Christmas, an occasional letter, and then on his elder sister's largesse he had gone to Pitt.

For his sister Clarice, who worked in television in New York, it was a question, she said, of sending young Donnie to college or going to the poorhouse putting up bail money for him. Donnie had, it was true, run afoul of the law more times than the average. Once, he had been witness to a brick thrown through a plate glass window and had foolishly climbed into the store to boost a television set, and another time he had, for a reason largely obscure to him as it was happening, wandered around the locked halls of the University of Pittsburgh, searching perhaps for wisdom after midnight but booked with breaking and entering. When Clarice, who had never lifted a box of pencils in the five and ten or kicked a telephone pole, accosted him with his misdeeds, Donnie said, "I'm a born petty thief and malicious mischief is what anyone but you would expect from me."

"But we both have the same mother and father, same as Kiley," Clarice pleaded. "They hit each other just as often when we were kids. They had fistfights on elevators. They called the cops on each other twice a week. They drank more when I was growing up than they do now. I grew up in Terrace Two too, don't forget."

"It didn't take with you and Kiley," Donnie said, respecting his elder sister more than anyone in the world. "The psychological tests showed I'm well adjusted, an ordinary guy with the bad fortune to have Tommy and Joanne Cunningham for parents. I'm lucky I didn't grow up worse." He thought for a minute. "It was an educational act my wandering in the halls at the Cathedral of Learning," he said. "Maybe I acquired my thirst for knowledge walking around Pitt at midnight."

In the old days, before students smoked marijuana to steel themselves for Biology 101 and fell asleep stony-eyed under palm trees near the Television Theater at Orion, the center of the campus was the Eunice Montcalm Leake Auditorium, called jovially "Leaky." There no one was allowed to fall asleep at the regular 8:05 A.M. convocation: it was an order from Dr. Farr, before he came to be a stranger on his own ancestral grounds, a ghost haunting the college he had founded, kicking over with his shoe spent prophylactics in the morning in the parking lots and in later years standing in an alcove watching students gulping capsules before class at the three new water fountains.

The Leake Auditorium, in the old days when Truman had been president, was the daily scene of an uplifting gathering, required attendance by every student not in class. One went there to hear flutists and piano players of limited means and large local reputations play duets by Schumann. Or ministers speaking of positive attitudes, ROTC colonels, former alcoholics, or the Founder himself discoursing broadly on the moment when he had observed the pastel buildings of his college rising like a mirage out of the swamp.

Now, the auditorium lay in a sullen heat all through most of the Florida year. Mrs. Leake, according to the best architectural standard of the time, had positioned her auditorium to catch cool breezes from the east, to seduce zephyrs from the north to enter through her great stained glass windows. But the wind over the years had rattled the windows and broken some, and Dr. Farr, who had founded Orion, had reluctantly ordered the windows leaded shut. Like other buildings at Orion, positioning the windows to catch winds on the campus had failed: the cool breezes which did come were not enough to alleviate the jungle heat which lay on central Florida.

At first, government loan dormitories had been built to accommodate returning veterans after World War II; then the extension to the cafeteria was added. Itself still not air-conditioned, Leake Auditorium lay as damp and dewy, as resplendent and luxuriant and useless as the masses of piled hair on Mrs. Eunice Montcalm Leake's head, a style already a quarter century in decline when Mrs. Leake had posed for the color portrait at the entrance to her auditorium. In the wet heat, Donnie thought, no large, raw-wristed center fielder from a major league team spring training in Florida would ever mount the stage again to tell students how right thinking had increased his batting average by sixty points. Dr. Farr in his welcoming address named each of those center fielders and their averages, some of the great flutists, a minister or two who had come before the students in remarkably unremembered admonitions to be better people.

Dr. Farr, now in his robust eighties, welcomed the teachers assembled in the old auditorium in grave tones.

At his right side stood Dean Donald Brace, the Dean of the Conservatory of the New Era School of Undergraduate Studies. The Dean, dressed in midnight blue, blinked his eyes and then opened them wide. He pawed the stage floor with his navy-plain shoes: he was a runner all right, Donnie thought, ready to burst from the paddock with the inside rail forever ahead in his mind. When in repose, the Dean jutted out his large chin. He obviously wished that people would ask each other behind his back, "Where does the man get his energy?"

Once in the auditorium, when Dr. Farr paused, the Dean, thinking his speech was over, somewhat in the manner of a daydreamer applauding between movements of a symphony, said loudly, "Well said, well said."

Some of the scholars from the traditional disciplines across the campus, all apparently by their sighs and downcast eyes, types given to depression or at least, no clinical eye here, profound melancholy, sat in the Leake Memorial Auditorium somnolent and impatient. They glanced at Donnie and the other new people only when there was no place else to look. Each, it turned out, had been offered extravagant authority, wings to take flight, if he or she would identify with New Era Studies. Now when the moment had come, they seemed uneasy in their listening, uncertain of what domain there would be to rule or whom they would command, something untrustworthy as teachers or subjects about Donnie and the rest of the newcomers.

Donnie found their apprehensions justifiable.

Among the new people listening to Dr. Farr were three ministers (only one from a recognizable Christian denomination), two women who lived within two miles of the campus, in fact, Orion graduates, three high school teachers from Jacksonville, Orlando, and Winter Park, respectively, a young man from Princeton named Popkin whose father had had a serious stroke in Orlando, and Popkin, coming home to fulfill his familial duties and seeking part-time employment, had been hired on the spot to teach at Orion in two days' time. He wore a badge denoting him as hastily anointed "Associate Dean Henry Popkin." And there was a seedy man with a bad toupee and trembling hands named Gundry. He wore a tag saying "I'm Morris Gundry, Assistant Dean." Another was a shaky woman who ground up a hundred Kleenexes merely listening intently that afternoon. An ex-coach who changed seats frequently as perfume, his own sweat, or the acoustics bothered him, had to Donnie, who had majored in American history, in his glowers and general belligerency the proud, visionary appearance of one who had been designated governor of all the lands acquired in the Louisiana Purchase. About everyone in the auditorium there was the aura of a new enterprise to Donnie, seemingly an occasion for dividing up future spoils.

The regulars did not intentionally look at any of them, wrapped in the dignity of their tenure, rank, studies, and even earlier ordained empires: from Television Lecturer, Grade One to Coordinator of New Era Summer Institute and Directors and Facilitators and Interim This and Deputy That and Acting Vice-

President. All their tags had emblazoned in red above their names and titles, somewhat hysterically to Donnie's anxious appraisal: HELLO.

"Good, good," Dr. Farr said gravely. He spoke for another hour about the history of Orion, recounting his joy at drain-spouts, each air-conditioner, planter, driveway, drape, and victory over negative thinkers who had thought none of it—the Founder threw his arms out to embrace even the blue skies and sunshine outside—would come to pass in such profusion of tended palms, plate glass, marked parking spaces, and now visibly rising Television Theater to accommodate the thousands of new students coming to register the next day.

"Thank you, sir, thank you," said Dean Brace fervently, then led Dr. Farr from the stage when the Founder ground to a conclusion like the last train from a town under siege.

Then a man named Branzman passed out insurance forms for comprehensive medical, life, and accidental eventualities. He asked in a deep sober voice that the forms be filled out and returned at the end of the first orientation. A woman whose name Donnie did not catch—it sounded like "Dr. Barton"—came to the stage and began reciting facts about registration. Donnie could not keep up. The woman had authoritative calves like bowling pins. She straddled confidently the small stage and rocked and barked information. But Donnie could not follow her.

"Make sure they get a seminar coupon when they get a TT coupon," she said and waved a piece of paper in the air. "They won't be able to take TT unless they take seminar, or vice versa. The Social Science Worldview seminar is voluntary, the SSTT is not. Can you folks back there hear me?"

Donnie raised his hand.

"Yes—back there."

"What's TT?"

He was not pleased to see people swinging about to observe him.

"Television Theater! TT!"

"And SS?" he asked.

"Social Science."

"What's New Era mean?"

"Where you draw your paycheck."

No one laughed. Donnie nodded. He started to sink into his seat when the Princetonian across the aisle raised his hand. He was a dark young man with a wide mouth and a bluish beard.

"Yes, Popkin."

"We've been here more than two hours," Popkin said.

"Yes," the woman said and nodded. "Now be sure that you're familiar with the waiver requirements. Are you all familiar with the waiver requirements? Please raise your hand if you're not familiar with the waiver requirements."

No one raised their hands.

Dr. Farr came forward again and said, "I join you young people on this great adventure," nodded, and returned to a chair on the platform.

Dean Brace said, "Dr. Barton will be standing immediately in the back with your assignment card for this afternoon. All the information you need is on the card."

The man named Branzman, who had a tendency toward spectacular public outbursts, a trait which caused him to collapse from excitement the first month of New Era, unfortunately in the cafeteria line where students walked over and around him en route to the mashed potatoes, iced tea, and peas, leaped center stage. Branzman cried, "Please do not leave until you fill out the insurance forms. We worked hard on this program for you new folks."

Someone called, "What if you don't want insurance?"

Branzman concealed his displeasure. "Mark the form where it says no," he said, "and sign it. But why should anyone turn down a plum like this? We put in long hours working this out for you."

But already the teachers were filing out through the rows toward the exit.

Branzman turned to Dr. Barton, but she had already vaulted from the stage.

"Wait," Donnie said when Dr. Barton handed him his assignment slip. "This says, 'advising.'"

"You get some lulus there," Dr. Barton said, winking.

Donnie put his suitcases into a locker near the bookstore. He carried his briefcase. The afternoon began to slip away in heat and yellow light.

He had never supposed that he, who had become permanently stiff-necked nodding his head at volumes of misinformation, would ever be called upon directly to give anyone else advice. "Never lie," his mother had said. "Be honest with everyone you meet."

Criminally bad advice, Donnie thought.

He packed in his briefcase the *Orion Bulletin* with its descriptions of all the college's courses. Then he packed a current schedule booklet. In a slim black notebook—he wished to indicate a personal interest—he listed three venereal disease clinics from the Orlando daily paper. Then he listed seven women's health clinics in the neighborhood. For himself he listed a pizza restaurant.

"Never buy a shirt unless it's marked wash and wear," he said.

"Do not eat gray meat."

He walked across the campus with his briefcase.

"Yes, sir," he said.

He saw a stoned girl leaning in a doorway. He said to her gently, "You're probably the best generation of kids of all time. Higher morality, better health, better-looking."

"What?" she asked.

Donnie was not tall but had a rather large head. And furthermore he had a short neck, but the effect was not turtlish, instead canine. He looked like a muscular, straightforward good dog, even honest. It was an advantage. The burly shoulders and the thrust-out welcoming face were useful: not the face of the receiver of stolen affections. He had heretofore not committed himself to honest work for various reasons.

The burden of being who he was: and, again, it always came down to that missing father and perhaps the government housing project where he had been born. He sat on common courtyard benches watching people grow up and out, either purchase a house somewhere or depart under a sheet on a stretcher carried by two men with thick forearms. It gave Donnie a sense of the transitoriness of human life: all that rent jumping and roller skating and ice hockey on the concrete floors upstairs, radios blaring all night, drunks in the garbage courts and the woman who turned from her boyfriend in bed one late afternoon before her husband came home to listen for the baby in the high chair. It was too late. She found the child had strangled herself on a strap. It all made for a belief in uncertainty in Donnie. Yet Kennedy had become president of the United States. Could there be anything more sure in a troubled universe?

Still, if that father had been there to tell him better he would not have stolen, he presumed, sought easy hours and counted on that bull-like heavy face and glib tongue to carry him first and last. He could represent his case for mischief better than most people told the truth. Actually, if the truth were known, in season, he held back, giving the rest of the world a handicap. He supposed, if his health did not desert him, he would have the last word on something important someday.

He had, however, thought with the rest of them at the Irish Club that no Catholic, for reasons he wasn't specifically sure of, would ever be president.

I hunt the truth, he thought, swinging his briefcase. He hadn't fought the idea of Kennedy in the White House as others did. Sitting about the Irish Club, they shook their heads. "No good will come of it," old Dolan said.

"The first bomb gets dropped," McGrath said, "they'll say it was the pope ordered it."

But not Donnie: he was, he thought, an optimist. He could see old John F. Kennedy at the bar in the Irish Club, the best of our own: one of us hits the jackpot now and then, me and Jacko. Now Professor Donnie Cunningham (I'll be vice-president here by the end of the month), he was determined to be counted with the hard workers, put in more than he got back.

The slip with an office number he had been given at Leake Auditorium apparently noted the wrong place. He sat in a classroom alone for two hours, waiting to advise students.

The room was air-conditioned. He knew he was expected somewhere else, but—habits of a lifetime: since no one would know the difference—he supposed he would, if anyone asked, claim to have advised students, who also had been given the wrong place to go.

At the Holiday Inn in Orion, where he stayed his first two nights, he called Clarice.

"Yes, I'm fitting right in," he said.

Registration, the next day, was held in the largest classroom at Orion College, a small room barely large enough to accommodate the seventy students who came to attend class there, but impossible for the three-thousand-seven-hundred-and-eighty-one students who finally registered in the Conservatory of the New Era in the fall of 1960. Florida weather, often capricious with hurricanes in season, occasional tornadoes, blistering heat, humidities and rain in buckets, cauldrons, eye-droppers, gusts, and waves, all in one day, conspired to make the first registration memorable with a single-mindedness almost intentional. The rain fell in broad hot sheets from Key West to Daytona Beach.

Every word written in ink on the registration forms the students carried, course numbers, signatures, addresses, all became mystical designs of whirlpooled, illegible ingenuity.

Rain from students' deflowered haircuts fell on the registrar's papers, causing puddles on the tables as the students bent over to hear instructions. The two open doors of the classroom and the assembled humanity broke down the air-conditioning. The humidity, the constant repetition of required courses to the students waiting in mile-long lines, the dizzying heat gave the instructors attending registration eventually a glazed-eyed mad look: they were pale with cold sweat, their clothes tight against them, rude, abrupt, hoarse, and still the lines of students came. Dean Brace at first nodded at the success of the new enterprise, patting students and questioning them about hometowns as they waited in line. ("Well, what do you think of those Orioles this year?" as bewildered freshman girls answered, "I didn't know it was going to be like this.") He finally fled, not to be seen again for days.

Donnie noted, like the novitiates in a mountaintop monastery or some recruits in a ferocious soul-testing Marine Corps basic training, that strange personality qualities, often surprising the host, bloomed and took root at registration.

Dr. Basil Carter, a gentle biologist, so soft-spoken he was famous for not being heard beyond third rows, roared. His voice cracked, but he roared. "Stand back there, you! Don't you crowd me! Don't crowd me, sir!" The soft southern accent (Donnie guessed border state, eastern Kentucky perhaps), snapping in apprehension, growling, breaking in assertion of his lordship behind the table where he stood supervising, gave the man the grandeur of an old general staring into the setting sun. "I will not be moved by you people," Professor Carter stammered as students en masse pushed against the table where he stood guarding natural science coupons. Donnie nodded in approval of himself as colleague to the failing Caesar, flicking aside water on the table before him.

In passing Professor Carter, Donnie said, "They have us outnumbered, sir, this is suicide." But the man looked at him with contempt, defiance of Donnie there too with the amazement, blankness with the surprise at his own ferocity.

"That man will die today," Donnie said to Mrs. Farber, who said, "I know."

A complicated schedule of points had been evolved to insure that the hordes of new students would not all take either morning or exclusively Tuesday or Thursday courses. At any cost, Dean Brace had explained that morning, the classrooms must be filled in the afternoons and every day of the week. At Orion it was all but stated in the catalog that Tuesdays, Thursdays, and afternoons were the time to drive due east and go directly to the closest local beach. The insistence on classes five days a week and all day was frantic, occasionally rabid or raving, always mean-tempered.

Dr. Bernice Barton, from Social Science, distinguished by those calves worthy of a decathlon runner-up and a bald spot directly on the crown of her head, sat at a table in an outside corridor checking points. She sat at a card table with Acting Assistant Dean Morris Gundry, who wore Bermuda shorts and crossed his bare legs, not nearly as muscular as hers, in a kind of synchronized unison with her movements.

There were extra points to be given for Monday, Wednesday, or Friday and afternoon classes. If the student did not have the adequate number of points—eleven was the first year's figure—he was sent back to rework his schedule with afternoon courses or courses for a five-day schedule. The line before Dr. Barton and Dean Gundry went out into the rain, a thousand miles of students with water-logged waiver forms and schedules.

If the student lied or, for that matter, told the truth, Donnie thought, and pleaded a job in the afternoons, a dying grandmother who had to be tended on Mondays, diphtheria shots to be taken only on Wednesdays at four, Dr. Barton signed the waiver form. But she listened intently to every case. She asked questions. She did not give waivers lightly. In fact, she gave practically no waivers: she requested, demanded as the day wore on, medical excuses, notes from terminally ill stepmothers, distances between various points certified by employers.

Occasionally, Donnie took over at her table when she reluctantly gave up the seemingly arduous chore. She stood blinking at the lines of students waiting for class coupons intertwined with her own waiver students, the lines of students waiting to ask where to pay and the waiver students, students just standing and not knowing they were in the waiver line.

Donnie decided immediately on a course of action. He would okay almost every waiver request. Not listen to the heartrending accounts, prompt few tears. He would keep the line moving. But in order to maintain the spirit of the day, he would turn down two out of every six requests. No favor shown. No class consciousness, no attention to race, clothing, sex, or manner. Okay four, turn down the next two. Breezy. He had majored in history at the University of Pitt, at Clarice's insistence, and thought now he was grateful: he knew something of historical inevitability, he thought.

"Next!"

"Sir, I have to use my sister's typewriter and she uses it every day except Friday."

"Sensible plan," Donnie said, signing his initials. "Next."

"My dog has to go to the vet's every week—he was hit by a car—and—"

"Say no more. Request granted. Take care of that old fellow."

"I work at the Medical Center, research—"

"Sorry. Bring a note from the head honcho there."

"But Dr. Bradley is—"

"Move on, please, we're running registration here."

"My mother—"

"Sorry. Get a note from her."

"She's dead, sir."

"Well, yes," Donnie said but stiffened his backbone "Try your father, I must have a note."

"Sir!"

"Save the tears, we're running registration here. This is college, not kindergarten."

Gundry, whose hands had begun to shake so badly that the table moved with his convulsions, stood quickly and ran away into the rain. Donnie stood to watch the student leave too. She did not commit suicide within a hundred yards of the table: he sat back down. "Imagine, trying to hand me that shit," he said to himself. "Next!" He was going to get a reputation as a hard-hitter, he thought: no drones were going to enroll in Donnie's classes. Tough, but fair.

"My car—"

"Goddamned things!" Donnie said, as the first of the next four arrived, the ones who received waivers for any excuse at all. "Here, let me sign that."

More than one observer noted how fast the lines moved when Donnie took charge. It was a rhythm, he thought, okay, okay, okay, okay—sidewalk! sidewalk!—okay, okay, okay, okay.

Sometimes he stood and shouted at the students to re-form their lines. Donnie began to believe that his organization was better than the other people working at waivers. But, thoughtful, he questioned himself. Never stop trying. He stood occasionally and had new hordes of students re-form their lines back to the original designs. Only the shouting and the authority remained the same, a constant thrill racing through his humidity-tired limbs. That and the unfamiliar certainty: that made him almost drunk with the afternoon.

He liked being a teacher. Unlike a physician, Donnie thought, no one will die from my fatheadedness. Not like an attorney: I won't cause anyone to lose money, time, status. What a job! Contributing to the world's fund of harmless nonsense, reveling in shouting, false dramas, blank stares, cosmic statements.

"Tell it to Sweeney!" he said to the next no-waiver student. "Next!"

"Here, let me show you," the student cried, exposing his forearm with a huge purplish rash. "I've got to get that taken care of—I get shots. I don't need a note, look at that."

"Belligerency—" Donnie started to say, defending the okay-forget-it rhythms, but changed his mind. "Don't get excited now, you should have shown me your forearm in the first place." That was the tack: never wrong. "Oh, Dr. Barton," he said as his nearly bald colleague returned, "look at that rash. Explain it, will you, son, to my colleague. She'll be happy to sign your waiver. Good luck. Take care of that arm."

He had not realized until the last hour or two all the gifts he had inherited from his father. To a social worker once coming to assess the amount of money the family would receive when Tommy had been stricken with a queer pneumonia-like disease and could not work, the old man had said, "You come into this house as a guest, sir." Where the bottle came from that restored him to health was as always a mystery. "And you have made yourself unwelcome here." He seized a cane and brandished it at the social worker, ordering him from the government housing apartment with a rage worthy of Lear on the moors. Barred for life, the only individual so honored, from the Irish Club; his cabdriver's license suspended thirteen times, a record with the Yellow Cab of Pittsburgh; managing when he was entitled to welfare payments from the state to alienate the hapless bureaucrat who had come to determine the sum: his father, white hair tossed like a ship on stormy seas, Donnie thought, certainly had passed on to his youngest a flair for cane brandishing, outrageous overstatement, and intemperate dramatics. And what an arena the sixties would offer his son, Kennedy up there in Washington confounding a million Irish sages who said it couldn't happen, this mission on the sands of Florida, profound, dedicated, bent and determined, and, resolutely, useless. It's a fine time to be alive, Donnie thought, putting together his books for his first class, lovingly putting them into the briefcase Clarice gave him for graduation.

The Florida sun was bright and hot on Donnie's forehead as he felt a warmth for the old man, a good feeling for the American people who had come through: nay-sayers would have to say good morning to the bright-eyed Irishman who could deal out imagination with the best of them, call back in all those people who thought the president of the United States was a social worker they couldn't trust. Kennedy knew a thing or two about the heroes who drank pitchers of beer at the Irish Club, though he'd never set foot there. The thought once more of Kennedy at the Irish Club bar made Donnie warm as the sun blazing away on the path to his classroom. A chance at the plate was what the young president was: types never left the dugout would now take their turn at bat. How good to have said so long, sucker, to malicious mischief and taken this long run all the way here where the breeze carried the scent of mango and youth and promise.

"Good morning, scholars," he said to his first class. "I'm a little late because I was lost in my thoughts on my way here. Never mind the particulars. Just be happy fate put you in those seats today and Mr. John F. Kennedy is your president. He won't let you down. I promise you. Let me introduce myself. I am Donnie Cunningham, a poor but honest seeker after truth from Pittsburgh in the great commonwealth of Pennsylvania. I'm going to tell you things like you never heard before."

He felt a sudden surge of elation soaring in him large enough to burst even his happiness at this new chance. "God damn it! Yes, I am!" he cried to the astonished class. "Forget anything else you ever heard and don't believe a word unless I tell you it's true."

Dr. Farr, treading carefully not to break an ankle, made his way over the troubled grounds of what had been his proud university, dealt cruel blows by big winds, sun, creditors, and declining enrollment. In the dark light of the Florida night he came often to patrol here on ground he had once considered sacred: a temple addressed to learning. Now it was all gone, bankrupt, the windows broken, twisted iron bars, rubble to trap and ensnare an old man pacing over the ruins of what had once seemed a bright future.

He jumped at the sight of another man standing near a pillar, a looter—but of what? Nothing remained.

"Dean Brace?" he asked. "Is that you? Watch your step. Watch your step."

"Donnie Cunningham, sir. Is that you, Dr. Farr?"

"Who? What?"

"A former teacher here: I'm between planes, I drove over and found this."

"Found what? What did you say?"

"I taught here. It was a good time of life for me, high hopes."

"I thought you were Brace. I never trusted him."

"Yes, there's not much to trust these days. Things died here for me, Dr. Farr. When Kennedy died, I knew it was curtains."

"Kennedy, eh, Kennedy? There was no Kennedy worked here."

"The president, sir, the fallen hero."

"If you see Brace, tell him they took the last of the toilet paper before they were through. Pictures from the walls, vases left us by benefactors. I suspect Brace had something to do with it."

Under the lowering sky a lizard leaped from a bent desk lying on its side to an empty, rain-soaked cardboard box. Its tiny claws made a swift scratching sound as it tried to catch hold and then it thumped softly as it struck the sand where the box lay. The wind was not strong, and nothing moved or stirred or fluttered.

FOURTEEN

The Inheritance

THE OLD MAN said to Edward, his grandson, on news of the job: "In the old days the closest one of us would come to flowers would be when there was a handful put on his coffin to decorate our departure, and here you are going to make an honest living among the flowers of the field."

"I'm plenty lucky, I guess," Edward said.

"That's the ticket," Grandpa Dorn said. "Know it's luck in who plays with flowers and who sees his first one the day he's buried."

First day on the job, truck shined ready for Easter, Edward made an early flower delivery out in East Liberty, dollar tip, and then swung back to Squirrel Hill where Forbes ran close to the golf course at Schenley Park. It looked like a lucky Easter; it was his uncle Ralph who had secured him the job with Bewitching Bouquets, much coveted by industrious boys in Oakland, and

Edward was going to make the most of it. Polite by nature, keeping his thoughts to himself, he saw at eighteen an opportunity here to make something of himself.

An orphan at twelve, mother gone last of tuberculosis, father when he was a baby, he lived with his grandparents, both of whom were old and these days without money to do anything for him. He was blessed to have them: he never knew, even without parents, a foster home. His grandfather had been a fireman, and his pension barely kept him and Edward's grandmother going. It had always been a fact of Edward's life that he would work through high school, after classes and weekends, and take a job the day after graduation and he did, not exactly the next morning, searching around and then Uncle Ralph, his father's brother, came up with the job delivering flowers and Edward felt on his way.

His grandfather, who said he was an optimist, despite the many awful things he had seen in his long lifetime, said he was proud of Edward. "No use holding on to the past like it'd be an electric blanket to keep you warm," he said. "Things happening right now is my motto: but the past's sitting there like a bad dog in the roadway—sorry news being an orphan at your age, but I see you coming through."

Grandpa had seen men with their heads busted in union disputes with companies when he was young and later as a fireman saw people sitting on a curb without a place to sleep and someone inside the ruined and charred house gone forever. It was enough to make him tired of life, he said, but at eighty he still saw good things happening if a person didn't expect too much. Every day he shopped for Edward's grandmother, who could not walk anymore.

In Squirrel Hill, Edward carried his ripe bouquet, purple cellophane and roses colored purple and red inside the wrapping, up to the front door of the house on Forbes. They were good, fairly big houses, stone not brick, and even for that expensive neighborhood had large yards and trim shutters on the windows, painted fresh and bright. "Good morning, happy Easter," he would say, smiling, tip to come or not, cheerful whether he was rewarded or not. Nory Grandelli, the owner of the shop, paid him ninety cents an hour, rain or shine, and all tips were his to keep. There were rumors some clever boys, hustling along, could make forty dollars on Easter Sunday alone.

No one answered the front bell. Edward rang again, and there was still no answer. Edward circled the house and knocked on the back door. He stood on a small porch and thought he would take wing across Murray Avenue to the next delivery in Greenfield and then circle back here to Forbes in about an hour. It was nine in the morning, a little after, and the people from the house had probably stopped for coffee after church.

He started back down the driveway when he saw a small tool shed in the backyard about fifty feet from the house and decided someone might be back there. It was a small brick building, and it had a shingle roof like a permanent installation. There was a door in front with a very dirty glass window. Edward knocked on the door. He peered through the glass window, an opening about two feet by two feet, and from bending far to the left and upward he saw unmistakably the legs of someone lying stretched on the floor, the entire body obscured by a work bench, only a foot or so of the legs visible. They were a man's legs with a heavy work shoe on the feet. Quickly, Edward pushed on the door, but it was locked. He was uncertain that if he broke the glass he would be able to push himself through the small opening to get into the one-room tool shed. He would have to clear the glass thoroughly to get through and then perhaps the opening would be too small. Edward was two inches above six feet but slender.

He ran around to the back of the tool shed. He gently placed the flowers on the ground, careful not to rumple the cellophane. The ground was damp, but he felt there wasn't time to run back to the porch at the rear of the house: the man might be dying at that moment.

There was a boarded-up window at the back of the tool shed. It had been filled in with a composition material of plaster and, to the touch, something like cardboard. He tried to push it in with his hand but could not. The closed-in window was waist level to Edward.

He ran back into the yard about ten feet and ran toward the boarded window and threw himself into the air and with both feet smashed into the board. He fell to the ground, unhurt, but the window still intact. Three times more he ran at the window, both feet off the ground, and he felt the material give each time as he gradually poked both feet through. Breaking the board, he fell to the ground. He felt himself scraped as he tumbled off the building's wall and onto the grass. He touched his cheek and saw on his muddy hand blood. He climbed into the window and ran around the bench to the man.

No doubts here: the man had been dead for a time. He had fallen and bumped his head and the blood was already dry there. And although Edward had never seen a dead person (his mother, of course, but she was rouged and powdered in her coffin and looked more beautiful and alive than the gray woman he remembered from the hospital), he knew by the man's bluish cast that this was what death looked like.

He climbed back out the window. He picked up the flowers from the ground of the yard and placed them on the front porch. They were addressed in a small card from a man to a woman, probably the dead man to his living wife.

He went next door to the house on the right and knocked on the door. He stood back and a small elderly woman opened it.

"Your neighbor next door is lying in the tool shed," Edward said. "Will you please call the Montefiore Hospital and tell them to send an ambulance?"

"Who are you?"

"I'm the flower delivery man from Bewitching Bouquets."

"I don't know the number of the hospital."

"If you want me to I'll call."

"No, call from somewhere else."

"Will you call the police then?"

"I don't know their number. I'm not from Pittsburgh. I'm visiting my daughter and I don't know you. I don't know the people next door."

She started to close the door, and Edward said loudly, "Call the telephone operator, she'll connect you to the police."

The woman closed the door. Hurrying to the house on the other side of the unfortunate man's home, Edward knocked on the front door there. No one answered. Not knowing what to do, he went back to the house where he had come to deliver flowers and lifted the bouquet in its cellophane and put it neatly back into the truck. Preserving the freshness of the flowers seemed important to him. He sat on the front porch steps of the house, thinking someone would soon come or he would walk into the center of Forbes Street and stop an automobile. But traffic was very slow; there were few cars on Forbes. It was not nine thirty yet.

As he sat on the steps, he saw on the street a police car coming up Forbes. He ran into the street and waved at the car. The police car stopped and Edward explained slowly to the policeman, a short muscular man, who he was, what he had seen. The policeman listened—Edward thought skeptically—and said nothing but pulled the car into the driveway of the house. As the policeman waited for Edward to walk over to the driveway, it occurred to Edward that the cop might think Edward had murdered the man. But why would he call his crime to the attention of the police, and the man's condition would surely indicate natural causes. Still, the cop observed Edward carefully.

They walked together to the tool shed and Edward climbed into the window, showing the policeman by gesture the actions he had taken before discovering the corpse. He opened with an inside key in the lock the front door of the shed, and the policeman strolled in. Standing very still, the policeman observed the room, looking into corners, then at the corpse. He stood over the corpse and said to Edward, "Did you touch the body?"

"No."

"Why didn't you?"

"I could see the man was dead."

"How?"

"His color, I guess."

The policeman said nothing. He bent and looked in the dead man's pockets. "Did you take anything out of the man's pockets?" he asked.

"I told you: I didn't touch the body."

"The body's not his pocket."

"Nothing," Edward said.

"He was just like this when you found him?"

"Yes."

The policeman thumbed through a wallet the dead man had carried. He put on the work bench about three dollars and some change. "He isn't carrying much change," the policeman said.

"Why would he?" Edward asked. "He was working in his tool shed."

"I can't find a key to the house," the policeman said. "I can't find any house keys."

"There's keys on that shelf," Edward said and pointed, "a lot of keys. Maybe the house keys are on that ring."

"You spotted those keys pretty quick."

"They're not hidden."

"Okay, I'm going to go into the house, see what's up in there, and make a call to the station. Don't go anywhere. There's going to be questions."

"Well, I'm working," Edward said. "I have flowers to deliver. I have a driver's license. I'd give you the business number, they're open today. My house phone. I'm not going anywhere. It was me who stopped you on the street, remember?"

"You mind if I ask you how much you have in your pockets?"

Standing at the front door to the house, Edward emptied his pockets. He had the dollar bill from his morning tip and another dollar and eighty cents. The cop looked at the money Edward had handed him. "Okay," the cop said. He gave the money back to Edward. "Leave me your name and where you can be reached," the cop said.

Edward went back to the truck and took two small blank cards from the glove compartment. On one he wrote his name, phone number, and address. On the other, he wrote, "Mrs. Hannigan, Sorry for your trouble. I'm the person who discovered your husband in the tool shed. I read the card in the flowers he ordered for you, and I know he must have loved you very much to order such beautiful flowers for you and to have written you such a beautiful card. Have as happy an Easter as you can. Your Bewitching Bouquets Delivery Boy, Edward."

He called Nory Grandelli, and Nory said he had done everything right. "You left the flowers?" Nory asked. "The dead man, Mr. Hannigan, he paid for them."

"Yes, I did."

"You ain't shaken up or nothing?"

"No, just thinking it's weird. My first day a dead man. I could work delivering flowers fifty more years and I'd never see nothing like it."

"I been at the profession twenty years, and I never saw a dead man in a private residence. Maybe when we deliver to a funeral home I could have, but I never looked and I never saw one. Other things, naked woman once in a window, but never a dead man."

There were times, it was obvious to Edward, when there would be days that passed, then maybe years, in which nothing much was going to happen, and then at the end of that period something big, like an explosion in a person's life, would occur to change everything that had gone before and make the future different. Then again, maybe skipping an explosion or two, for good or evil, a person could live life out with nothing much happening to transform things in the future and what was written to begin with would happen and nothing more.

That night he received a telephone call from Mrs. Hannigan. Her voice was composed and friendly. She wanted to thank Edward for his lovely note. He said he was sorry he could not do more.

Two days later, going to the mailbox, he discovered a check from Mrs. Hannigan for a hundred dollars.

"I knew it," his grandfather said. "Even in this old world there's still kindness in places people hardly look. See that check: it's more than money, Edward."

The old man worked on a complicated jigsaw puzzle on a card table in the living room, seated near an open door so that he could hear Edward's grandmother, who had a bedroom on the first floor, if she called. Then he would stand slowly, careful not to dislodge one of the pieces of the puzzle, and hurry to her. Sometimes Edward worked at the puzzle with him: a cottage with vines and blooming flowers, a thatched roof of different colors, goats, cats and a dog in the front yard, a big tree with branches filled with leaves in many shades of green, in the far distance a mountain with snow at the peak and the rest of its crevices and boulders and pathways in gray and black and silver. Watching Grandpa's puzzles take shape over weeks and months he thought the picture there colorful and even beautiful, but, he admitted to himself, there was nothing to learn from it except that a roof was in one place, a tree bloomed, and the top of a mountain was white with snow, all things he knew before his grandfather had spent months at deciphering the puzzle.

Edward called Mrs. Hannigan to thank her for the check, and she asked him if he'd come to dinner Friday. He said, "Sure, it's good of you to invite me," and his grandfather said, "Look sharp, son, this woman means you well."

In the next two months, Edward went to the Hannigan house several times for dinner, sometimes alone with Mrs. Hannigan, who showed him photo albums of her life with her late husband, trips to Hawaii, Texas, the Grand Canyon, and Canada, and at other times with her two nieces, both women older than Edward.

Edward could tell by the preoccupied look the nieces put on when they observed him as he talked that they did not like him: he hoped they did not see him as expecting anything from Mrs. Hannigan. He was, after all, just the flower delivery man who had been there the day her husband died and who did what anyone under the circumstances would have done. The nieces barely spoke to him at dinner and when Mrs. Hannigan asked him to chauffeur her around on weekends, paying him more than he made at the flower shop, he knew he had crossed a line with the nieces. They were enemies.

Mrs. Hannigan still looked like a woman who might be interesting to men, but not within close distance of her obvious corsets or her very lined face and the scarves she wore at her neck. She was old, and standing near her, her eyes seemed red and tired and the sturdy good looks faded to a facsimile of a healthy woman. Too close, and it was apparent to Edward that Mrs. Hannigan was not healthy or strong, and these were her last months, maybe a year, of walking quickly and decisively and standing in command and erect with a sense of herself. She was once probably attractive in ways that made heads turn. She was now only touched by the last of her formerly fine appearance.

"We never had any children," she said to Edward on their drives after shopping. "You're the son I wished Freddie and I had. You remind me of Freddie when he was young."

Dutifully, Edward told his grandfather about her talking of sending him to college and paying for it, making him a lawyer like her late husband, setting him up in practice later. "She said," Edward said, "I'm the last link to her husband, Freddie."

"I'm not looking a gift horse in the mouth," the old man said, ever the optimist, "but you were not a link with the man dead. You never knew him in life."

"She says I was the last person to be with him."

"Don't make sense."

"Not to me either."

"Edward, you had your share of bad breaks: you're due for a turnaround."

The nieces became more removed, not attending the dinners Mrs. Hannigan and Edward enjoyed. Their talk now centered on schools where he would attend. Never a good student, no trouble to anyone, though, Edward sent away for pamphlets and Mrs. Hannigan did the same, and they discussed Pitt and Notre Dame and Southern Cal and Yale. Particularly did Mrs. Hannigan enjoy showing Edward brochures in different parts of the country where he might be living.

"And I'll visit you," she said, making a motion as if she was going to clap her hands in pleasure.

About two weeks before Easter, almost a year later, Mrs. Hannigan did not phone Edward. He decided not to press her over the neglected weekends. He worked at his delivery job those weekends, the boss easy and understanding. He called her in April and discovered the telephone had been disconnected. He did not know what to tell his grandfather. The old man had listened quietly to the names of colleges and places and said only on occasion, "Beats me."

In the delivery truck, when he was on his way to turn in for the night on Good Friday, Edward drove into the driveway of the Hannigan house on Forbes. He saw no one there, nothing of life about the lawn. A quiet lay on the yard and house Edward had come to feel a friendly place. The windows seemed to be boarded. Nothing stirred. The welcome mat was not there at the front door and the porch swing had been removed. On Easter Sunday he stopped there before he began his day's deliveries.

He saw a man walking around the house.

"Hi," Edward said, "what's up?"

"What do you mean?" the man asked. It was almost cold out and the man wore an overcoat and a muffler.

"I'm a friend of the lady of the house," Edward said. "Mrs. Hannigan."

"Yeah. She's selling the house, moving to Arizona, one of her nieces married and going to live out there."

"Mrs. Hannigan's okay? I mean her health."

"I guess: I didn't talk to her, my partner did. We did some work for her husband, died awhile ago, seemed fine, the lady. Made all the arrangements. You know this can be a lousy climate for an older person. Lot of people moving from this neighborhood to Florida, Arizona, you know?"

"Any place I can reach Mrs. Hannigan?"

The man gave him a card that read "Brandt Realty Associates."

"That's my partner, Morris Brandt. You could ask him."

Edward called the next day and could not talk to Mr. Brandt directly and left a message about his business with a secretary. He waited three days and knew Mr. Brandt would not phone back. He knew the nieces' names but did not call them: as he passed the house that week in the delivery truck from Bewitching Bouquets he saw the For Sale sign for the real estate company on the lawn.

He did not know how to tell Grandpa. The old man had thought there was something ahead for Edward in the future.

Maybe there was, but Mrs. Hannigan would play no part in it. Finally, knowing something was up (there had been no talk of Mrs. Hannigan in a month), Edward told Grandpa about the missing woman and the disconnected phone and that Mrs. Hannigan was moving to Arizona with a niece.

"She may contact me yet," Edward said. "This is probably a quick decision. She has a lot of odds and ends to put together."

"Don't hold your breath."

The old man sat at the card table with the jigsaw puzzle, the roof of the cottage forming in corners and a chimney.

"Well, I haven't lost anything," Edward said. "This didn't cost me anything. And I know about colleges now."

Grandpa didn't look up from the card table. "I was a few years younger than you," he said, "when all that hatred and murder was boiling over there in Homestead, just a kid really but Carnegie worked us like we'd be men. Not a bad job for the times, but then there was a union starting and Carnegie always had said unions were for him, liked the ideas of working men getting together and taking pride in their work. Well, he left the country for Scotland, Edward, left the steel works with his man Frick— I know they come to hate each other, I know that, know that story—and Frick hired the Pinkerton detectives to take back the plant in Homestead where the union was asking for rights and money. Men were murdered there: men were shot by the Pinkertons. And then it came the Pinkertons' turn. They were swamped by the workers there, beaten some of them till they might have died an hour later for all anyone knew—no one kept count on what we did to the Pinkertons. Women, children, throwing rocks at them in a gauntlet, I never hope to see a day like that one again. And what was Mr. Carnegie doing that day, the man the workers thought was their friend?"

When Edward did not answer, Grandpa asked, "Well?"

"I don't know," Edward said. "What was he doing?"

"I don't know either," his grandfather said. "There's not a soul on earth except maybe his wife or a groundskeeper knows what he was doing. I know where he was, though: Scotland. And that's a long way from Homestead, Pennsylvania."

Edward felt sad for Grandpa; the old man tried hard to put a sunny face on things and sometimes he just couldn't. Edward loved him for trying, with all that ran through his mind, things seen and never able to be willed away. Looking up from his puzzle, the old man asked, "What's Mrs. Hannigan doing this minute?"

Edward saw Grandpa was smiling.

"I don't know. What's she doing?"

"I don't know, to tell you the truth," Grandpa said. "I'm at sea when it comes to knowing what people are doing or thinking. But I know she'll be doing it in Arizona. She doesn't know what we're doing either. If she'd been at Homestead, luck being what it is, she might have maybe been chucking rocks at the Pinkertons, knocking out their eyes while the poor bastards were weeping and sobbing, sent there by the owners. Cheer up, Mrs. Hannigan's gone, but the Pinks aren't at our door either."

"But isn't there something to be aside from throwing rocks or getting hit by rocks or hiding out?"

"Jumping off a bridge, I guess. But my point is money will give you more places to duck, keep you off the bridge while things are going on, general ups and downs, rock throwing and such." He sighed and asked, "How you feeling, Edward?"

"Grandpa, it's not me or you or Grandma in the tool shed with Mr. Hannigan, and I'm tops, I feel good. How are you feeling?"

"Good," the old man said. "Good as can be."

The jigsaw puzzle on the card table was almost complete, and his grandfather, holding the little cardboard cutouts up to his eyes, went back to filling in the missing pieces.

One Easter, a year after Mrs. Hannigan had deserted him, Edward pretended he had a flower delivery to her house. He carried a dozen roses to the front door and said to the woman who answered the bell, "Roses for Mrs. Hannigan."

He knew she would not be there, but the feeling inside himself that moment was what he tried to guess. He supposed he was trying to find what was real about any of it: there was a house, a woman stood before him shaking her head no.

"They're the people who lived here before we did. They moved awhile ago. This is some mistake."

"Sorry. Mistake."

He walked down the path slowly, trying to hold on to the idea that things happened, promises were made, then vanished as if no one had been in places, talked, made sense; and Edward, for more years than he cared to remember, drove a flower delivery truck until he no longer enjoyed the lilies or the roses or the carnations he had once savored and hardly saw them, scarcely cared to know their scents one from another. He was courteous, kept his eyes open, and caused other people as few problems as possible. He never saw a dead man again on his deliveries.

When he passed in his rounds the Hannigan house, particularly on Easter weekends, he stared hard at the house, trying to determine why in the stone and mortar of the place and things that had happened there, despite all his good and high intentions, even to the look on his face while he was listening to the miracles that were waiting for him as Mrs. Hannigan spoke, he had somehow gone wrong. Maybe he should have said he was interested in art. He could have told her he was more religious than he was. Did he not laugh right at things she said were supposed to be funny? With a woman's beloved husband dead and she even thinking there was a link between the three of them, he had missed a golden chance somehow through nothing he had done or said and maybe a lifetime would pass and he'd never again have the opportunity to be loved and welcomed to good times by a rich woman.

PART THREE

The Drums of Morning

FIFTEEN

Shannon Made of Sunlight and Bones

A STORY, she thought, only beginning but already receding to her who was living it: surely, not at twenty-four a life to be called over because of what hadn't happened. Shannon had not loved her husband of two years and then he had gone to war, never to return. Perhaps they could have found when he came home from Europe love in the matter of years passing between them, taking on with the passage of time feelings of comfort and habit and that being defined as love in the absence of anything else. There were never the outward signs of hatred and neither of them capable enough at expressing contempt toward each other by the small demonstrations of distaste she saw in her mother and father. But she knew there was no love.

She had a terrible basis for judgment, having had an experience with a man before her late husband; and that had so embarrassed and confused her that she knew she'd accept anyone who asked marriage and the late Gary Kinch was there at the right moment. The other man, her first romance of bedrooms and phone calls at midnight, ten years older than she was at the time, eighteen, overwhelmed her with feelings she could not bring together afterward to re-form the person she had been before him. He was not friendly or even kind, not really concerned with her at all, but he had a manner that was diffident and he was quick to fill in a silence with something smart, and he was her first. Having contained herself in what in her youth had once been called "saving herself for marriage" till she was eighteen, she abandoned with him everything she thought she stood for, or was, or aspired to be. When she started with him and was whirled away into what he wanted of her and the things her body gave him she saw the handwriting on the wall and knew men, even less sure of themselves than he was, could be the ruin of her.

Seemingly, if her first was to be considered remotely typical, they did not care in ways women might understand. For her part, she felt fire inside her when she thought of him and tried, without success, to tell herself that she hated him—he was married and did not tell her—and when she had to assume distaste as a tactic for forgetting him could not save herself from specific memories, almost flexing her fingers to touch him sometimes when she thought of him, and she turned to other thoughts to rid herself of him. She prayed, but it sounded like a sermon on her end.

She decided she would think of him as someone who had taught her things about herself, a sort of person in her growing up, but there too he lingered, unalterable, the same as ever, a heat and a passion and a lost cause because, if she understood the game at all, there'd never be another like him. Not just that he was first; she could easily enough dismiss him as taking advantage of her inexperience, but however her thoughts tried to shape their time together, winning with him because of how glorious it had been, losing because he had been married and probably working his expertise on her—even innocent himself, he did know more about their situation than she did—or regarding it as a draw, he was there, she was there, she still ached with her memories. But why place meanings at all on a hopeless time? Let it stand for nothing except what had happened. Then at night she dreamed of his hands and the shadows on the wall he cast and she saw him in her dream states with other women making love and fled down long corridors and woke remembering things said while she had slept.

In the mornings she drove with her father to work selling hardware at a store her father owned. They spoke of little; it was almost as if her widowhood allowed her mother and father a relief from talking to her. They had not done much of it before Gary's death; now it was sanctioned out of respect for her feelings. As the car drove through streets with snow drifts higher than the car, she was quiet coming and going to work and her father seemed satisfied she grieved honestly for her husband. Occasionally with his gloved hand he touched her hand, and she nodded, smiling faintly. She mourned: for the lost world a bad person had opened to her and then slammed the door, not for Kinch whom she barely knew.

In the summer of 1947 people said it was a way to forget, not that they would understand the ripe memories of sheets and dirty windows and flame in her temples from a shadow up to no good—she enrolled in a night class in design at Carnegie Tech. The students all seemed to be people trying to forget, mostly women, somewhat dry from a day's work behind them, their eyes focusing too quickly or remaining blank. They were cheer-ful and drank coffee at the breaks and talked and one was a bookkeeper and another an assistant buyer at Kaufmann's and another woman was a widow like Shannon; but she, it seemed, genuinely missed her husband. She cried and there was bitter-ness in it and amazement. Shannon maintained her secret— it was a deceitful lover she mourned, not her husband, with whom bed was the trial women warned each other about in her childhood.

There was one of the women, though, that Shannon particu-larly liked.

She was a tall woman, perhaps thirty, with dyed red hair and a slow, slurred speech that made things she said seem modern or funny. She called Shannon "Baby" and said, "Baby, I know it's rough, but rough ain't till it happens at least four times: then you know you've been there. Once ain't nothing but training."

Shannon laughed: a woman like this would know what to do with memories unwanted and painful as falls down stairs in childhood.

All through the spring of 1947 Shannon went with her new friend, Lucy, to a bar near the campus of Carnegie Tech. There artists sat in sweatshirts and jeans and argued and drank and some of the young women had paint in their hair. Shannon was only a few years older than they were but felt almost motherly. She enjoyed the noisiness and the sureness of the students who seemed to believe their youth would go on forever and never, as she did, looked back. No one had told them panic might lie in wait for them at discoveries about themselves and they lived as if they knew all there was to know about what to expect.

Shannon was short, two inches over five feet, and she had a very large bosom, and she knew that some men looked at her, estimating what her chest would be like without the concealing clothes she wore, and sometimes it pleased her and sometimes it did not. Her legs were too short and she often felt awkward. She was not the sort of young woman men would particularly want to be seen with to impress other men, a cheerleader on display, flash and interest and commanding, but she knew other men wanted to have her and did not care that she was not a show horse. She wished she could have been more ornamental. With her first man she had felt none of the disabilities she felt in rooms where people looked at her as if they understood she wished her legs were tall or she had eyes more clear and not an obscure dark. Even with her husband she had somehow, nightly, been reminded that she was not the love goddess of movies. She raged at herself after the two nights a week when she went to have wine with Lucy at the University Grill that she had had her one great opportunity and it had been brilliant and terrible and passed, everything else to be judged by it and pale in comparison.

Often, standing where she knew she was an object of calculation, she felt as if she were a photograph in an X-ray, nothing there but the bare bones of her, a woman with something dreadfully missing, but what? In herself, no matter what was not there, a heart, a soul, a capacity for love or laughter like the staleness in her mother and father, she woke some mornings thinking the reason no one could really see her was that she was made of sunshine, a peculiar idea of childhood. Her father was a secretive man, silent and removed, and her mother was lost in her own thoughts; and Shannon occasionally thought she too was not there either but because she was as invisible as sunshine, not absent as her mother and father, but not there in a warmth no one could see, a brightness too quick to be taken in with the male sweep of vision accorded women. And when people looked, what they saw were the bones of her, walking, talking, even laughing, but missing something.

And in the year she had known Malcolm she learned that she had for the first time felt complete and it was a man who inspired it. Men, she knew, if she searched for her false lover among them, could betray her. There would be repetitions, attempts to re-create moods and moments, and at the end she knew it would be Malcolm who came to stir her in her dreams. She had ended it with him when she drove past him where he walked with his wife and a child with another child in a stroller on Fifth Avenue near Mellon Park. She knew married people when she saw them. He saw her in the car with her father, and he never called her again. When she called him at home, pretending she demanded an explanation but praying it could be maintained between them, he hung up on her, and each time she went to the phone to call she remembered the dead phone in her hand and did not ring him.

On Saturdays Shannon took the afternoon off from work in the hardware store to walk with Lucy in Schenley Park. They took long strolls and talked of men and marriage. Lucy had been married twice and said as far as she was concerned it was an impossible situation between men and women. Each of her husbands had demonstrated to her that men did not care to be friends with women: they hardly spoke the same language. She was pleased, she said, for the time being to be done with them. Maybe someday, but for now she was happy with herself and her work, selling cosmetics in a department store.

"What about children?" Shannon asked.

"I'm raised Catholic too," Lucy said, "and I have the same feelings you do about having a family, but whoever made the rules left out that there were men in the deal."

"But you can't go through life ignoring half the human race."

"So far so good. I'm not interested in them, maybe later, not now."

Walking in the open air in the park, Shannon felt rid for the moment of her oppressive father and mother, their long periods of stillness, not the quiet of people lost in thoughts of something good or valuable but almost seething. Enraged with each other, what fate had put them to, fearing death or sickness: she could not tell, only that in a room with them she felt happy and relieved she was neither of these morose people. At work her father was cheerful, each customer a friendly occasion; he smiled and was attentive. As Shannon watched the leaves turning with Lucy, she knew the world was larger than her mother and father: there was a freedom to her, almost becoming visible like a plant in April, that Shannon had never understood, except through Malcolm.

Could it really be that with him gone she would never know that freedom again unless it was with a man who broke rules? He was, she decided, so corrupt he hardly understood that what he was doing was wrong. Still, there was no touch, no moment of bodies naked in each other, like that she had known with him. But how could she know? Gary Kinch had not betrayed her: he was the way men were, she supposed, in love, gentle, considerate, confusing in their lack of spark and danger. They apparently, using that awful standard of her late husband, did not know what they were doing.

In the fall, after the course in design ended, Shannon went one night with Lucy to the Carnival Lounge downtown. It was still the grieving widow: it's him, she knew, it's him, I hope to find, it's the rotten one I want, not the decent Kinch buried in a graveyard in France. I am a very bad person, she thought, listening to the music of a three-piece combo. There are people who do bad things, knowing no other, and there's someone like me who knows better and has to live with wanting bad more than good.

A man came to join Lucy and Shannon at a table, and it seemed the man knew Lucy from somewhere, but not well. The music was loud, not allowing talk.

Across the street at the Tropicana, Frankie Laine, the singer people said imitated a Negro, was appearing to large crowds, and the man talked of his friendship with the star.

The man sang "Shine" as Frankie Laine might and "That's My Desire," and he was not very good in himself and nothing at all like Frankie Laine.

Lucy, who usually looked at people as if she found them funny or distasteful, listened respectfully to the man singing. Shannon thought he said his name was Milt. He paid for drinks and tried to rush the women's orders, signaling more as if he wanted to make them drunk. Shannon tried to catch Lucy's eye. Wasn't this guy a scream! What was his silly game? The singing, the drinking, the bragging about knowing every show at every club in downtown Pittsburgh: if Lucy did not seem sort of interested, not exactly smiling but not unhappy either, Shannon would have suggested they leave immediately. The man was a pest, thick-necked and pasty, laughable as a seducer. His shirt at the collar was soaked in sweat.

"Frankie Laine makes thirty thousand a weekend in Vegas," he said at a lull in the music.

"Yeah?" Shannon asked, a little high. "More than you?"

"That's peanuts," the man said and began to make Frankie Laine scat sounds.

Lucy said nothing. The club was dark, and Shannon had no clear picture of Milt but she knew the evening had gone on too long. Quick and ready, Lucy was perhaps not herself because of the wine, and Shannon had not come downtown to sit at a table with a strange bird.

Around eleven, Shannon stood and said, "Lucy, let's go."

"Wait a minute," Milt said. "Wait a minute."

He took Shannon's arm. She pulled away. "Come on, Lucy," Shannon said. "Let's go."

Lucy stood and said something to Milt and walked with Shannon to the door.

"I feel like I need a bath," Shannon said.

Outside in the fine crisp air, downtown alive with scents and fragrances unknown to her, Shannon felt freer than she had for a long time. In the open air, not enclosed in the noisy club, her funny friend with her, it suddenly seemed life held prospects. Maybe it was the wine, maybe the goodness of the evening lay in that part in the Carnival Lounge being over, the smoke and inane talk.

"Let's go somewhere else," Shannon said.

"I can't," Lucy said, and her eyes were hollow, and she did not look away from Shannon.

"What do you mean you can't?"

"Milt's my boyfriend."

"Your boyfriend? What are you talking about?"

"I told him about you, how good you look, how you're lonely, and he said bring her around."

"Yeah, yeah, I'm gorgeous," Shannon said. "But I don't understand. I don't know what you're talking about."

"He likes you, he likes you."

"But you're his girlfriend."

"He likes you the same as he likes me, Shannon. That's the way he is."

Shannon stepped back, speechless for the moment, the air still charged with a big city's promise but now alleys in it and shadows and doorways filled with menace. Rooftops were blank and deceiving and there might lurk there crouching enemies spying on her. The death of Gary and herself impaled on emotions never to be understood and in it a life gone before beginning surrounded her, and Shannon caught her breath at the recognition of where she was and stepped back from the frightened Lucy.

"You too?" Shannon asked.

SIXTEEN

A Day at the Lake

IN THE SUMMER, on Labor Day weekend, Scratch Baily and one or two others usually hitchhiked the four hours up to Conneaut Lake, Ohio, away from the usual places in Oakland. There, in bursts of suntanned youths from Ohio State, Waynesburg, Slippery Rock, and other colleges as far away as five hundred miles from the resort, they fell into step with other people, acting nonchalant, and tried to pick up girls. They might be anyone on that weekend. Walking about in shorts, shirtless, their skins burned by the unaccustomed outing, they came to think of themselves as belonging with the festive crowds. The college students there said repeatedly to each other that they were resting from their studies, going back to school after the weekend. But Scratch and his friends, he knew in his heart, were already in the middle of the long time between high school graduation and death in which no institution recorded their progress and no one bothered to keep score. But, all about them in the sunshine, even listless and bored, tired and hungover, the college students waited for another time to arrive, better things, grades, cars, new friends, jobs on graduation. Scratch felt the contrast keenly.

At the end of the summer of 1972, Scratch enlisted in the army and went once again for the last time, the week before he was to be sworn in, up to Conneaut Lake. He hitchhiked up with a rummy like himself named Zero Noonan who frequently said, "The Beatles wrote my song: I'm a nowhere man."

The boys prowled around the rides at the amusement park at Conneaut, making cracks at girls. They tossed a volleyball they had found to each other over people's heads, hiding from each other their lostness when they ran into someone from Oakland who had other things to do.

Scratch had left high school a year earlier at the end of the eleventh grade, falling for a scheme that took him down to West Virginia to sell baby portraits on an installment plan. But the people in Morgantown and Charleston were too poor to put down five dollars on a hundred-and-nineteen-dollar combination portrait and gold frame set, and Scratch returned to Pittsburgh to live with his widowed mother on Zulema Street. Both of his elder brothers had graduated from high school, one an honors student at Central Catholic, and gone on to Duquesne and to hold jobs with IBM and Chrysler and sent money home from Detroit and New York to their mother. But Scratch—defective, he guessed—now slunk about watching the kids he had gone to high school with, some from elementary school up, prepare to graduate Schenley High in 1973. Knowing he had to make something happen or fall over dead one day from staying in one place too long, Scratch enthusiastically embraced the army. He was, at least—small men in black pajamas ready to slit his throat in a far country—going somewhere.

He avoided at Conneaut the students he had known from Schenley: damnable, the streets of the resorts were jammed as if he were there in the midst of a crowd attending a football game at Pitt Stadium, and there the old students were too, pretending the same as he that they were college students. But now they were all graduates of high school at least. They said hello to Scratch and Zero, then moved on.

"Cupcakes," Noonan said, bouncing the volleyball. "Fairies." He had never gone past the tenth grade.

"That Mary Hughes has nice lungs," Scratch said.

"You go for that?" Noonan asked, as if in confused concern. "Moon Gourley told me he had her and there was nothing there but an uplift and a prayer."

"He says that about every girl."

"She's shit!" Noonan said vehemently. "She's shit, and I wouldn't waste ten minutes of my time thinking about her." He bounced the ball on the sidewalk, hard, hard again, and when the ball flew into a young man walking with his arm around a girl and the boy looked up, surprised, Noonan asked, "What's the matter with you? I wasn't trying to hit you with the ball. What are you making out of nothing?"

The boy said something to the girl and she laughed and both continued to walk.

"Retard faggot," Noonan called.

Scratch felt low. He spotted a six pack of beer in cans inside a car, opened the car door, and quickly put the cans inside his shirt. They cooled him. He drank one after another. He walked in a large aimless circle with Zero Noonan around the amusement park, then down to the beach, then up to the sidewalks crammed with young men and women. Zero drank each beer Scratch handed him as they strolled past resort cottages. They tossed the empty cans into the bushes lining the sidewalk at the guest houses.

In front of one of the small hotels, a place called Monticello's, Zero and Scratch saw a boy from Oakland. "Hey, Paul!" Zero said.

Paul said, "Zero, Scratch, when'd you guys get in?"

The boy had bright slightly protuberant blue eyes and never held a job, but his clothes were neat. His hair was short and well-trimmed. It was said he sold drugs but no one had ever bought any from him and it was said he was homosexual but no one had any specific information. If he made walk-around money at playing queers, that was nobody's business but his: still, Scratch could not believe anybody he knew was homosexual.

At the Irish Club Paul occasionally danced with a stray young woman, and some said it was a cover-up and others said he was normal. He floated in the places where Zero and Scratch drifted in Pittsburgh, seeing them around sometimes five times in an evening in bars and on corners where air wasn't expensive. No cover charge kind of places, they were called.

"We hitchhiked up this morning," Scratch said. "I'm going to the army on Tuesday. Where you staying?"

Paul waved them close. "Inside here," he said. "You guys know a guy named Okle-fadocle? Guy with a face red and round like a tomato?" He blew out his cheeks and tucked his head down into his neck.

"Big belly," Zero said, pulling his pants down over his hips and thrusting out his abdomen.

"The one," Paul said.

A Day at the Lake

"Is he queer?" Scratch asked.

"I never asked," Paul said. "He's got a room in here and Barrett, you know, and Markie, and Rich and Gary, we're going to stay here. You guys have nowhere else, come stay."

"What's Okle-fadocle going to say?"

"I'm not going to ask," Paul said. "What's the difference? You know, a guy gets to be his age—he's got to be thirty-one, two—he takes any kind of company he can get. He came up with Gary and Markie, and, you know, guys invite their friends."

Zero said, "We'll look in if nothing better turns up."

Wandering about as night fell, Scratch began to feel as if his feet were weighted down with being all that he hadn't become since he was a boy. No priest had particularly liked him; no nun had singled him out as someone with a nice smile—the way nuns did; no special choice of anyone's as each of his brothers had been. They returned home at Thanksgiving or Christmas and were clapped on the back at the Irish Club as if they had killed a dozen Communists in Vietnam. Feeling proud of them, Scratch still ached from being hard luck and hoped the U.S. Army where everyone wore the same uniform would allow him to escape into its khaki-and-olive drab anonymity. If the price of living somehow not a fool was to spray the enemy with napalm and risk their machine guns and slow torture, it was—given the dizzying round of nothing happening in Conneaut Lake, Ohio, and the rest from grade school up—a small price to pay. The Irish Club itself, moving around to locations, Gustine's, Lasek's, it was an annual rumor, was said to be folding. He hoped it would go on somehow. Flourishing at least in some good bar's rental hall until he came home from basic training to show people he had not disgraced the family name by being nothing at all.

Two hours later, when dry discontent only had come of the endless greetings they had thrown to passing girls, numb, Scratch said, "Let's see what they have over at Monticello's Hotel."

"You think some girls?" Zero asked.

"You never know," Scratch said, somewhat quickening his pace.

At Monticello's in a long bare room with two beds and two chairs, Scratch found two boys sleeping in each bed and Okle-fadocle sleeping in a chair, his feet up on an ottoman. In another chair Markie lay half-asleep. The floor was wet with beer. A boy lay stretched out and soaking wet in the bathtub. Someone knocked at the door, and Zero opened it. "Say, man," a voice said, "I'm looking for a place to stay. Guy named Gary sent me over."

"Come back later," Scratch said and closed the door.

The room was brightly lit. No one had turned off the overhead light.

"We can sleep on the floor," Zero said.

"There's things been spilled on that floor will kill you," Scratch said.

Zero took off his shirt, rolled it up, and laid it on the floor. "I don't need the Waldorf." He lay down on the floor, curling in on himself. "It's the middle of the night out there."

"I'll see you later," Scratch said, but Zero already had his eyes closed.

Okle-fadocle said from his chair, "Shut up over there."

Scratch closed the door, then counted the change in his pocket. He had a dollar eighty-two. Maybe he could climb the chain-link fence to one of the rides in the amusement park and go to sleep in the caterpillar or on the Ferris wheel. As he was walking along, trying to remember his plan, two policemen pulled up in a white car. "Hey, fellow," one said, "where you going?"

"To get a pack of cigarettes," Scratch said. "I'm back there at Monticello's."

"I don't want to see you an hour from now," the policeman said, and the car pulled away.

Scratch walked with his head down and made up his mind that, even if it were two in the morning, he would go out on the highway to hitchhike back east to Pittsburgh. Who knows? Something lay out there: a dreary night was here.

Eyes to the sidewalk steady pace, he passed a man and a woman putting suitcases into a car parked at the curb, and someone called, "Harold!"

Scratch looked up. In the indistinct illumination from a low streetlight he could not make out who had spoken his name. It was a young woman with the two people at the curb. "Joan," she said. "Joan Corcoran."

Fatigue and the night had robbed him of an answer, but he had never known what to say to her. She had joined his class in the ninth grade at Schenley, having gone to Mt. Mercy and other good schools, and she glittered in rows across from him, somewhere behind him in art, alone with a chosen friend or two in the cafeteria, wanted, spoken of, too remote even to be a cheerleader, a small bright sports car at her bidding. Her father was said to be a banker. They were Irish, but he had never seen them at St. Agnes.

"What are you doing here?" she asked as he stood mute.

"I was going to go out on the highway and hitchhike home."

"At this hour?" the man asked.

"What time is it?" Scratch asked, and everyone laughed.

"Late," the man said.

"We'll take you," Joan said. "I'm being abducted. I'm being taken back to Pittsburgh as a prisoner."

Scratch could feel the silence that fell was more at her invitation to him than the ill will which lay between the three people.

"Where's your suitcase?" the woman asked.

"I only came up for the day."

Everyone laughed again, and Scratch thought, so I'm a clown—it doesn't take a nuclear physicist to recognize one: this bunch is not so smart.

He got into the car, and Joan said, "Everyone calls Harold 'Scratch.' Is it okay if we call you Scratch?"

"Sure," he said, and all three laughed again. It was amused contempt: Scratch laughed softly to himself.

Her parents had come up to take Joan home to Pittsburgh when Joan had called to say a cousin hadn't been able to make it to Conneaut and she'd be alone. It was a four-hour ride, but they came instantly. Her father worked for Mellon Bank and Scratch could feel disapproval from the front seat where Joan's parents sat, but he could feel their attempt to be pleasant to him too. To pass him off as a friendly joke between them, easing things.

"Scratch, that's beer in that case back there," Joan's father said. "Help yourself. It's probably warm but you're welcome to it."

"I'll have one too," Joan said.

"Joan!"

Watching her in the back seat, sitting well away from her, Scratch saw the long, straight nose and the small mouth. But her lips were full and her neck was long. There was a preening to her even as she sat, amused, occasionally looking at him, then out the window. She did not touch the beer, but Scratch opened one, then another as they drove along. Sometimes he dozed, awakening each time more leaden but more himself with each new round of full consciousness. He listened. Her father was in investments and vaguely knew one of Scratch's older brothers. Scratch had another beer, thinking himself fortunate to be sitting in a comfortable car and not trying to sleep on the hard floor of a hotel smelling of mildew and spilled alcohol.

The family quarreled softly as if he weren't there. "I'm going to be eighteen this month," Joan said, "and you treat me like a child."

"Joan, we do it for you," her father said.

"None of us knows everything," her mother said.

"I'm going to live my own life," Joan said. "Do you expect to drive up to Radcliff three times a week to check on me?"

"No, dear, you'll be away from home," her mother said. "Conneaut Lake isn't Radcliffe."

"Oh, brother," Joan said. "Are you two out of touch!"

Scratch felt the beer and agreed with all parties: it seemed an unsolvable problem to him.

"Trust us a little while longer," her father said.

"You haven't given me one bit of advice that wasn't to my worst interests," Joan said. "You humiliated me up in Conneaut Lake. I'm your prisoner."

At their house in Pittsburgh, as Joan was being let out of the car, Scratch got out too. There was daylight in the sky. I'm going to the army tomorrow, he wanted to say, but even after four hours in a car with him, sort of knowing he was normal, they'd all laugh in some way to turn his enlistment into a joke between them.

"Can I take you somewhere?" Joan's father asked.

"No," Scratch said. "I don't live far, Zulema, I'll walk."

Joan's father reached in the back seat to lift out the beer case and said, "What the hell! This was a full case." He opened the brown bag on top and counted. "Scratch," he said, "you drank eleven beers between here and Conneaut Lake."

Scratch tried to look blank, and when he asked, "Did I?" no one laughed.

Joan's father, a handsome man in white-and-brown shoes, put his hands on his hips. "I'll be damned," he said.

Scratch said, "I'm sorry," and started for Zulema.

"Wait," Joan said. "I'll walk down the block to Forbes with you."

The Corcorans' home was a long distance from Zulema, almost an hour. The Corcorans lived in a house with a porch that had white pillars and red brick covered with vine two blocks from Carnegie-Mellon University. While Joan walked friendly with him, falling into step with him, Mrs. Corcoran asked, "Are you sure you don't want a ride?"

"He doesn't," Joan said. By the morning's light she still held the glow she had cast in the car. He noticed her teeth were very white even in the pale dawn.

Joan's father waved and continued down Forbes away from Scratch and his daughter.

Joan stopped and said, "Come inside. Let's go back to our house."

Scratch looked down Forbes at the Corcorans' Chrysler rounding a corner near the Carnegie-Mellon tennis courts. "Where are they going?" he asked.

"I don't know," Joan said. "They wanted to drive you home so they got in the car. Now they have to pretend they're going somewhere. They're like that. They'll drive now and he'll buy a pack of cigarettes. They won't say they're trying to run my life."

She took his hand. "Come inside." They walked back to the house, and Scratch said, "You live in a nice house."

"Phooey," she said.

Inside in the living room Scratch put his arm around Joan and kissed her. The morning was a dream anyhow; if he woke would he still be trudging like a slow, beaten horse on his rounds at Conneaut Lake, Ohio? Or would he open his eyes to a room with the stench of sleeping boys where Okle-fadocle lay sprawled in an armchair?

He peered about quickly, hiding his surprise at the beauty of the tapestried couch in the large living room, green and white with a silvery weave. On a table near the couch, solid and carved in ornate seashell pattern, was what looked like a dazzling silver ashtray, but it could not have been an ashtray. No one would poke cigarettes into that polished surface. He stared at the intricately wrought silver dish and looked away quickly. The drapes were of a green and white similar to the couch and Scratch would have liked—for a moment—to fall on to the thick white carpet and lie there and think of where he was and marvel.

Joan held him close, and Scratch ran his hand down her back and pulled her close. "Let's go upstairs," Joan said.

"Won't they be back soon?"

"They're not going to ruin my life," she said. "You don't seem like the type who scares easily."

She took off her clothes quickly in a room indistinct with freshly pressed white frills, the curtains turning white to become a bedspread, white pillows merging into a coverlet stitched and dancing with patterns of flowers. He took off his clothes too and she reached to turn off a small lamp, happy and white, morning outside the curtains. He felt himself slide into her easily, kissing her, and smelling the scent of starch and her hair. Her blond hair lay spread on the pillow behind her. She kissed him as if she wanted to hurt his mouth, then gasping said, "They can't tell me what to do."

It was over too soon and he stirred quickly when he heard the car downstairs in the driveway. "I'll let you out the back door," she said. "Wait until you hear them come in the front, then leave."

"Where?"

"Around the side of the house."

He dressed quickly, putting his socks into his pockets and not buttoning his shirt. Wait, he wanted to say. Let's say something else. He followed her down the stairs and stood quietly in the kitchen. On the kitchen counter lay a dish of cashews and four credit cards. Scratch looked away. He heard her parents come in. He left quickly by the back door, around the side of the house. The tennis courts down Forbes shone in the early morning sunlight, dew on the steel fence around them and on the ground itself. Unsure of where else the day was going, he walked the long hour down Forbes, looking out for a bus, but none came. He opened the door to his house, old smells, tired, thankful for the sleep that pursued him now in small aches and calls behind his eyes.

"Harold?" his mother called. "Is that you?"

"It's me," he said, and wearing his miraculous clothes from the brief hour earlier fell into bed.

Both his brothers called later in the day and wished him well and told him to send an address as soon as he had it, and Scratch went up to Oakland at dusk. He walked around the Carnegie Library and drank a beer in the Oakland Cafe. He watched television and thought of Conneaut Lake and wanted to call Joan, but he knew it would be a short conversation and anyhow over too quickly for him no matter how long they talked: sifting through his mind he knew it was best to let it lie there as if something could come of it the day he appeared in his army uniform back home, rather than risk the matter collapsing at the black telephone on the wall near the men's room. Maybe he would write her, send a funny card. He drank beer with Billy Bryce, who had gone to Schenley with him, and worked into the conversation Joan's name and was pleased to hear once more of her inaccessibility, her beauty, her father's job with Mellon while he turned over her long slim arms in his mind, the lamplight gleaming in blond hair probably even she had never seen quite the same way as he had. He walked unsteadily home at ten that night, woozy with a sense of accomplishments behind him, and fell into bed and in the morning went down to the U.S. Post Office on Grant where he was to leave. His mother kissed him before he left and reminded him that his uncle John Flood had learned an electronics trade in the U.S. Army after Korea. He had never regretted his army experience. It had helped him open three television repair stores in Morgantown. Scratch promised he would write and at Fort Jackson in South Carolina the army cut his hair and gave him a uniform and set him with thirty others to cleaning a huge mess hall. He did it happily, feeling at peace with the blacks who mopped the floors with him, even feeling superior to the other soldiers, white and black, because only he knew the burdens he had left behind.

The second night in camp a soldier came to where Scratch lay on his bunk and said, "Baldy, you look like a good guy, people, you know, I got something I want to talk about."

The young soldier had his name, "Kuyinski," on a tag on his fatigue jacket and he said that was his name when he shook hands with Scratch. "Harold," Scratch said, and Kuyinski showed Scratch a revolver tucked into his waistband. "I'm putting myself in your hands, Harold, because I trust you. These guys up here—hayseeds, you know, kids—they're holding these big crap games every night in the latrines. It's too much money for kids. There might be four, five thousand around the game, too much for jabones who don't know how to handle it. I do all the work in this deal: I heist the game. I walk in, wearing a ski mask, you know, and shout 'Stick-up!' or something like that, and you throw whatever money's around at me. Take it from the floor, anywhere. I grab everything I can, put it into a sack, and see you back here the next day. You're in a panic, see? You stay in the panic when I leave, cause confusion—they'll all be doing it anyway. Say, 'Don't shoot, soldier. Take the dough, don't shoot.' Then I split with you."

Scratch sat up on his narrow bunk.

"Why'd you pick me for this deal?" he asked.

"I don't know," Kuyinski said. He had a long chin and very pale eyes. "You had a good look to you."

"Guys get twenty years for what you're talking about," Scratch said and lay back in the bed. "You'll get five for that gun, for carrying it."

"Hey, you think I'm an amateur: I thought this through. Everybody in this camp stays around here three days, processing, even you and me—we split whatever it turns out to be and maybe we never see each other again. I'll buy you a drink you ever get to Cincinnati. Maybe we'll hit a couple of games. They're all over."

Staring up at the ceiling, Scratch said, "Forget about it."

The other soldier stood. "You looked okay to me," he said and quickly walked out between the beds to the door. Scratch heard it close with a numbing sense that he still carried about with him that going-nowhere atmosphere, reaching even to strangers to announce who he was. He turned over on his side, his eyes hot and hurting. He could not sleep for thinking the army was just another mile of that long road on which no certificates or diplomas were ever to be given for anything he did and nothing good waited.

Listening to the sounds of the men moving about in their sleep, Scratch turned on his back and put his hands behind his neck, staring up into the rafters of the barracks. Marked out for the small time by something about himself that pulled in people like Kuyinski, he thought. And there's not one of them now blowing bubbles in his sleep not better than me in some way. I can't ever guess the code. No one hustles them or thinks them open for illegal work that could get a soldier hard labor at Leavenworth with the only time off being for hanging yourself till dead by a light fixture. Then in small movements of good feeling the rafters turned gray above him and a light broke. Why, there ain't one of them in their ill-fitting underwear twisting and turning in their sleep in these hundreds of barracks with these thousands of soldiers in South Carolina and dreaming of home who has Joan Corcoran on the brain this moment and forever more. Not in the whole U.S. Army. Like a holy medal around my throat or a secret kind of word of protection spoken to me by a priest who liked my face and which I carry into battle on alien shores with Vietnamese. And it took me a half hour, less if you counted the falling away car of the father and mother as they went down Forbes and left the fool boy there with their lovely daughter. Scratch, it was you who did it! Turned it, touched the long, white thighs and leaped to prominence in less than thirty minutes with the queen of all that was most desired in the graduating class of Schenley High School, 1972. He smiled into the darkness. And another thing, he said in his mind to all those people who would condemn him without knowing his triumph, there was that matter of four credit cards lying in open welcome on the kitchen counter and a silver dish in the living room my mother would have loved and I was man enough not to lift any of it.

SEVENTEEN

Why He Never Left His Wife

ONCE there was a famous lawsuit that momentarily, like a passing breeze, hardly stirred dust on the windowsills of the Ancient Order of Hibernians, Division No. 9, but caused sharp comment among people never involved in the car accident outside the front doors of the club. The man who was struck by a taxicab in 1953 was a man alternately known in his career as Sly-boots or Big Picture Cogland. He was known as Big Picture because of the quality of blatant and transparent deception that he threw off around him, invoking larger plans that he was following that a victim might never know. He was called mostly Sly-boots because he was endlessly evasive in his cruelties, as if he were not an open book in his shameless games: he was known as a worrisome presence because he confounded people from their accepted composure that truth might lie at the core of the universe, natural order (a comforting thought with its moral implications), with his insistence that up was down, the heavens were beneath a person's feet. And no consequent punishment, Joe Shields saw, fell to the bum-boy for his deceptions!

Sly-boots had in his youth publicly one night at the Ancient Order of Hibernians set out his plan for marrying a rich woman, never to work a day in his life. There were several people around the table when the sallow boy explained in detail how he had looked at the proposition from all sides, weighed, measured, considered everything that could go wrong in how he would choose the woman, by what stratagems he would seduce her, winking and licking his lips in anticipation, how to investigate her family wealth, testing her for hints of loyalty; then, jumping to his feet, not terribly agile, he showed the young men at the table in the Irish Club how he would pounce, his arms wide, in the process knocking over three beers on another table.

"Well, I know where I'll go for a sly boots," old man Canty said, lighting his pipe, "if the occasion ever comes I need a master schemer."

Sly-boots, a hunched, dumpy U.S. mailbox of a man, came to work for years in the County Courthouse downtown in the Relief and Welfare Office where there was no problem brought to his attention that he could not contrive to make worse. He was safe from scrutiny because there was little concern with his manipulations of the hapless people who passed through the revolving doors into the lobby from Grant Street since, it was asked, what personal profit did he get from any of his misuse of the poor people who needed public service? The regulars at the Irish Club knew that it was not money or acclaim or ideas that impelled him. Seeing himself, apparently born with the notion, as a martyr, he enjoyed making other people suffer, anyone, anywhere, all the time.

Considering his character and the hysterical need the un-
gainly boy had to devise peculiar labyrinth tricks, the name Sly-
boots became as indelible a part of him as the peculiar smile that
hid what he thought of as his secrets. He could not contain his
glee at some foolish inner thought. Watching him, it was possible to note the very second the idea came to him that he was
putting one over on someone, usually a lie with what he imagined was a straight face. While given the nature of easy accep-
tance and dismissal in those days of the strangest of traits and
physical characteristics, his lies and atmosphere of fool-all-the-
people-all-the-time protected him from gibes at anything more
than those qualities of character. He was also known as a coward
and a braggart and boring. But few peered beyond his inability
to hide his joy at others' grief.

Protected from scrutiny of the specifics behind his slight smile
by his obnoxious conduct, he managed to cause Joe and the others discomfort when he was struck, perhaps staggering drunk
(there were no witnesses there except Sly-boots, his wife, Dorene, her brother, and the cabdriver, under the circumstances, in
other words, no credible witnesses), leaving the club on a fine
St. Patrick's night. Never in the history of the club did anyone
prior to that moment choose advocacy of a vehicle against a human being: people on the occasion of the collision of cab and
man argued compassion for metal and bumper, headlight and
tires against the blessed body of a creature made in the image of
God. Fairly steady men, themselves known to fear runaway tax-
icabs in the night as a threat to themselves and the fortunes of
their families, expressed sorrow for the Yellow Cab.

The driver was said to be a respectable student paying his way
through college, known as a Catholic boy of good reputation on
the South Side where his brother sang in a choir, a youth with a

career of mechanical engineering responsibility in front of him, and then Sly-boots walked into his car, causing somehow the windshield to shatter, two doors to flap in the wind, the cab to jump the curb and tear down a telephone pole down the street from the Irish Club on Oakland Avenue. Sly-boots's wife, Dorene, in her own right as notorious a deceiver as her husband (he was her sixth husband), claimed the Yellow Cab was ripping down Oakland Avenue ninety miles an hour. To get to ninety the cab surely needed a far longer track than Oakland Avenue to reach that speed only one block down from Forbes, but she stuck with her story, and her brother verified it, insisting that Sly-boots was cold sober and the Yellow was going closer to a hundred. The cabdriver, who was fifty-five or so years of age and had not graduated high school, as it turned out, insisted his brakes had gone out as he had slowed to three miles an hour to stop at the curb. And Sly-boots, on the sidewalk, standing with one foot on the pavement and the other in the street, had moved quickly toward him, maybe intentionally seeking the accident, and the damages to the vehicle had come from the taxi bouncing off him.

Sly-boots wore a neck brace for a year, and, as he was the chief source of information about the settlement, it was assumed correctly the truth would never be known. But more than one person at the Irish Club, when the subject came up, said sincerely, "I pity that taxicab. It must have done something real wrong in its time to collide with Sly-boots Cogland on the sidewalk."

While Joe Shields, a Democrat by choice of soul and a truck driver's assistant for money hire, listened, old Harvey Malrose said to Pal Mahoney one night at the Irish Club about a month after the tragic assault on the Yellow Cab, "Well, Sly-boots didn't die, hardly scratched. Real good form. The taxicab is out there in eternity, but Sly-boots is here to tell the tale. I saw him eating a whole ox sandwich two days ago."

"Old Cogland, most hated man in Oakland, worse than John Crumpton, who threw his mother and old aunt down the stairs," Pal Mahoney said. "Do you know the rat, Joe?"

"I do," Joe said. "I had occasion to call him down at the Allegheny County Courthouse for an old lady living in our neighborhood who was seeking a shortcut to getting welfare payments—you know, Sly-boots has been down there at the welfare office since the time of George Washington—and I called on him as a neighborhood guy to do what he could, even knowing his reputation. Well, he set up more roadblocks than the highway patrol looking for John Dillinger. First, it was her not talking English like Roosevelt or knowing who was her state senator, then dates wrong on her citizenship papers, then it was her name misspelled three ways out of nervousness. But he's one of those fellows like the fireman who sets a building on fire, then runs to get a pail of water to be the first to quench the blaze. She eventually got her welfare money, but he made it look like him that done it and not the Commonwealth of Pennsylvania. You know, every time I go down there to the courthouse I think they're going to find something on me in the files and I'll never go home. But it's Sly-boots's kind of place, secrets in every brick and schemes and wrong alleys for the innocent."

"Passing on the street down there," Pal said, "you think that old castle holds prisoners haven't seen daylight in a hundred years."

"Built to last," Joe Shields said, "and beautiful, like they're always saying, but it's cold stone against human beings and there's no beauty ever impresses me more than all the weeping and moaning the wretches do down there: nothing painted like a sunset in it for me."

"The bridge that takes the prisoners from the courthouse to the jail," Pal said, "is called the Bridge of Sighs and I can see old Sly-boots lining up to see men starting their first fifty feet of a trip that's going to take them ten years to walk back. A sadist is what he is. If he can he turns the screw when he can get away with it. You not looking over that old woman's shoulder, Joe, he'd have seen her out on the street left up to him. It's the twisting and turning the man lives for: like making other people argue or hate each other or suffer and it's all eyes not on him, except as a hero come to straighten out things."

"Four voters in her family," Joe Shields said. "You know I was going to tend that old woman's family, Democrats every one, like they was orchids."

"Bad as Crumpton," Pal said. "I never heard a man laugh as loud at other people's miseries as Sly-boots Cogland did—till, was it Tutti Dunne? says to him, 'I hear that phony laugh one more time, Sly-boots, and it's your last hee-haw at another person's misfortune.' And it was the last time we heard it, but I guess he does it in private, thinking nobody's on to him. Working out designs down there at the courthouse to make the rich get richer and the poor more confused who pushed them in the quicksand."

Rubber Hughes was at the table at the Ancient Order of Hibernians, Division No. 9, that night, and he said, "Pal, that's pushing it. There's no one worse than the late John Crumpton. He threw his old aunt down the steps and then he threw his mother down the same steps. He stole things up at St. Agnes. I don't think there's a worse person known to humankind, even Sly-boots Cogland."

"We have an interesting case here," Pal said to the assembly at the table, seeing the Jesuitical twist the conversation had taken. "Who's the second worst bastard any of us know if John Crumpton is the first by acclamation?"

"Sly-boots!" Rubber and Dickie said in unison, while old Harvey Malrose, slower to comment, said, "Undoubtedly Sly-boots. In a lot of countries, a lot of cities, maybe on whole continents Sly-boots Cogland would be the worst anyone ever saw. But us? Being blessed with John Crumpton and Sly-boots Cogland in one lifetime, and don't forget Spots Gallegher, in a little city like Pittsburgh, in a parish like St. Agnes, I guess we got blessed with more choices of worst people than anyone ever knew."

Pal tilted back on his chair. "And more," he said. "There's other candidates."

"Who?" Dickie asked. "Not yourself? I knew you forty years and I'm not near as pleased with you as you with yourself, not even thinking how low you are."

"I'll make my preferences known," Pal said. "I think I'll keep my counsel for the time being. I know some lousy people in my time. But it'll be Sly-boots near the top with that happy light in his eye for other people's sorrows and the wife with the wrinkled face and all those husbands behind her. Pray for me that God forgives me what I did in particular and general and ask that Sly-boots and his wife come to roost somewheres aside from my bedpost before I go."

Shields, a dark boy, was barely twenty-one: he had been working for the Democratic Party in Terrace Village, the government housing project overlooking on a high hill Oakland, since he was sixteen. He drew comfort from running errands for Bill Cary, the precinct captain, feeling at home and good in the party of Roosevelt and Jefferson. Sitting among the group at the Irish Club that night, he felt the same sense of being part of larger things when he thought of the company at the table and turning out voters for the Democrats at election time. He regarded as the greatest sorrow of his life Eisenhower's and Nixon's victory in 1952 but held the Democrats only responsible for nominating Stevenson, no kind of recognizable Democrat that Joe understood. What were men on their way out of the steel plants on the South Side to make of a divorced man named Adlai offering to represent them and the country?

About a month after that, as Joe was gingerly making his way down the steps from the Irish Club, a full, rich summer's night on Oakland, himself neither here nor there, like the twilight outside, better than day in subtlety of color and not yet drooping with night, he passed Sly-boots on his route up the stairs. "Hello, kid," Sly-boots shouted, extending his hand.

Joe shook hands with him, to his knowledge the first time he had ever spoken to him directly, no telephone between them: Joe was about fifteen years younger than he was, and Sly-boots and his wife and her brother were all legends to Joe Shields. "Let me buy you a drink," Sly-boots said.

"No," Joe said mysteriously. "Business calls."

To be in his company was to be marked a pariah. When Joe saw him at the club Sly-boots was usually alone at the bar, his wife elsewhere, and attended only by men of the most esteemed courage, reputation, and charitable character like Harvey Malrose, Pal Mahoney, or old Doc Pierce. Sly-boots was notable for

bringing bad luck as well as lengthy guilt by association, so broad
was his victimizer's history: for that matter given Joe's own su-
perstitious nature, he was not sure, witnessing him ascending the
stairs in a bright orange T-shirt, he had not fallen under an evil
spell.

But Joe overcame his fear of the unknown and took a walk
around the block in the ripe air of fulfillment in the coming
night, the weight of bounty on the streets, and decided that it
was not a night to be absent from the Irish Club. Sly-boots,
sailing up the Irish Club stairs, boldly dressed in the bright pri-
mary colors (pants of the strongest electrical blue to go with his
sunburst shirt), spoke to him of journeys to ports of untruth
soon to be revealed.

"A last punishment on me brought you here," Dickie Trent
was saying to Sly-boots, who, unbidden, had seated himself with
Dickie and Corny Sullivan, who sat at a corner table. "Harvey
Malrose told us you were cured from malice and pride and lust
and envy up at the hospital; I was hoping you were safely home.
Resting up for your new life."

"Hell, it's true I'm not myself, Dickie. I thought I'd look in
on the old boys for an hour or two, the night being fine. My
health generally isn't what it ought to be."

"Can you sit in one place for ten minutes without trying to
manipulate anyone with fables and falsehoods?" Dickie asked.
"Shields, you put a watch on it. Let's break a record."

Hinky Sutter pulled up a chair to the table and said, "Gentlemen, you're sitting tonight with the worst human being in the
Fourth Ward, counting Schenley Park."

"Hinky! Good to see you," Sly-boots said. "Don't let this neck
brace fool you. I'm in good shape."

"Don't give me that, Cogland. It ain't never good to see you. I know a man who thinks he's a martyr out of the Bible when I see one."

Sly-boots did what was a frequent thing with him, boy and man: he began to cry silently, twisting up his face. "When I went out for football in high school," he sobbed, "guys there at Schenley tried to hurt me. A psychologist explained to me that it was a fear of what they saw of themselves in me, because I cried when I was hurt, my feelings showed. Done me no good to hear it. The psychologist, bastard tiny like a bird, white as an albino—I thought he would understand, but the damned freak he didn't like me either, thought himself too good for me. White everywhere, eyes black and deep in his sockets, damned Halloween mask, he thinks he's better than I am. You all think you're better than me because I try to live a good life, help people."

"Cogland, don't start confessing your terrible life," Corny said. "Another lie you're telling." He stood and left the table and the others, except Dickie and Joe, followed.

This time Cogland sobbed in wild audible gasps. "My father told me a long time ago," he said, "nobody was going to understand me. My old man told me once a week I was superior to people who laughed at me. He says, 'Be your own man, Craig, them who understands will love you, them that don't ain't worth wanting?'" His father had been a friend to one of Mayor David Lawrence's secretaries, maybe a cousin, and that was how Sly-boots had come to be on the public payroll. His father had been well-respected but often himself stood up in haste at the Irish Club and said the hour was late when Sly-boots or his wife appeared and quickly left the place.

Sly-boots stood and offered to shake hands with Dickie.

"If you knew me better," he said, wiping his tears, "you'd treat me better."

Dickie stood and said, "God help us," and left Shields at the table with Sly-boots.

When Dickie came back he said, "I saw you shake hands with him, Joe. I told you: you're a liberal with all the lefties. I knew it the minute I saw you."

Joe said, "I was sorry for him. Sometimes I think he and guys like John Crumpton are in the world to make the rest of us think we're better than we are, being better than they are."

"Liberal," Dickie said. "Sly-boots'd eat your heart you give him a chance."

Joe, these days, often had to listen to slogans like "twenty years of treason" about the Democrats, now that they were the out party and people said Stevenson was a communist, but between him and Dickie there was none of that. What Dickie meant, teasing, was that kindness could only go so far: the dividing line was Sly-boots Cogland. It was, Joe thought, like the people who said they were against hanging or the electric chair, but given this special murderer they'd relinquish their spiritual beliefs, most people drew the curtain on their charity when it came to Sly-boots.

To Joe's bad fortune, Sly-boots began to regard him as a friend. He fled him, but not before he'd listened each time to the whole litany of calamities that had befallen him since he had been misunderstood in knee pants. Never caught in the middle personally of one of Sly-boots's complex fabrications, welfare obfuscations, losing mail, promises of political jobs, and crooked payoff games not meant to be honored on this earth, Joe had no profound commitment to detesting him.

Sometimes, it was obvious, Sly-boots invented criminal schemes to entice the listener, pull him in, form a compact on a nun or a priest, something adverse that a person would be ashamed later he had agreed about, suggested he knew the whereabouts of a stolen carload of wine, and then never again mentioned the subject, knowing he had made his obscure point: Sly-boots had achieved his largest goal—he proved he was not the only skunk in the cabbage patch. *Look at you excited! You're mean as I am.*

After his trip to the hospital, he cornered Joe one night and told him he had had a vision while lying on death's doorstep after a recent collision with a taxicab. The lights from the Briar Bowl on the corner of Forbes and Oakland Avenue where nightly lunatics of all degree gathered to harangue each other and passing visitors, their complaints, free as birds, Sly-boots's face was as mottled as Joe had ever seen it. Perhaps he wore powder. Some days Sly-boots looked pale, but the sweep and the absurdity of his assertions never waned by artificial illumination or cosmetic.

"It come to me," he said. "There's a Heaven, Joe, I know it."

Shields was uneasy: his researches told him that the speculation trade in heavenly futures was good enough, but people on welfare needed the Democrats, and so did coal miners and women who picked celery and people not making money from munitions.

"I expect I'll see you there then," Joe said.

"No, Joe," he said, "that wasn't what come to me. What come to me is that Heaven isn't for everyone, not even a good guy like you. You're a good guy, people like you. I admire you. But the point is: Joe, you don't need Heaven. Even fine fellows like you, good in the sight of the Lord, you're not going to make it. Not going to Hell either, not to Purgatory either I'd guess, Joe, but somewhere different than me and a few others. Joe, Heaven is for those who suffered down here below. Not being liked because I was gray-faced and not pretty like guys like you, people inferior to me laughing up one side and down the other, never honored for my love of people down at the Allegheny Courthouse. Doing my bit, day in, day out, helping out, crying my eyes out for all the sick and tormented I see and not a tear for myself: I'm ready for my reward. It has to be that way, otherwise nothing makes sense."

"I still hear it's God who judges."

"Right, that come to me early as a fact. But unless Heaven is like the civil service, which I'm under now, it's going to be this one higher up through length of time in grade, seniority, veterans' benefits counted in, political pals, nothing there for me, and the same mess as here. So it come to me as another fact: people always think Heaven is a payback for a bad life down here—it's true! It's only the humble going to get there. You, a good boy, a fine boy loved by all, but you haven't suffered, Joe. Do you get me?"

Joe said, "Well, I guess I won't be seeing you in Heaven."

He left Sly-boots on the corner, anxiously looking around to find someone else to listen to his amazing theories of himself in the afterlife.

In Joe's rounds, the fortresslike Allegheny County Courthouse and Jail, a prison and a warning to passersby on the sidewalk, where Joe went on his errands for Bill Cary saving Democrats in trouble with the law and to the state welfare offices and out to Blaw Knox Jail where long-term convicts were held, Joe had seen enough to know for himself that Sly-boots had only been chosen as the second worst man anyone ever knew because nobody knew everyone else in Pennsylvania. Given the general makeup of the human race, the dreadful offices where people sat with their petitions for shoes and toasters and the bars of justice where daily there were lined up souls contending for the worst and the second worst awards, the stalwart, age-old building at Fifth and Grant, a pride and terror erected to strike awe, was a constant reminder of who else briefly strolled the sidewalks waiting for critical judgment.

Each time they talked Sly-boots affirmed for Joe the truth of every lie the man had told that had caused him to be regarded as the second most contemptible man in Oakland. And Joe—he would not hide it from himself—found him despicable; he feared him and his wife.

And they were not compatible with each other either, as it became clear with the passage of time. The better Joe knew him—if anything about him was ever more coherent than the facts of his ambush by a taxicab—the greater his turn to talking morosely about Dorene, his wife, became.

Sly-boots dreaded her leaving him. It was not love, as people understand the term. It was to Sly-boots's mind apparently a final repudiation. She, who had known many men, regarded as the most irrational of the Schlagel sisters, drunk in high school and forced out in the tenth grade, married five times before Sly-boots, if she called an end to the contract, what had he left? Her face lined with connecting passions too overlapping to be read simply, she was perpetually in a rage, eager to confirm a lie or to set one spinning. She was the second most despised man's last grasp of what he thought was normalcy. And she knew it.

She cursed him in public, went places with her brother and started arguments in barrooms, elbowed policemen who came to quiet her, was reported to have affairs with men and women and perhaps the brother who was named Derek. She often sat in repose, like one drugged, still as a tree, and when someone thought the look on her face was composure she erupted into curses and shouts. She had been brooding until her general wrath could speak through her. Passing Joe on the street, she made a small sound in her throat, like a dog growling. He had never spoken to her; he did not know who else she growled at, ashamed to ask.

Often she twisted her mouth to indicate distaste for strangers, and her hair was dyed a strange purplish hue, black in certain lights, simply purple in others. She was blunt in body, shapeless in men's clothing she wore, sleeves always rolled up high on her forearms, and she had a stride like a baseball coach coming to call in a failing pitcher from the mound, final, measured, quick, and relentless. When he saw her in her abrupt pigeon-toed trot, even at a distance, the child in Joe Shields wanted to run, but he met her head-on on Forbes and Fifth, and she made that mouth motion as if she intended to spit, and they walked past each other, some vestige of childhood frightening Joe into a pounding heart, throbbing temples, sweating palms.

Joe, knowing that smiles and a handshake were the key to the ballot box and good will among all nations, nevertheless never tried to talk to her. But one could hear her after two whiskeys declaiming at the Irish Club memories of the grandeur of her husbands: respectively a mailman, a driver for the old *Sun-Telegraph,* a self-employed Alsatian painter who spoke no English, a fourth either a hairdresser or a bartender, and the fifth a waiter at a local Chinese restaurant who had died two months after they were married. Two other husbands had died too while married to her, the mailman and the hairdresser/bartender, and the others had disappeared, but she turned them into wealthy businessmen and entrepreneurs, not quite polo players but world travelers, men who had left her, as she said, "well set up." She held her social status over the head of poor Sly-boots Cogland. Sometimes she put on an English accent through her narrow, almost closed lips.

Sorry Sly-boots worked his entire adult life as an intake clerk at the Office of Pennsylvania Welfare at the grim Allegheny County Courthouse and Jail where daily he created emergencies for the destitute and generally wretched and then professed in a series of dramatic telephone calls and letters to them to have staved off disaster for the unhappy, anxious clients. Papers had not cleared, letters had not been written or were lost, affidavits were not properly signed, but Craig Cogland, heroic and preposterous, their man against the bureaucratic storms, was there in the nick of time to save a suffering humanity. Joe heard there were complaints about him at every step in his career, inflating his clerk's job to pathological dimensions; there were charges, but his resources of activity and inertia, knowing when to act or conceal himself among a tired bureaucracy, were vast. He had the will to continue himself without changing; others were there only for the job, some even aspiring to offer comfort to the endlessly troubled at the front door. In his high voice he proclaimed he was only working as his good heart led him, frightening, ominous, bewildering, hiding behind the institution's missions, and in the great faceless machinery of the welfare associations, who was there to care about how a certain low-paid clerk amused himself?

The building held murderers and slashers: Sly-boots was safe in that haven for the masked perpetrators against the common good when and if rascals were ever to be counted in a local census.

Still, holding on to his lies and Dorene, his job with its joyless satisfactions, he yearned for something better and began a long affair with a woman named Grace Kelly, the same name as a prominent movie actress of the time. The local Grace Kelly was a small woman, not at all as aggressive as Dorene, did not drink, unlike Dorene, had a pleasant speaking voice, and was a waitress in Gammon's Waffle House on Forbes. She had been an eager Democrat, and Joe looked forward to having a cup of tea with her on election days. Her house was clean and she did nothing with men as so many women on Robinson Court had in the war years with their mates thousands of miles away. But her husband had come home from Korea filled with tics and hallucinations and could not hold a job, and she left him a few years after his return, and Sly-boots began to visit her frequently at her apartment in East Liberty. There was no explaining it, Joe thought, what some women saw in a man other men found wretched— indeed, other women too. But they saw something there.

When Joe knew her she was a fairly young woman on his route in Terrace Village Two, where he lived with his mother and father and during election campaigns joyfully enlisted soldiers for the Democratic army. Her husband usually sat in a darkened room, not looking up at Joe, lost in other battles not known to Joe and the other Democrats saving the nation from rapacious Republicans.

The affair was apparently not known for a long time to Dorene. In his remarkable sweating presence Sly-boots could have been noticed by an Airedale as a man in misadventures, but somehow he managed to bring it off and not reveal it to anyone at the Irish Club in his boasts of sexual magnetism. The first Joe knew of it was one night in the Atwood Cafe where he sat waiting for the seventh inning of a Pirates night game, to take his place perhaps in a vacated box seat behind first base, when other less devoted patrons left for the night and Joe Shields could slide through the ticket stalls with a wave to a crony and resume his continuing interest in the local baseball fortunes.

Sly-boots arrived at the Atwood Cafe, largely disheveled, looked around at the nearly full house, and saw Joe at the bar. He rushed to Joe and put his arm around his shoulder. "My friend," he said, "I need a favor. I have to be home. I have to be there this minute and there's a small blond woman going to be here in a few minutes. I was supposed to meet her, but I can't be here and I won't be able to telephone, a little trouble at home. Please tell the woman Craig will call her at home or see her at work tomorrow. Can you do it? Will you do it?"

"Sure," Joe said, "but I'll only be here till the seventh inning," heavy with his burden of following the Pirates.

"She'll be here, she'll be here," he said.

"What's her name?"

"Her name? She's little and blond."

"Look around: there's two fit that description right now, three if you count that woman asleep in the back booth."

"Grace," he said, "oh, Grace is her name," and fled.

About twenty minutes later, Grace Kelly came in and Joe walked over to her at the door, gave her the message, and prepared to leave. But she looked so shaken Joe decided to stay for a few minutes. He missed the end of the Pirates game that night.

She and Sly-boots, it developed, planned to marry, he to run away from Dorene, she to wait patiently for the divorce. She sipped a rum and coke and talked slowly as if reciting a lesson long ago learned and gradually recovered for her as she stumbled on words and ideas. Only now, as their grand love was culminating in marriage soon, could she talk about it since she and Craig feared Dorene as if she were a demon. She beat Craig. She hurt him, twice stuffing a pillow over his head and trying out of simple malice to murder him. "She has a killer in her," Grace said. "She wants to kill someone and she married Craig because she wants to murder him. I see him days he's black and blue and she's scratched him and clawed him and tried to burn him as if because he cries like a big baby she has to rip at him to tear him apart. I don't know why he married such a person."

Telling Joe of her love affair, she occasionally wiped her eyes. "He brings me a dozen roses every time he comes to see me," she said, "and we sit for hours and he tells me things she's done to him, shows me the marks on his back from her fingernails, the burns on his neck where she threw hot coffee into his face. Once she tied all his clothes into knots and dumped them over the Panther Hollow Bridge and he and I went down there and collected them and untied them and took some to the dry cleaners and destroyed those we couldn't save. Now it's all but over but a happy ending for him and me. I've been through terrible things, Joe, and so has he. We found each other. Maybe we don't look right to the world, but we're right for each other. Suffering brought us together. Maybe he doesn't look right to the world all by himself, but what I'm saying, Joe, is he looks right to me because of what he's been through. Being good to him is like winning back some of the bad been done to me."

The Pirates lost that night to Philadelphia, and Joe read about it in the paper the next day. He had been given two weeks off work because things were slow at Gimbel's Department Store, and he enjoyed the leisure to think about politics and sports and men and women. He thought, as he studied the night's statistics over a cup of coffee in Thompson's Cafeteria on Forbes, about the world of love and pain and smoke and waited to hear that Craig Cogland and Grace Kelly had married.

But no one heard of such a marriage. When Sly-boots was anywhere in Oakland he was alone or with Dorene, she in her triumphal pinch-mouthed public assaults on decorum, and he himself, bragging as gusty as the wind off the park on Forbes. The hurtling cab was hardly a memory, the queer confluence of bum guy and automobile to pass like a dream from conversation. No longer did even some people committed to a life of convivial company question the propriety of drinking and smoking and the terms of association of free souls in communion with each other, knowing Oakland Avenue itself was unsafe. And Grace Kelly continued on at Gammon's Waffle House, moving out to East Liberty with the chain when the Oakland restaurant was closed. Sly-boots grew heavier, thicker in the shoulders until he seemed to be slumping forward, and Dorene daily over the years twisted her mouth at strangers and acquaintances and was of note only in a single instance in the following decade when it was alleged she tried to drown Sly-boots in a washtub where he was bent over, presuming to work on the plumbing. But the charges were dropped when Sly-boots would not testify against her, and they stayed married.

Joe saw Grace only once more, at a bus stop downtown, when he was leaving the Allegheny County Jail on Fifth. He had gone there that late afternoon for Bill Cary, who told him there was a young man being arraigned down at the massive structure for lifting a suitcase and a wallet at the Pittsburgh Airport, and what was curious was that it was the very afternoon he arrived for the first time in the United States from Dublin. "Crazy time to turn crook when you've been in a foreign country for no more than an hour," Bill said.

"Not if you were a crook all your life in Dublin," Joe said.

"The rest of the family ain't and I've known them, cousins and aunts, more than forty years and there's not one smart enough to steal."

Joe took cab money from Bill and in a Christmas time of wet streets and a chill wind took the bus down to the courthouse, saving the cab money for the criminal, who, while not knowing which bus to take to Oakland, still felt confident enough to estimate which suitcase was right to lift feloniously in the land of plenty. But at the courthouse Joe discovered someone else, a member of the family, had collected the visitor earlier that day, and Joe, oppressed by the building, left quickly and in the cold was debating whether to wait for a trolley or use the money in his pocket for a cab when he saw Grace.

She called to him, and he did not know what to say to her. It was two days before Christmas and the lights in the stores below on Fifth were too bright for the approaching night and the dark old building hovering over them. Built to last a thousand years, the stone edifice had few windows and in the clearest daylight was a looming dark presence. It had been erected to announce to people on the trolleys and sidewalks, in the little houses on the hills, of payment for crime, retribution, the remorseless threat of long years of judgment and revenge.

"Damned busses," Joe said. "Never on time."

"You know Craig and I didn't marry," she said. "I know you're wondering, I remember our last conversation. Craig and I went almost to the altar and it didn't happen. I was supposed to be in Atlantic City waiting, and we were going to run off and start new in a place like Dallas or Kansas City. I was there and he came, happy and good to me. He loves orange juice, we drank gallons of it every day on the boardwalk. We had a time, I tell you. He can be fun. He really can, people don't understand him, roses and candy. I never met a man like him. But after three days, we're laughing all day long and holding hands on the boardwalk and room clerks are calling me 'Missus,' he tells me he's going back to Dorene."

"I said to him, 'Craig, this isn't you talking. This is someone else. You can't go back there, not after what she does to you. Craig, honey, she's going to kill you. She hit you with a shovel and tried to drown you. She said it was an accident, but she spilled gasoline on you while you slept and would have set you on fire but you woke at the feel of the liquid on your chest. Craig, honey, listen to me, I'm not speaking for myself. I'm talking for your best.'"

"He takes my hand, Joe, and he looks at me, and he sighs like it's his last sigh, like a moan, and he nods his head as if he was agreeing with something I said, and he says, 'Grace, honey, I deserve her.'"

The Allegheny County Jail is a famous shrine to justice, a landmark in Pittsburgh known to all from childhood, designed by the great Henry Hobson Richardson to be intimidating and beautiful in its relentless statement of final authority on right and wrong and completion somewhere. It speaks in stone of retribution, and the monument knows nothing of the good who are punished here, Joe thinks, and the bad who are rewarded, only that there is payment. In its huge stone building blocks Richardson had embodied the power and majesty of order. It is in stone limitless in antiquity and grave with promise beyond humankind, not to be taken lightly. In the season when Joe stood with

Grace in its shadows, there were hints down below on Fifth of renewal in green and red Christmas lights hung from telephone poles, electric bulbs in white with silver tinsel. Somewhere a tinny store's recording spoke of sleigh bells and snow fresh and white with innocence.

"He deserved her?" Grace Kelly asked. "To get hit in the face with a shovel and set on fire, Joe?"

Joe Shields shuddered in the cold, reluctantly drawn back to the old year, winter's grip, and above him the imposing gray and unyielding building stronger than the frail and lost company of Grace on the sidewalk. His teeth chattered. His fingers were numb. He felt bathed in ice. He tried to escape the building's call, hearing her speak dimly through ears ringing with cold and promise of penalty for Sly-boots and the good and the bad and in a corridor where no sun ever shone Dorene Schlagel waiting with a shovel like the strong right arm of God.

EIGHTEEN

Caught

ONCE Dennis and Head Dougherty worked for Head's older brother Bambam, known to everyone as a gangster. In those days, just after the war, the way to tell a gangster was by the white hat he wore with a wide brim, a loose, flopping handkerchief in the lapel pocket of his double-breasted overcoat, and his hand in the right pocket of the overcoat as if he were packing heat. Bambam did that and more: not shaving for two or three days at a time, looking at people a long time before he answered the simplest questions, and occasionally making a mock punching gesture at another person's jaw, male or female, and tapping them gently with his knuckles. He liked Dennis, he said, because Dennis, who lived with his mother in a government housing project, was a kid from the wrong side of the tracks.

Bambam operated a vending machine business. His candy bars and cigarettes were placed in bars from Troy Hill on the

North Side through Carson Street south, Hill District, Oakland, and Sharpsburg. He showed Head and Dennis around the dirty, abandoned warehouse in Soho, brushing aside cobwebs. "The reason I have two of you here," he said, "is one keeps his eyes on the other. Something goes wrong it's two guys have to get their stories straight. And you know this neighborhood: I was hearing I was held up every week, two hundred dollars in pennies stolen like it was water running through my fingers. One guy, what am I going to say? You're lying? There's no witnesses. Two, I have a witness on the thief."

"Bambam," Dennis said, feeling the warmth of being a trusted gangster-in-training, "you got the right two guys."

Their job was to put pennies into cigarette packs by running the cigarette packs through a device that shoved the pennies under the cellophane. Cigarettes cost seventeen cents at a machine in those days and a customer putting two dimes or four nickels into the machine expected his three pennies to be returned. They worked fast, sitting at a little table in the old warehouse down in Soho, banging away like boys possessed, reloading the machine with pennies as the upright tube needed replenishing. They smelled of pennies and tasted metal with every meal for weeks, but the pay was good: fifty cents an hour and they were both thirteen at the time, below hiring age, and it was gangster-good of Bambam to give them well-paying work. They made an easy four dollars a day and that was good wages for many adults.

"This has to be the best job guys our age ever had," Head said often, stretching after their day was done. Their backs were stiff, but Dennis felt as if he were making an investment in a future whose promise of hats with broad white brims, double-breasted overcoats and being well known was going one day to be built on rock as was Bambam's own reputation. Men who were not remotely gangsters put on the slick hair and fast walk like Cagney. It showed you had the class of a movie star but not soft, a tough guy and respected on the street too. A great beginning, Dennis thought, for the only child of a widow having a hard time getting by: he'd get her out of waitressing and see her in jewels.

"Shoot some pool?" Dennis asked.

"Sure, we got the cash for it."

Pool was five cents a game, and they had the money.

Bambam was damned kind to them: he gave them each thirty-five cents for dinner in the mornings before he left them with the pennies, the machine, and the boxes of cigarettes. At first Dennis sometimes had for supper only a Coke, saving thirty cents from dinner to add to the sum he gave his mother weekly. She was very proud of him: working three days a week, he was bringing home more money than his father when he was living did. Not home most of the time, his father while he lived may well have made millions in some other city, in some other state, but they had seen nothing from him.

The bust-up with Bambam started slowly. The boys took ten cents apiece one night and instead of using Bambam's thirty-five cents for a sandwich, fries, and a Coke they each bought a hot dog and a Coke special for fifteen cents, adding a nickel of their own to the ten pennies each they lifted from Bambam's money.

"It's not like stealing," Head said. "He's my brother, you know. He'd give us it but I don't want him to think we're dissatisfied with the money or the job. So we show our thanks we don't give him no headaches."

He was tall and thin like Dennis but softer, paler. Dennis had learned how to swim in settlement summer camps and had a sturdy quality in his shoulders. Head's shoulders sloped and his stomach was round even though he was a kid. But both of their necks were long and their ears protruded. Their shadows on the sidewalks when they came to work after school were elongated like the telephone poles' shadows in the late afternoon, long and slender like fine lines drawn on the streets that moved with them when they walked. Judging by the shadows, Dennis thought, bending and twisting into unnatural shapes, someone would think Head and me are twins, but we're not, couldn't be more different.

Perhaps someone else could not have worked for hours with Head, Dennis thought. He talked about strange subjects and himself as part of an ongoing story of mysteries. He said he had seen when he was a child stars collide in the night sky and in the fallout of the explosion showers of bright flame, streamers come to earth from unimaginable distances. He had watched the gigantic fire show from his roof when he had been awakened by the soft murmur the stars made as they approached each other.

"They were whispering up in the sky to me and I didn't want to miss it," he said, "and I wasn't there ten minutes when the stars started to dance and there wasn't a sound except for them humming, getting ready to bang into each other; the street was all asleep, all the people and cats and dogs. And the lights coming down to earth and the roof where I was was hot up there for a long time but by the time they come down they were a fine ash, like a powder for babies but finer."

"It sounds like a dream."

"It was no dream, I know a dream. I was eight years old. I quit telling people about the things I'd seen. It was a dream, they say. Oh, you took a medicine and you seen things, like I don't know when the one time I saw the infant Jesus asleep in the corner of St. Agnes Church and the other time I saw those stars in the sky hit each other like a couple of trains."

They worked diligently while they talked, pressing with a swift bang the pennies into the cigarette packages and refilling the cartons from where they'd taken the packs. They worked from three thirty in the afternoon until past midnight, only the two of them in the warehouse, as the weeks passed Head trusting Dennis more and telling him more incredible events he had witnessed and places he had been. A tiny car he had built in his garage and then had driven to California and back all in one night while everyone else slept, a moment when he was trapped on a Ferris wheel and an angel had swooped down and carried him to earth, and then he told him how the seven deadly sins had been coming to him in various horrible forms since he was a child at St. Agnes and they were a horrible lot. Some were hunched over and lurching at him as he walked home from elementary school at St. Agnes and others waited until he had seated himself in a movie theater and then sidled into an empty seat next to him and terrified him until he thought his heart would stop: such horrors as he could hardly bring himself to express to Dennis, but finally leaping from where they were pressing pennies and showing him with his hands the gargantuan shapes the sins had taken, wizened little misers, bloated frogs, toothless old women with snakes at the corners of their ugly mouths and twisting down around their wrinkled necks.

Fortunately, he alternated these events and visits from metaphysical places with long accounts of baseball games his brother Bambam had taken him to at Forbes Field, and their nights mostly passed pleasantly with his voice droning away the long hours while he stood to illustrate a play at first base.

They had been working there for two months of the summer when Head handed Dennis a dollar one night as they started to press the pennies into the cigarette packs. "What's this for?" Dennis asked.

"It's because I like you: you're my best friend."

"You don't have to give me a dollar."

"You never laugh at me."

"That's no reason to give me a dollar."

"I took a hundred pennies for myself," he said, "right under your nose last night. You never saw a thing. I put two cents into the packages instead of three. I quit when I had a hundred and changed it for a dollar bill. Then I thought of what a friend you are and I decided you deserved the dollar."

"Look, it's Bambam's."

"No, it was mine and I gave it to you."

From there over the next two weeks he began to give Dennis gifts of money in a sort of game: they were to be accepted only if he stole the money while Dennis was almost watching him for theft. And after awhile Dennis pretended not to see him stealing, turned away at the right moment, left the room when he knew a theft was in the air. He started one day for his part with two cartons of Camels that he hid under a raincoat, sold them for three dollars, and insisted Head take the money because, as it turned out—money at the core of anything he'd ever been taught to value, friendship, love, and honor—Head was his best friend too, giving him those sums that after awhile amounted to twenty dollars more a month than the job paid him. He consoled himself that if they were caught Bambam would not do anything serious to hurt his brother and he'd be safe too, no jail, no beating like Cagney or George Raft took from time to time.

They stole cartons of cigarettes weekly. They kept no

accounts. After work they went to a pancake restaurant and ordered blueberry pancakes and pancakes with walnuts. They ate club sandwiches with extra bacon until two in the morning and still had folded bills in their pockets. Head bought himself a wristwatch for forty-two dollars and Dennis bought his mother a necklace for the same amount. Touched by his generosity to his mother, Head bought Dennis the identical wristwatch he had purchased for himself. He engraved it "To my best friend, from Andy, his pal forever."

Dennis bought him, in return, from their crooked gains a thirty-eight-dollar alligator belt, then a rarity.

But they did not keep it in the family, recirculating Bambam's pennies into necklaces for mother, wristwatches and alligator belts for each other, eating huge meals at one restaurant, then at midnight ordering up again at another, because before the summer was out Head had expanded their larceny to include a young woman named Norma De Shance. When she saw them around Oakland throwing money at movies, in bowling alleys, strutting in their wristwatches and belts, she moved in. She was perhaps a few months over twenty and had been married and was—or was not—divorced. Her past was murky, and they were no match for her drift through her past shrouded in mists of evasions and phantasms of imagination (her husband had been a sailor, an aviator, a head chef at the Pittsburgher Hotel). Head alternated talking about kissing her for two hours straight and descriptions of a terrifying visit from a small, toothless woman—"I could see she was more than two hundred years old by her wrinkles"—who had accosted him that morning at a bus stop and said, "Unclean boy, you are an unclean boy." Dennis, who wanted nothing more in life at thirteen than to be a gangster like Bambam, did not understand what passed between

Norma and Head. As far as Dennis knew, given the climate of ardor and romance in black-and-white movies in the late forties, this was true love.

Head began to give her money regularly, for this purpose or that, her teeth, *her* aged mother, shoes to look good when she went for a job at United States Steel: the sums grew. Head and Norma De Shance never went beyond kissing but were going to be married soon, Head said.

They named dates, then postponed them, literally because of rain one Sunday, hail another. And of course neither Head's family, especially Bambam, were to be let in on the secret that Head Dougherty, not yet fourteen, was going to take a wife. All in all, if she had not insisted that Head rob his brother of a big sum, the end might not have come so soon; their other thefts were so transparent that Dennis wonders to this day if Bambam knew about them all along and dismissed them as family business, a small loss to pay for boys who hadn't enough wisdom, guile, or desperation in them to put him out of operation. But Norma demanded that Head pretend that the warehouse had been broken into—a certain Ron Marconi, a rival gangster, was suggested as the murderous invader—and no one would be the wiser and who could prove what had really happened or find the missing four hundred sixteen dollars Head and Norma had marked out for theft. Bambam could hardly ask the Italians where they had spent his money, and it was them or strangers against the word of his brother and his best friend.

Only Dennis's cooperation was uncertain but of course necessary. Money was no incentive: his high idealization of gangsters and Bambam particularly was edged with scores of movies and radio programs about honor among thieves—he could never openly, before himself and the world, admit he was doing anything but lifting some pennies for lunch or a game of pool from a friend's brother. This big plot with hundreds of dollars in it smelled of back stabbing, and Dennis, who frequently went to confession, refused any part of the proceeds. He agreed to do it because he had become persuaded that soft and brittle Head, the kissing fool and observer of strange visions, and he were friends forever.

For four days they discussed whether they both were to be tied up by Norma, a small dark woman with eyes as alert as a cobra's, fast and darting at each opportunity on the warehouse air. They decided that Head would be tied up—as Bambam's brother it would look bad if he ran even with two gunmen with bandanas on their faces after him—and Dennis would claim to have jumped from the second story where he and Head thrust the pennies into the machine. Dennis, of course, wouldn't really jump, just pretend that he did, fleeing for his life from the two armed men. With no other witnesses, Bambam would have no choice but to believe them and Head would have enough to marry Norma in Maryland; they discussed their stories by the hour, Norma asking questions to trick them. Dennis would set the conspiracy in motion by phoning Bambam that he did not know what had happened to his brother, who had been overwhelmed by two hoodlums. Going together to the warehouse they would—Bambam, whoever else came with him, and Dennis—discover the bound Head Dougherty: Bambam's relief would be so great he would not question the boys' honesty.

Norma and Dennis wrapped Head in rope, tightly, rolled him around on the dirty floor of the warehouse, opened a window, sealed shut from years of weathering and disuse, and left the building.

Norma listened, her small eyes licking at Dennis's face, while he called Bambam.

"They were wearing masks."

She nodded in approval, quick, enthusiastic. "No, I'm not hurt. We got to go get Head. They could have killed him, they were mean, Bambam."

She held the money in a small purse. When Dennis was done with his conversation with Bambam, Dennis and Norma solemnly made plans to meet the next afternoon.

At the warehouse, Bambam seemed very tired as he and Dennis and another man named Rollie untied his younger brother. When Head was unbound, Bambam went to stand by himself in a corner of the dilapidated building. He leaned with his back against a moldy board and watched Dennis and Head talking about the holdup. Dennis energetically dusted off Head, who looked as if he had been painted in floor dirt. The other man with Bambam said nothing at all but stood back from Dennis and Head, across the loft from Bambam. It was obvious to Dennis that neither man accepted the story of criminals breaking in and taking money. From opposite ends of the floor the two older men watched the two boys, restless spectators at an awkward performance. As he spoke and listened to Head, the words sounded more false to Dennis with every recitation.

"Were you scared? I almost let go."

"I never saw a man move so fast through that window: you could have beat Jesse Owens."

"The little one was mean: his eyes were like a killer's with that gun."

"I ain't ashamed to admit it. I cried, Bambam."

Bambam said nothing, listening.

Head said, "We should have fought, right, Bambam? But it was only money, you know, those guys could have killed us."

Bambam came into the light that fell from an overhead naked bulb onto the penny-stuffing machines. He stood looking at the two boys, first one, then the other. "Rollie," he said, "it's only money. I'll see you in twenty minutes, at the Atwood Cafe. I'll be twenty minutes, no more. This business is not going to take more than twenty minutes."

Rollie left, shaking his head in theatrical wonder, playing at being astounded and amused, and Dennis was filled with a cold alarm. There was no story that would stand up, never would be. He and Head were in a hard, relentless rain, wet and exposed, nowhere to hide. He fought back tears. He held back words. We didn't mean nothing by it, Bambam, we're just kids! Okay? Let everything be the way it was, back when we didn't take a nickel didn't belong to us.

Bambam said, "Don't say nothing further, Dennis, this is between Head and me, a family situation. Just tell me what you did, Head, what you and this other traitor cooked up, get me the money, and out with the garbage, the two of you. Where's the money?"

Head said, "I don't know. We didn't take it."

Bambam asked, "Where's the money?"

"I don't know."

Dennis felt his mind unmoored. It flew from his skull into the dusty rafters of the warehouse, dropped, caused him to tremble. *Tell!*

"Stop saying that," Bambam said. "I'm giving you the chance first because this is a family situation. You know what your father did for a living? I'll say it straight in front of Dennis: he was a Western Union boy at fifty-five years of age. You hear what I'm saying to you? It falls on me to put the straight and narrow on the Doughertys, including you. He ran mail on a bicycle rain and shine and they called him 'Kid' and 'Boy' and he was old enough to be their father. Okay? He's gone now and I'm lifting up the pack of you and you did this. Okay, it's done. The old man is done. It's all history. Don't make me turn to a stranger for an honest answer, you jug-eared bastard. Where's the money? And out the door."

"Honest, Bambam, Dennis and me never took the money."

"Oh, Jesus. Okay, fellow rat, what's it about? Where's the money? I know nobody else is in it with you because there ain't nobody else as particularly stupid as you two. Dennis, let's start with the truth. Forget it, Head, you had your chance, a family courtesy, you little bastard."

Dennis listened to his own words from a far distance. "We didn't do wrong."

Bambam sighed. "It's five minutes and I'm done with you," he said. "I'm asking you like a man who's in the family. Head, save yourself. You ain't neither going to ever work for me again, for nobody. Just say the truth."

Head said, "It is the truth."

"Dennis, last chance."

"We never took a dime, Bambam."

A long time ago, as Dennis remembers it, Bambam turned from them almost as if he were crying and left, but that meant he would have departed before the two criminals. They must have all walked out together, and Bambam locked the door behind them.

Dennis often thinks over the years back to that strange moment in the warehouse when the truth wasn't in him but a good thing anyhow possessed him, a lie maybe but something else somehow called from somewhere higher or deeper or more himself. Finally after years of night school at Duquesne and later listening to crooks and angle-cutters while he peddled a belief in the law and himself as an honest lawyer, he is puzzled by Bambam. Didn't he know the hallucinatory criminal's code of not squealing on a friend had taken grip of the two trapped boys in the warehouse? Perhaps no one really believed in a code of honor among thieves, Dennis thinks, but who could speak with assurance of what lay in the hearts of two adolescent boys?

He thinks of those walks to the warehouse in the late afternoon where Head's goblins and personifications of the seven deadly sins reached out to grasp them in the shadows of their own scrawny bodies, parked cars, and lamp posts. The neighborhood is gone and the cars and the telephone poles and everything else that could cause shadows to fall on the old streets, including the two boys sauntering along the sidewalk into the world of good fortune. It was true that in the district of shabby warehouses there had been nothing finally to retrieve them from the clutch of the innocent, ravenous appetites inside themselves, redeem their descent, except trust in each other, one a dope, the other too smart for his own good. They were no better, in one summation, than Head's delirious dreams of punishment by visitation of evil spirits for wrongdoing, but, inexorably, there was more to it.

As far as he knew, Head saw Norma perhaps once or twice after the theft, but never the stolen money. He would not have wanted it anyhow, more interested that Norma had her teeth fixed with their ill-gotten gains. Dennis, sure-footed these days among criminals and lawmen, victors and victims, oppressed in the courtroom and their oppressors, thinks maybe Bambam wasn't a gangster at heart after all, a matter of clothes and expression but not much else there, not to know that at thirteen Head and he, wrapped in movie code decencies and soaring dreams of perfection in friendship, would have rather died than tell on each other. Only later, where there are no overnight trips to California in midget cars, does the field of love and friendship come to embrace the bargain and the deal and the turning over and the strategic retreat and the sweet compromise.

Dennis has regarded his thefts from Bambam for a long time with shame. He used to flush at the memory of the naked discovery of his disgrace at unbidden moments, and only now when he is at comfort in a world of deceit and mistrust is he proud of himself and Head and their brief sunny bravery in the dark old warehouse. He could have lied among the cobwebs and thievery, at least, in the name of common sense. He is satisfied that he was true to reasons knit by threads of impossibility and colored with the nonsensical idealism of boyhood.

NINETEEN

Outlaws of the Purple Cow

THE SUBJECT of talking and listening came up one evening, and Fancy, who had finished work late and joined us at midnight at a table near the window at the Irish Club, asked Pal Mahoney, when Pal paused in a lengthy oration, had the Catholic Church ever canonized anyone for being a martyred listener. "It seems to me there ought to be a reward for not stoning people who bore us with old shoes and cobwebs masquerading as the word from on high," Fancy said. "I think I myself ought to be in line, listening to you for more than twenty years, man and boy, without leaping out a window and landing with suicidal intention on my head."

Mahoney had been talking when Fancy O'Toole sat at the table and had hardly stopped to catch his breath, barely acknowledging Fancy, nodding his head in recognition faint and irrelevant, and continuing on with his monologue about lies, eavesdropping, false witnessing, and probably one or two angles on the main discourse I've forgotten.

"You know, O'Toole," Pal said to Fancy, "your interest in Church lore in its smallest detail would be a delight to the nuns who gave up on you at St. Agnes in your youth. Seeing as how some of the major points like confession and communion and being of a clean mind and spirit seem to have eluded you. I can tell you this: whatever saint it is that the sinner calls on for help in being cursed with the sin of not listening would sure be your man or woman. There's such a thing as a half listener, just as there's a half truth, and Mr. O'Toole is a perfect example, a man born to listen with half a mind."

"You saying all these years I've been listening to you, Last Word," Fancy asked, "I've only been hearing half of the applesauce? Bad as you feel about my moral condition, imagine how sorry a creature I would be if I heard the other half of your misunderstanding of what the Jesuits taught you."

"Cite me an example," Mahoney asked. In the flow of the exhilaration that we traded off each other like dark flashes in the smoky loft of the Ancient Order of Hibernians, Division No. 9, sometimes it seemed all the currents came to rest in Mahoney. He was large domed and quick as a switchblade in the night, when the arguments were about God and the World. Mahoney, the agent of the supernatural, was invulnerable and tireless. He was ready, as Dickie Trent said one night, to talk God's Son down from the white mule entering Jerusalem, having decided there was a better way to make His argument aside from a death Mahoney hadn't sanctioned.

"How about humility?" Dickie Trent asked. "Don't it seem someone grabbing the floor and holding it ain't your picture of a man without pride?"

"False pride, the very definition of it," Mahoney said. "A man with something to say has an obligation to speak. I'd be lying I pretended I hadn't more to say than you, Dickie."

Corny Sullivan, usually very still, said, "Well, Mahoney, I got to speak. They sent you home from the Jesuits because they were sick of listening to you. My cousin in the Trappists went two years without a word: sentence of death for you."

Mahoney's departure from Jesuit seminary was usually a subject seldom addressed, obviously a source of great pain to Mahoney, who had wanted to be a priest from childhood. Mahoney had a punch like a mule, but only in a theological argument was he ever aroused to physical anger. He laughed. "God's will, I might suggest," he said. "He knew where I'm needed most. Let's get back to eavesdropping and lying. I think I'm among God's chosen in that field this very night. He didn't need me where people made sense. There are people snooping is their main line of work; and I guess eavesdropping on their neighbors is their hobby too."

I let it pass. "God's chosen" could mean me since I'm Jewish. Often Mahoney asked me, "And what has the anointed to tell us that will help us with our dilemma, Clifton?"

Vernon Scannell, thinking himself under attack with the pointed references to eavesdropping and being chosen and generally shy, said, "It's getting hip deep around here. I think I'll call retreat." He stood, and Mahoney said, "I wasn't speaking of you, Vernon, you know that."

"Good night," Vernon called.

"Mahoney," Vinegar Root, a fair boy at the table, said, "you talk too much. It's no dollar in anyone's pocket to listen to you. You know you run on like a motor going full blast in an empty room."

"That's it!" Fancy said, standing, patting young Root on the shoulder. "Next we'll hear the rain shows a tendency to water or the wind blows air too much. I'm going home. I just learned from Mr. Root the news Mahoney talks too much. You drove home Vernon, Mahoney, now it's me. Soon you'll be talking to yourself like Mr. Root's motor and not know the difference."

"I didn't mean Vernon," Mahoney said feebly. "I wasn't speaking of him. He had no reason to be put off. I was speaking on the whole of a human failing."

At the Irish Club, and in Oakland generally, a favorite expression was to say at a table in a bar about someone at another table that they were "on the Erie" or "riding the Erie." It meant they were listening into things that should not have concerned them. "Erie" was a synonym for "ear"; they were, according to our code, listening to subjects that were no business of theirs. Be careful, was the point: the walls have ears. Secrecy was like gold. A man's privacy was our top claim on the street bill of rights. As we had few secrets someone might be interested in, our passion for what we knew and had done took on a mystical proportion, having no rational basis for our retention.

Three years after the war ended with Japan, Vernon Scannell, who had won a bronze star and three battle stars in the Pacific, acquired among us at the Irish Club notice as great as the government's recognition of his wartime service. He was, in daily performance, said to possess an almost superhuman ability to hear conversations at a distance and, better, to break the code of other people's secrecy and explain what he heard to an eager audience.

Vernon did not brag about his extraordinary skill, and he was justifiably offended when Mahoney seemed to mock it. Reticent about his gift to a degree unknown to the rest of us braggarts with no worthy attributes at all, even humble, he accepted our praise for his faculty with a small smile and a tilt to his head, hardly agreeing he had the ability. He was called "Submarine" because he seemingly heard conversations a hundred feet away over the sound of a jukebox, listening through thirty loud conversations in the Irish Club to get there, people talking to each other at the table where we sat and often while Vernon himself, as happened, was shouting over the noise. He was at first credited with extraordinary hearing. Occasionally, someone would want to test him and would detach themselves from a group and go sit across the room and hold a conversation there. Vernon failed every time.

His skill, we discovered, was not one of good hearing. It was also not very reliable. His gift was the talent to make out, from the way people sat, what he knew of them and their history and a word caught here and there the meaning of what they were saying to each other.

He could recite what people were saying by surrounding them with his own sense of their conversations. He acquired a reputation for good hearing, even occult powers, but it was guesswork. It was filling in blanks with a talent for reading the varieties of experience in the ordinary life around us. He was, for all the flaws in the limited accomplishment in his gift, still a phenomenon in the shadowy outlines of the Irish Club, haze, lights in the smoke: he was right an amazing amount of the time as frequently as he was wrong about the secret world under the rhythms of the polka bands and pop songs on the jukebox, but his dubious gift gave us strength, an irrational knowledge of abilities beyond ourselves.

It was not a universally known fact that he had this knack. There were perhaps a dozen of the regulars who knew about it.

For it to be common knowledge, it would lose its power: who would say a word to another with Vernon Scannell on the premises either at the Ancient Order of Hibernians, Division No. 9, or any of the other places on Forbes or Fifth where we congregated? On some off evenings, nothing doing otherwise (to say it directly, most evenings of our lives), we insiders huddled around Vernon while he sat, his head in his hands, concentrating on a conversation at a far table. Sometimes he looked up to see the objects of our interest; other times he stood and casually found a reason to walk by the targets, trips to the men's room, the cigarette machine, the jukebox, or merely to elaborately stroll to a part of the bar closer to the people whose conversation we were pursuing. He took his oracular ability very seriously. He was, in his way, of course, an artist.

Thus, one night, in April in 1948, we came on the facts, or was it the face of the dim but brave glory in untruths? of the situation on Tennyson Street.

The source of our information was, all unknown to them, the Huddleston brothers, Jackie, Billy, and Eddie, and their cousin, Alfred Lynch, from Connelsville, Pennsylvania. The three brothers and their cousin when he came to Pittsburgh sat in a distant corner, bent over their beer and wine. They talked in tones so low it was remarkable that they heard each other. They enjoyed their small community and spent enough time in each other's company that none of the four found it necessary to raise his voice to be heard. They might have been shortwave radios tuned precisely into each other's wavelengths. They nodded, they smiled, no one knew what they said to each other, in larger groups or only themselves to hear the words.

But one night while Dickie Trent, Pal, Fancy, a boy named Rufus Riley, and two older men, Richard Norby and Joe Carrier, and I were sitting at a table with Vernon, it was suggested that Vernon try out his great gift. First, though, I was asked to try to hear the Huddleston brothers and their cousin, sitting, as was their custom, at a remote table. I tried, but I could hear nothing. Then Fancy tried with the same results. Vernon agreed to concentrate on them, but looking at them intently and trying to listen he admitted there was nothing he could pick up in the air from them. They talked intently; he could ascertain nothing of their subjects. The evening went on to other subjects and Dickie left and then Riley and, as I was preparing to depart, having a test in American political parties and leaders the next morning at Pitt, Vernon made a gesture for us to be quiet. I sat back down: *The Federalist* essays would have to wait.

"They're talking about Tennyson Street," he said.

We held our breaths. Within short walking distance of the Irish Club on Oakland Avenue the neighborhood changed its character completely. From the government housing project where I lived with my father and mother and where Fancy lived with his mother and sisters, down Robinson and Darraugh and Dunseith and Terrace with their shingled houses and wooden stairs and porch swings, out into the center of Oakland with the University of Pittsburgh's Cathedral of Learning and the Carnegie Library and the Mellon Institute, there lay a neighborhood called Schenley Farms. The houses were built around the turn of the century. The streets, a block from Pitt and the then exclusive Pittsburgh Athletic Association, were named Ruskin and Tennyson and Thackeray and Lytton, for nineteenth-century English literary figures. We considered them then, and indeed they seem so today, posh. Hedges and driveways and stone and brick and lawns and locations with no stores near. The people there had money, servants, cars, places to go nights, and days we could not imagine. We never had a reason to be on those streets, although coming home from Schenley High School after school we sometimes wandered past the houses, idly talking to each other before we veered back to our homes in the government housing projects. At other times, after school, we walked past the fine old houses on our route to adventures in Oakland. Never, though, did we think we had any business on Tennyson, Lytton, or Ruskin.

Yet, as those things go, there was a celebrated belief among us that one or more of these houses held servant girls, sometimes said to be eager maids fresh from Ireland, other times hot-blooded young Polish girls, who were ready for anything—particularly what we, marked for romance, from the streets of Oakland and the tables at the Irish Club in our beauty, wisdom of life, sex, and love, had to offer. In support of our unlikely expectations, we had been lately assembling in twos or threes, in the flush of the end of World War II where everything was possible, at the corner of Forbes and Atwood where we took any trolley going downtown. On the streets of downtown, passing young women and old women and women in between, beautiful or squat, easy or not, we made our way to a restaurant called the Purple Cow on the first floor of the Roosevelt Hotel on Penn Avenue. There we had coffee with congenial young men like ourselves from the Hill District, East Liberty, Crafton, or the South Side.

At the Irish Club among ourselves, and in our tales now at the counter in the Purple Cow, we were corroborated a thousand times a night by others from the far corners of Allegheny County. We assured each other that anything could happen to young men capable of making their own decisions about things in general, laws and society be damned. Working was for mules and they turned their backs on it. Women were there! Somewhere! It was a matter of finding them: over eight cups of coffee a night, prowls through the downtown streets in search of those same ready women, a hunt at its beginnings as exhilarating as too much caffeine, at its end like cigarette ashes in cold coffee, we made our way through the educations of our new manhood. Everyone lied: money, family, women, the war, peace, school, and what had happened that very morning. Coming from Oakland to downtown, it must be said, we were fertile ground for anybody's story, we lied less than the others, having hardly any basis to launch a tall tale, so little had happened to us. It was not that we had few lies of our own. We had plenty, but we were no competition to what we heard. Wheat and barley could grow in the rich brown depths of our inexperience, even at the art of lying. But money and women would come to us if we had the boldness to take what was out there waiting: who, with our armies triumphant, said otherwise in 1948?

Vernon murmured, as we sat not stirring a muscle in terror of disturbing his visions, "Oh, it's some rancid and racy matters. It's descriptions between the Huddlestons of nights up there on Tennyson, boys, nights unbelievable. Nights of lust like nothing I heard."

Joe Carrier said, "Go ahead, Vern, we're listening."

"Yeah," I said, "don't leave out a syllable," while people made gestures at me to be silent, lest the harmonies in place at the Ancient Order of Hibernians that had assembled to bring us on the receptive air the accounts of magical, illicit nights be disrupted by my intrusion.

"There was, I make," Vernon said, "more than a bit of deception in the business. There was not one woman there on Tennyson but two."

"Two!"

We hushed the intruder, while Vernon bent his head in his hands, lost in his telegraphy.

"There was a younger woman and an older woman. And the older woman, on what I'm hearing, was a great thing herself— it was Jackie, the youngest Huddleston, came on the conspiracy. He had gone there, lured by the young woman, he seen her in Oakland and went to the Isaly's on Forbes for a malted with her and she invited him to visit her in the dead of night, saying, 'Don't appear before midnight. I'll leave open the back screen door.' Well, he follows the directions and, you see, he already knows what's coming—it was Eddie, the middle brother, told him about the girl, she's a maid there. But it's Jackie now explaining to Eddie what's going on: it's Eddie doesn't know that it's an older woman who creeps into the room from time to time, using the younger woman to attract young men."

"Does she have scars, the older woman?" Mahoney asks. "It is some kind of horror story the Huddleston boys are cooking up to be ribbing Alfred, the cousin from the country."

"No, the older woman is just fine, a rare dish, but she's the lady of the house, and it's not parading around Oakland picking up boys she's doing by her preference. She has her position to maintain. She's well born, you see, but hot as a firecracker. She lets the young woman do it and Jackie says it was the two of them had him last Thursday night. And Eddie is saying he'll be damned he'd seen only one woman there. He'd swear it was only the young woman there he took like his brother for a malted and then given the same instructions to creep in by the back screen door."

"Two women," Vinegar Root said. "There was two women. You're saying it was two women up there on Tennyson Street?

There was the maid and the lady of the house? Bless me, Vernon, those Huddleston boys are demons."

He was about eighteen years old, and he played American Legion baseball with some fairly good prospects. There were times he did not shake hands with people in fear of injuring his pitching hands. He'd say, "Sorry, too much to lose."

"I'm not saying there was two women," Vernon said, "I'm saying Jackie Huddleston is saying it. And Alfred, down from Connelsville, is saying, 'None of it happened, you two are lying.'"

"Oh, no," Rommy, an older man, said. "Them boys who were there aren't lying. I know the truth when I hear it."

He had worked on trucks unloading freight at the old Pennsylvania and Lake Erie Railroad until he hurt his back. He went to chiropractors and physicians at the Montefiore Hospital and weekly said he felt himself returning to the old powers, but nothing much had changed in the eight years I knew him.

"Quiet," Vernon said. "Eddie's describing the room where it all takes place to the cousin. It's a room with music coming in like a phonograph is playing and there's markings on the wall, like hieroglyphics or signs."

"Signs!" Mahoney said. "Signs like what?"

"Signs. Designs. Markings like lit up in pretty pale yellows and greens, Eddie is saying. He's relating how the room is spinning around, total black except for the signs, and there's a big, cool bed and by the light from the signs he is able to make out the naked woman in the room. Then Jackie said it was two women coming at him and one was reaching for him to take him by the neck and the other was approaching him from his feet, rubbing against him, you know."

Just then someone played "Ghost Riders in the Sky" on the jukebox, and Vernon sat back. He said, "I can't hear a word over that racket."

Vinegar leaped to his feet and said, "I'll pull the wire out from the socket," but before he could move, Mahoney took his arm. "Vinegar," he said, "the music is real. That's good, old Vaughn Monroe, you're not going to make what's real go away because of a story of Vernon's. It's a story, boys, maybe true, maybe not. But it's just a story, and maybe Vernon's hearing it right and maybe he's not. There's no witnesses to any of it, only the Huddleston boys and Vernon repeating it."

"It was me," Rommy said, taking a deep breath as if he had gathered the will to confess. "It's a true story. I was the one. The Huddleston boy is telling my story. I was in that room with the woman. It happened like Submarine said. I'm brought back there this minute at what I'm hearing. I'm living it. Three months ago I was in the room with them women."

We were quiet for a moment: old Rommy was hardly the man we contemplated in such rare, ripe times. Clothes never quite right, shoes with a hole here or there, heavy white socks winter and summer, a fine man for company in a discussion on almost any subject, but not women or love or the longing that burned in us. "I know the room, I know the house," he said. "It happened just like the Huddleston boy said. She made me forget my back, she did. Maybe it was two of them, I can't swear."

Our sudden preoccupation with the turn old Rommy's passion had given the account of the tales of intrigue on Tennyson was immediately shattered again.

Richard Norby, not known as a man often taken by hallucinations, said in a profound and melancholy voice: "It's a double magical occurrence, Vernon hearing those boys the length of the club and the subject of their experience. Boys, it happened. It happened to me too. It happened like Huddleston is saying and Vernon is repeating. I thought it was only me who blundered into the ladies or the darling or whatever it was up there on Tennyson, but now I heard it with my own ears, out of this war hero's mouth, my exact experience. It's all true. I met her on Forbes and been in that dark room with the music playing and the signs on the wall."

Pal Mahoney said, "Someone tells you roisters of the word of God and you say, the criminal gang of you, 'Old wives' tales. I'm going up to the Pitt Tavern for a beer. Never heard such fairy tales,' and then you catch these rumors of Vernon's out of the air like they'd be ripe strawberries and hold on for dear life. You tire me, all of you. I'm ready to find a cave."

Joe Carrier said, "All true, Pal, all true, I was there myself. Vernon heard right. I'm a witness. And never there was another night like that with the whirling lights and the sweet perfumes and the music coming up from all sides. It was a night like no other. I'll be reliving it on my dying day."

Pal waved his hands in the air, threw them out in a circular motion to dispel the heat and mysteries gathering at our table, and said, "Enough! Enough!" But he should have known better: there's never anywhere, never any time when shouts or cries or indignation or pleas for lucidity can roll back the tide of belief when, called, it sweeps everything before it.

Restless later, I let O'Toole persuade me to take a trolley downtown with him to the Purple Cow. "You'll do your studying tomorrow morning," he said. "Let's see what's happening downtown. There's things out there. You'll get up at six, plenty of time for books."

In the dark we rode toward town, hope in our hearts, past the funeral home on Craft and the old carbarn, through Soho with every doorway harboring mayhem, through lower Fifth and Duquesne University perched on a hill. Fancy went there to night school, planning to practice dentistry one day and live off the fat of the land. But he could not pass the manual dexterity tests for entrance and moved down to Texas and I lost track of him. Still, as he and I ride through the sooty streets, young and in a time of faith, we hold high our expectations. Back doors will open and admit us to fairy lands of fulfillment, only because we walked a certain street one day where came the swooning daughter of old Ireland to redeem us. Armies of job holders will move aside for us to sweep their careers before us, making them ours. The telephone wires overhead in Oakland, Soho, East Liberty, Squirrel Hill, and the rolling hillsides of Schenley Park announce our coming, and we know, whispering among ourselves, outrageous things. Nothing is what it seems, our chant, our message of reward to ourselves. What is there for us to lose with maybe it is and maybe it is not, as Mahoney might say. But we too have traveled to that room of the black arts on Tennyson and plan to return until we are no longer boys and must face for what they are the lies that once caused our blood to race.

"Did you ever hear such bushwaw like what that pack of lunatics back there were peddling?" O'Toole asks, his hand shaking as he lights a cigarette and reaches over with the match to light mine.

"Never," I say, trying to quiet my trembling hand.

"Mahoney makes out he's the only man in Pittsburgh has a pipeline to God."

"He was right about one thing: Mr. Vaughn Monroe. That's real."

"Even Mahoney knows that. And what about the Ink Spots and Frank Sinatra!"

On the streetcar, empty except for the two of us and the motorman, I did my imitation of Vaughn Monroe with a particularly good "Tie-yipee-i-o," and then Fancy did his, and then I did Bob Eberle on "Brazil," followed by Frank Sinatra on "All or Nothing at All," holding the long note at the end. On Penn Avenue, a block from the Purple Cow, Fancy did his best, the night being memorable for what had been, however flawed, a confirmation. He sends up into the cool April clouds over Pittsburgh where promise hasn't died yet from deep in his throat his spectacular version of Harry James's trumpet solo on "Sleepy Lagoon." I was there, and you'd swear it was a man playing a trumpet on the sidewalk in front of the Roosevelt Hotel.

Outlaws of the Purple Cow & Other Stories

was designed by Will Underwood;

composed by G&S Typesetters, Inc.,

in 10.8/14.5 Adobe Garamond;

printed by sheet-fed offest lithography on

50-pound Glatfelter Supple Opaque stock

(an acid-free paper with 60% recycled

content using 10% post-consumer waste),

notch case bound over 88-point binder's boards in

Rainbow 3 cover material with 80-pound Rainbow endpapers,

and wrapped with dust jackets printed in four

color process on 100-pound enamel

topped with polypropylene

matte film lamination

by Thomson-Shore, Inc.,

and published by

The Kent State University Press

KENT, OHIO 44242